Freud Upside Down

THE NEW BLACK STUDIES SERIES

Edited by Darlene Clark Hine
and Dwight A. McBride

A list of books in the series appears at the end of this book.

Frǝud
UPSIDE DOWN

African American Literature and Psychoanalytic Culture

BADIA SAHAR AHAD

UNIVERSITY OF ILLINOIS PRESS
Urbana, Chicago, and Springfield

C 5 4 3 2 1
∞ This book is printed on acid-free paper.

Library of Congress Cataloging-in-Publication Data
Ahad, Badia Sahar.
Freud upside down : African American literature and psychoanalytic culture / Badia Sahar Ahad.
p. cm. — (The new Black studies series)
Includes bibliographical references and index.
ISBN 978-0-252-03566-1 (cloth : alk. paper)
1. American literature—African American authors—History and criticism. 2. African Americans in literature. 3. Psychology in literature. 4. Psychoanalysis in literature. 5. Race in literature. 6. Race—Psychological aspects. 7. African Americans—Psychology. 8. Psychoanalysis and literature—United States.
I. Title.
PS153.N5A398 2010
810'.9352996073019—dc22 2010016581

To Ma

(1953–2007)

Contents

Acknowledgments

I recognize that any published text has many authors and without the love of support of a very generous and dedicated community, this book could not have been written. This project bears the mark of many scholars whose work, whether in the form of a manuscript, a conference paper, or a casual conversation, has enabled me to think more intensely and broadly about my own. Among all of my influences, I am truly indebted to Glenn Hendler, who is at once my sharpest critic and most ardent supporter. He has been an invaluable mentor, advisor, and friend at every stage of my academic career. I also thank Toni Irving, Ewa Ziarek, and Kate Baldwin for reading the manuscript in its earliest stages and for their honesty about what worked and, most importantly, what did not. I would also like to extend my gratitude to the Department of African-American Studies at Northwestern University for awarding me a postdoctoral fellowship, which allowed me valuable time and extensive resources to revise significant portions of the manuscript. Perhaps the most important "resource" to which I was privy during my year at Northwestern was the intellectual and personal relationships I developed with rigorous scholars who helped me extend the scope of this work beyond the "literary" and take seriously this study's interdisciplinary elements. I thank Richard Iton, Sherwin Bryant, Krista Thompson, Jennifer DeVere Brody, Sandra Richards, Barnor Hesse, Celeste Watkins-Hayes, Mary Pattillo, and Tracy Vaughn for pushing, challenging, and encouraging me to push my scholarship to its limits. I owe a special thanks to Dwight McBride and Darlene Clark Hine for their mentorship and for realizing the potential in this book. I am grateful to my editor, Joan Catapano, and the staff at the University of Illinois Press for bringing this project to fruition.

The actual writing of this book could not have been possible without the support of those colleagues who sat with me week after week in writing group sessions as I made plan after plan to "get it done." I thank Michelle Boyd, Helen Jun, Amanda Lewis, Dave Stovall, Sacha Coupet, Noni Gaylord-Harden, Ruqaiijah Yearby, and L. Song Richardson for sharing many hilarious moments, making me accountable, and for serving as my personal, career and social advisory council. This book would have been difficult to produce without a consistent flow of lattes—thanks to the staff at Iguana Café, Kristoffer's, and Efebina's in Pilsen for keeping my cup full and allowing me to occupy a big table, even during the lunch hour. Kerry Ann Rockquemore deserves so much more than a single line for her generous time and spirit, specifically spending hours upon hours guiding me through the tenuous and, sometimes mysterious, paths of this profession, and for being a really good friend above all. I greatly appreciate the support this project has received from Loyola University Chicago, especially my colleagues in the English department. I am indebted to Paul Jay, David Chinitz, Jack Kerkering, Joyce Wexler, and Pamela Caughie for their helpful suggestions and careful reading of parts of the manuscript. Thanks to Deborah Oliver, Emily O'Keefe, and Gillian Nelson for meticulously editing and proofreading the entire manuscript when I could no longer "see" it. I thank the very helpful staff at the Beinecke Rare Book and Manuscript Library at Yale University, the Schomburg Center for Research in Black Culture (New York), the Library of Congress, and the Ransom Center at the University of Texas at Austin for expertly navigating me through their archival collections. I have greatly benefited from conversations with Stephanie Batiste, Stephane Dunn, Margo Crawford, and April Langley. I owe a very special thanks to Reanna Ursin, Lauri Dietz, and especially Liz Fenton for their willingness to give hours of their time to read and reread drafts, and take as much as time with me as necessary to help talk through any obstacles along the way. Because of them, this project is stronger and more compelling than I could have ever accomplished alone.

A warm thanks to my circle of friends: Dina Best-Williams, Sandi Thompson, Michael Leslie Amilcar, and Muneerah Abdul-Ahad, who completely understood when I needed to go underground, yet were always there to remind me what really mattered. Without the unconditional love and support of my family, I simply would not be. I am grateful for my aunt, Romi Lowe, who has over the years encouraged me to work hard, do my best, and watch the rest fall into place. I greatly appreciate my dad, Michael Toney, for teaching me to approach life and work with dignity, integrity, and a smile. My grandparents, Eddie and Annie Lowe, brought with them from Livingston, Alabama, to Chicago, a sense of purpose and possibility that they could create a new and better life for their children. I thank them for teaching me to fearlessly travel open roads and to create new ones when there is no visible path to follow. And lastly, I thank my mom, Anna Lowe, who inspired my love of literature by example and who has been there every step of the way.

Freud Upside Down

Introduction

In a letter to his mentor, Sigmund Freud, Carl Jung surmised that every subject maintains an intersubjective dependence on his perceived Other: "Just as the coloured man lives in your cities and even within your houses, so also he lives under your skin, subconsciously. Naturally it works both ways. Just as every Jew has a Christ complex, so every Negro has a white complex and every American [white] a Negro complex. As a rule the coloured man would give anything to change his skin, and the white man hates to admit that he has been touched by the black" (*Collected Works* 10:508, par. 963). The "complex" dialectic Jung imagines relies upon the notion that African Americans desire whiteness and that whites systematically negate blackness. As such, Jung's Negro becomes inextricably linked to, and even informs, the psychic life of white Americans and vice versa. Jung's 1930 analysis of black-white relations both reveals his daring to place the thorny matter of race within a psychoanalytic frame and places his conjectures about the psychic underpinnings of race and racism in dialogue with then-contemporary modes of African American sociopolitical discourses of race pride prevalent in the early twentieth century. At the same time that Jung conceived of the white complex suffered by African Americans, black intellectuals were producing a psychoanalytic counterdiscourse to Jung's paradigm.

One such example is Hubert Harrison, popular journalist and founder of *Negro Voice*.[1] Harrison is an obscure figure compared to his contemporaries Alain Locke, James Weldon Johnson, and W. E. B Du Bois, but his broad range of knowledge and expertise in the areas of politics, psychology, cultural criticism, science, and drama made him privy to key occupations within mainstream and black media outlets, including the *New York Times,* the *Boston Chronicle,* the *Call,* the *Messenger,* and the *Masses.* I invoke Harrison here as a counterpoint to Jung because Harrison appropriated psychoanalysis as a way to expound tenets of black nationalism and trouble the logic of white supremacy. In March 1924, the *Boston Chronicle* ran Harrison's "Race Consciousness." In this article, Harrison conjectured that the race consciousness of subjugated people emanated from their experience of white domination:

> The general facts of the outside world reflect themselves not only in ideas but in our feelings. The facts that make up a general social condition are reflected in social *states of mind.* Thus the feeling of racial superiority which the white races so generally exhibit is produced by the external fact of their domination in most parts of the world. That same fact, by the way, produces in the minds of the masses of black, brown and yellow peoples in Africa, Asia and elsewhere what is called in psychology a protective reaction; and that is their race-consciousness. So that race-consciousness is like loyalty, neither an evil nor a good. The good or evil of it depends upon the uses to which it is put. (3–4, my emphasis)

Jung and Harrison contextualize black responses to white hegemony in two distinctly different ways: Jung insists that white domination produces the desire for the black man to change his skin, while Harrison reads white racism as producing a protective reaction among raced persons that manifests itself as race consciousness. Indeed, Harrison posits race consciousness as a defense against white subjugation that both engenders a feeling of racial pride or "loyalty" and serves to bond ethnic subjects across the Diaspora. Further, in Jung's view, the psychological complexes that dog "the Jew," "the Negro," and the "American [white]" are expressions of the "social states of mind" to which Harrison refers. In both cases, racial dialectics inform individual interiority as well as the collective psyche of the social world. While Harrison and Jung were not in conversation with one another about the psychical consequences of racism, their theories about such processes points to a dialogue in which the language of psychoanalysis frames larger cultural debates around the implications of racialization.

Using Harrison's example, I suggest that just as mainstream and white America was obsessed with psychoanalytic logic in the 1920s, so too were African American writers and intellectuals, who believed that the new science could further the cause of racial inclusion.[2] Black writers and artists were as anxious about the possibilities of psychoanalysis as their white modernist counterparts for whom the psychoanalytic model proved liberating. But Harrison was not singular. The era of the Harlem Renaissance produced a body of intellectual work that deployed psychoanalysis as a way to create a productive space for the expression of black interiority. Indeed, the coalescence of black intellectual and psychoanalytic discourses in the 1920s and 1930s produced both a counterdiscourse to mainstream psychoanalysis and, more significantly, a legacy of conversations between these seemingly disparate communities that has continued to evolve into the twenty-first century.[3] I am interested in how black authorial engagement with psychoanalytic thought coincided with emergent cultural ideas and uncertainties concerning racial and sexual subjectivities. Though the study of psychoanalysis was originally explicated in Sigmund Freud's 1899 text *The Interpretation of Dreams,* the evolution of American psychoanalysis produced a series of paradigm shifts throughout the twentieth century that parallel and are reflected in the works of major African American writers. Since the beginning of the twentieth century—perhaps originating with Pauline Hopkins's appropriation of William James's notion of the unconscious or the "hidden self" in her novel, *Of One Blood: The Hidden Self* (1902–3)—there have been a coterie of black writers and scholars who have maintained an interest, and I would argue an investment, in psychoanalytic thought.

In an effort to address the mutually informative relationship between psychoanalysis and African American cultural studies, this book provides a loose chronological narrative of African American literary and print interventions within psychoanalytic discourses that roughly parallel the evolution of American psychoanalysis. For example, Freudian protégé (and dissenter) Otto Rank appealed to the artistic sensibilities of Nella Larsen and her Renaissance counterparts because of his conception that the artist possessed a unique ability to find relief from the death drive by immortalizing himself in the creation of his art; Ralph Ellison and Richard Wright witnessed the exponential rise of psychoanalysis in the United States during World War II and applied it in their literary productions and intimate lives as evidenced by their establishment of the Lafargue Mental Hygiene Clinic in Harlem; and Frantz Fanon's psychoanalytic accounts of colonial trauma resonated with and deeply informed black nationalist discourse in the 1960s to 1970s, including the plays of Adrienne Kennedy, who provides a concrete engagement with Freud and Fanon in her 1992 play, *Dramatic Circle. Freud Upside Down* examines the works of Nella Larsen, Jean Toomer, Richard Wright, Ralph Ellison, Adrienne Kennedy, and Danzy Senna and their various investments in psychological ideas as a means to undermine black essentialism, to advance the project of developing an interracial discourse (or in some cases a discourse of racelessness), and to create a space for black interiority to emerge in the American consciousness. Specifically, the writers in this study were less concerned with the exclusion of blackness from classical Freudian and Freudian-derived paradigms but located a space both within and outside its frameworks to create a psychological narrative of African American experience. Collectively these psychoanalytically engaged texts produce an intellectual history of black literary and intellectual negotiations with the concept of race. The title of this book, *Freud Upside Down,* is taken from Richard Wright's essay "Psychiatry Comes to Harlem," in which he describes the work of Harlem's first mental health clinic as the "turning of Freud upside down." This notion of turning classical psychoanalytic logic on its head so that it might account for the specificity of black subjectivity functioned as the explicit and underlying imperative of black writers for whom psychoanalysis provided both a vocabulary and a model to examine the paradox of race.

Though this intellectual history maps the shifting, and sometimes parallel, discourses of race and psychoanalysis throughout the twentieth century, it is essential to note that these writers do not produce a unifying narrative of blackness, or of psychoanalysis for that matter. Instead, the authors studied here construct competing articulations of racial interiority that are attendant to and invested in the rethinking of class, gender, and sexuality. Contrary to psychoanalysis's own claims to universalism, for many writers it proved an inventive space that produced multiple and often conflicting ideas about race. I argue, then, that African American writers did not simply appropriate the model and language of psychoanalysis to destabilize conventional, and often inferior, notions of blackness—they relied upon it.

Given psychoanalysis's troubling history—particularly its contribution to racist discourses of blackness and primitivism and its denial of race as a constitutive factor of identity—why were or are African American writers at all interested in and, especially, attracted to the discipline? In what ways did African American writers appropriate the ideas of Freud, Jung, Rank, and Lacan? How did they revise these ideas to speak for the black subject? And, most significantly, to what end? In "'All the Things You Could Be by Now, If Sigmund Freud's Wife Was Your Mother': Psychoanalysis and Race," Hortense Spillers points out that "little or nothing in the intellectual history of African Americans within the social and political context of the United States would suggest the effectiveness of a psychoanalytic discourse, revised or classical, in illuminating the problematic of 'race' on an intersubjective field of play" (376). While the psychoanalytic model may have proved ineffective in unearthing the problematic of race, the fact that it could potentially offer insight into the complexity of race proved ample motivation for black intellectuals to employ psychoanalytic models as a guiding methodology. To be certain, this project does not make any claims about the value of psychoanalytic devices to unveil the inscrutable nature of race. However, I do suggest that psychoanalysis emerges within black intellectual and literary history as a fundamental stratagem to trouble racial logic and to interpret racial dialectics unique to the United States.

Significantly, the black intellectual and literary imperative to embrace psychoanalytic thought in clinical and creative contexts was integral to the formation and possession of U.S. citizenship. As Thaddeus Russell persuasively argued, in the years during and immediately following World War II civil rights advocates argued that black heteronormativity was essential to its program of integration and racial inclusion. In the 1940 and 1950s, psychoanalysis was deployed as a way to normalize black subjects in that it provided a means by which black people could make the transformation from "citizen victims," in Lauren Berlant's terms, to "citizen subjects" (48). The denial of full rights of citizenship was indelibly linked to the denial of black humanity, and more specifically, black interiority. As such, the deployment of psychoanalysis for African Americans was a strategic method by which they could address the "trauma of citizenship" (to return to Berlant). Framing the difficult road to full and uncontested citizenship as a traumatic process underscores the extent to which the sense of national belonging is intimately tied to matters of the psyche. Especially useful in conceptualizing the relation between citizenship, psychoanalysis, and race is Gwen Bergner's notion of the "racial symbolic," which examines how racial ideology and the symbolic order work in tandem to produce racialized subjectivities (44). In doing so, Bergner underscores the significant relation between the social and material realities of race and racial fantasy as a way to emphasize the significance of the unconscious in the production of "raced citizen-subjects" (48). The notion of a raced citizen-subject highlights the salience of models of citizenship as integral to the psychic processes by which one becomes raced. This inextricable linkage between the machinations of national and communal belonging and interior subjectivity posits the ways in which the psychoanalytic functions as a salient social and political category.

Along these lines, Anne Anlin Cheng's *The Melancholy of Race: Psychoanalysis, Assimilation, and Hidden Grief* investigates, through the lens of a Freudian model of melancholia, the social, the political, and the psychic as a complex dynamic that possesses real material consequences in the lives of raced subjects. Cheng reads *Brown v. Board of Education* as a historical moment that produced a space for the psychical response to racism, grief, to reside in the context of the law. As a momentous response to "racial injury" (15), *Brown v. Board* generated a model by which social and political subjugation played a significant role in the formation of racial subjectivity on the strength of its psychological proof that racism was psychologically damaging to raced subjects. According to Cheng, the "psychical experience is not separate from the realms of society or law but is the very place where law and society are processed" (x). My investigation of the Lafargue Mental Hygiene Clinic in Harlem explores this dynamic between law, society, and psychical experience, revealing how although the clinic was established to promote the psychic health of poor and minority subjects who were regarded as victims of an uneven American democracy, its therapeutic responses to the problem of racial and economic inequities relied upon some disturbing cultural assumptions—one being that the promise of legitimate citizenship could only be accessed by submitting to heteronormative cultural and social ideals. I discuss this phenomenon more fully in chapter 4 of this book, but I broach the example of the Lafargue clinic here to shows how Cheng's model elucidates the sometimes contradictory underpinnings of psychological methods, and like Bergner, demonstrates the "politics of race in psychic development" (xix).

While a number of critical works acknowledge the presence of psychoanalytic paradigms in certain African American novels, the general resistance to psychoanalysis has created a critical lacuna in the historical and cultural relationship between African American literary and psychoanalytic communities. Claudia Tate recognizes that many critics remain skeptical about psychoanalysis as a critical lens through which to examine black experience. Such uncertainty is largely due to the belief that "the imposition of psychoanalytic theory on African American literature advances Western hegemony over the cultural production of black Americans, indeed over black subjectivity" (*Psychoanalysis* 192). Such arguments are historically valid, as Jean Walton points out: "In much of the early psychoanalytic literature, 'femininity' or 'masculinity' was coming to be understood as a 'mature' stage one attained after successfully completing . . . a developmental sequence that culminated in heterosexualized, gendered adulthood." However, she contends that "a racial subtext informs this developmental model" in which "one's subjectivity will inevitably be marked by the way in which one fails to be fully white" (5). The Jeffersonian notion that blacks lacked psychic interiority resonates with the ways in which the psychoanalytic institution approached, or failed to approach, the matter of black subjectivity. If whiteness was emblematic of a heteronormative ideal, as Walton makes clear, then blackness emerged as an inherently pathological site of subjectivity. Despite the ways in which psychoanalysis has proved oppositional, and even antithetical, to the articulation of racial interiority, concepts that are fundamental to psychoanalysis, specifically "self-division; the mimetic and transitive character of desire; the economies of displacement . . . ; the paradox of the life-death pull," are "stringently operative in African American community" (Spillers 139). The supposed universality of psychoanalysis draws the most criticism from scholars who contend that the field fails to account for identities, racialized and sexualized, outside of its normative, predetermined framework. However, psychoanalytic paradigms have historically played, and continue to play, a significant role in the ways in which African American writers imagine social, cultural, and personal transformations.

Spillers is also concerned about broad and blind applications of psychoanalytic theory to the study of African American literature, noting that "one must proceed with caution" to avoid succumbing to the enabling discipline that makes us "want to concede, to give in to its seeming naturalness, its apparent rightness to the way we live" (138). Black writers' deployment of psychoanalytic ideas as a way to address individual racial dilemmas is symptomatic of a larger issue regarding the attempt to reconcile individual subjectivity with the sometimes incongruous demands of social law and custom. Claudia Tate's seminal text *Psychoanalysis and Black Novels: Desire and the Protocols of Race* explains the insidious ways that "racism condemns black subjects to a Manichean conflict between their public performance of an essentialized, homogenous blackness, which is largely a by-product of white 'ideological formations' of racial difference, on the one hand, and a private performance of individual personality, on the other" (6). Psychoanalysis, then, becomes the method by which "to demonstrate how a black text negotiates the tension between the public, collective protocols of race and private, individual desire" (13). The conflict in making the "private" public emerges as a dilemma specific to black subjects for whom the concept of individuality has been especially fraught. In each chapter of *Freud Upside Down,* the contradiction between individual and communal desire emerges explicitly and implicitly as an issue that psychoanalysis is deployed to resolve. Spillers carefully distinguishes between "the individual" who often serves as a mere "synecdochic representation" of the black masses, and "the one" who is an "agent," a "position in discourse," the "'one' who 'counts'" (395). The emergence of the "total Negro," as Ralph Ellison puts it, was an effort to resolve or reconcile the largely sociological depiction of the black subject within the public sphere with one that acknowledges his psychical nature ("Harlem Is Nowhere" 321).

This study builds upon and is indebted to the critical methodologies of scholars like Hortense Spillers, Claudia Tate, Gwen Bergner, and Kalpana

Sheshadri-Crooks, who have done much in the way of articulating the mutually informative and theoretical possibilities made viable by the intersection of psychoanalytic and African American literary and critical discourses. These studies, among others, produce a body of African American literary and cultural works that subvert and complicate classical and contemporary psychoanalytic theory in its attention to the racially and ethnically specific circumstances that inform black psychic character. This book contributes to the body of criticism that regards the intersection between psychoanalytic thought and African American studies as an important and distinctive intellectual and social project that can potentially transform the ways in which we consider and interpret both black interiority and the history of psychoanalysis. Attention to the way that African American writers approached psychoanalytic thought in their personal lives offers yet another dimension to the study of race and psychoanalysis that has been relatively invisible in critical scholarship. One of the central and common claims raised by the aforementioned critics concerns how to straddle the line between psychoanalysis as a theoretically useful methodology for deconstructing the psychic underpinnings of the concept of race without succumbing to its persistent tendency to universalize individual subjects. But historically, at least, psychoanalysis's systematic universalizing actually served the interests of black subjects, so it becomes worthwhile to trace the ways in which revisions of psychoanalytic theories have shifted in tandem with evolving ideas about race. As such, this book offers a historical trajectory of the transformational relationship between African American writers and psychoanalytic thought, and demonstrates how psychoanalysis has clarified the psychical impulses within African American literature and how psychoanalytic concepts are also operative in the lives of its authors. The historicist imperative of this book complements existing scholarship that has sought to bridge the divide between African American and psychoanalytic communities.

I begin my exploration of African American negotiations with psychoanalysis with an analysis of Floyd A. Calvin's column, "The Mirrors of Harlem: Studies in Colored Psychoanalysis," which appeared in the *Messenger* magazine in 1922 and 1923. The content of the *Messenger* adhered primarily to the socialist imperatives of A. Philip Randolph and his successor, George A. Schuyler, and its articles generally emphasized the similar class positions of black and white laborers in order to fashion interracial solidarity and make the case for integrated labor unions. However, the narrative of interracial solidarity began to take on a more intimate character once Schuyler asserted his editorial influence. In 1922 and 1923, the *Messenger* published a number of articles that explicitly engaged the language and conceptual framework of psychoanalysis to further advance the magazine's and Schuyler's agenda of race mixing. The articles I examine, in particular those written by social theorists William Pickens and Robert Bagnall, employed psychoanalysis to revise predominant eugenicist claims that asserted the value of racial purity. Essays like William Pickens's "Color and Camouflage: A Psychoanalysis," published in the July 1923 issue, used Freud's theory of repression to suggest that white violence against blacks was largely the result of repressed sentiments of affection toward African Americans, and the release of their inhibitions would enable whites to reveal the natural affections they once held toward blacks. The *Messenger*'s contributors constructed similar narratives in which intimate relations between blacks and whites are easily imagined through the deconstruction of racial categories, which is made possible through creative revisions of Freudian ideas. The example of the *Messenger* reveals how the universalizing tendencies of psychoanalysis appealed to black subjects who were attempting to emphasize similarities between the races and downplay external or epidermal differences.

While it is widely acknowledged that Jean Toomer and Nella Larsen were interested in the ambiguity of racial identity, this has been generally linked to a larger fascination with the phenomenon of "passing" that was popularized during the period of the Harlem Renaissance. Chapters 2 and 3 contextualize Larsen's and Toomer's engagement with psychoanalysis within a larger cultural context, specifically the influence of Otto Rank's theory of birth trauma on Larsen's construction of interracial subjectivity in *Quicksand* and Toomer's tenuous negotiation of the racial politics of the 1920s and the psycho-religious philosophies of Georges Gurdjieff in Toomer's unpublished story "Transatlantic." In chapter 2, "The Anxiety of Birth in Nella Larsen's *Quicksand*," I argue that the paradigm of Otto Rank's theory of birth elucidates the mysterious "lack" at the source of the protagonist Helga Crane's mounting anxieties throughout the text. Specifically, Rank understood psychology as a "process oscillating between a striving for individualism and an urge to merge with some larger social entity," (*Psychology of Difference* 4) which underlies the fundamental dilemma for the novel's protagonist, Helga Crane, who desires recognition as a subject who is not wholly defined by race and gender yet seeks a communal experience that acknowledges both. Reading *Quicksand* through this lens makes clear the ways in which Larsen challenges and complicates the *Messenger*'s idyllic model of interracialism and Rank's theories by pointing to their inattentiveness to the matters of gender and race, respectively.

Chapter 3, "Art's Imperfect End: Race and Gurdjieff in Jean Toomer's 'Transatlantic,'" argues against prevailing critiques that assert that Toomer dismissed the concept of race after the 1923 publication of his novel *Cane* to suggest that Toomer attempted to shift racial perceptions through Gurdjieff's philosophies. Gurdjieff advanced the logic of "individualization" which stressed the notion that most people exist in a state of mechanicality and are thus unable to think objectively (Friedel 41). In Gurdjieff's view, people disregarded the cultivation of their own interior states and as a result were ill-equipped to form connections with others. While Gurdjieff decidedly and consciously avoided the topic of race, Toomer's social imperative differed. He adopted Gurdjieff's logic and applied it to the problem of race in the United States with the hope that his goal of racial transcendence could be achieved. In the case of Larsen and Toomer, each strategically deployed existent psychological paradigms to de-concretize racial categories.

In chapter 4, "'A genuine cooperation': Richard Wright's and Ralph Ellison's Psychoanalytic Conversations," I investigate how psychoanalysis became a more radically politicized space for black writers in the years during and immediately following World War II. In that chapter, I discuss Ellison's and Wright's relationships with analysts Dr. Harry Stack Sullivan, Dr. Benjamin Karpman, and Dr. Frederic Wertham to demonstrate the extent to which these writers desired to move beyond appropriating and revising existing psychoanalytic approaches to producing texts that would inform that discourse. Each writer believed that the deployment of psychoanalysis could potentially work in the interests of analyzing and correcting social problems (the psychological effects of racism, migration, displacement, urbanization), exemplified by their development of the Lafargue Mental Hygiene Clinic in 1946. However, this effort misses how the emancipatory or liberatory potential of psychoanalysis would come at the cost of enforcing a normative subjectivity with a repressive effect on black subjects. Perhaps this contradiction is inherent to psychoanalysis itself, but chapter 4 articulates how Wright and Ellison were implicated in the regulating practices of psychoanalysis. The chapter's most pressing concern is with the extent to which both Ellison and Wright became trapped within the contradiction between the emancipatory and the normalizing impulses of psychoanalysis, endorsing a discourse that, in fact, pathologizes and even scapegoats so-called "minority behaviors," particularly blackness and queerness. I examine how the democratic impulses of Ellison's and Wright's psychoanalytic interventions are undermined by the normalizing, regulatory qualities of psychoanalysis.

Ellison's and Wright's engagements with psychoanalytic thought were largely confined to rearticulating the terms of black male subjectivity. In *Dramatic Circle* (1992), playwright Adrienne Kennedy broaches the subject of black women who are generally misinterpreted or rendered invisible within psychoanalytic discourses. Kennedy satirizes the figure of Sigmund Freud (in the guise of a character named Dr. Freudenberger) and directly invokes Frantz Fanon's *The Wretched of the Earth* to construct the traumatic experience of her play's protagonist, Suzanne Alexander. In chapter 5, "Maternal Anxieties and Political Desires in Adrienne Kennedy's *Dramatic Circle*," I discuss Kennedy's approach to psychoanalysis via Freud and Fanon as an enabling yet problematic framework through which political desires are imagined and produced. For Kennedy, the shaping of political desire by way of the psychoanalytic imagination is even more complex for black female subjects who have been marginalized within psychoanalytic circles. I am particularly interested in the way Kennedy addresses this lack of recognition by exposing the critical gap in Freudian and Fanonian analyses and their relative failure in imagining black women as political subjects. Put simply, in *Dramatic Circle* Kennedy attempts to recuperate black women within the schema of a radical psychoanalytic politic by calling into question its very limitations. As such, Kennedy's drama broaches the contemporary relevance of psychoanalysis and the ways in which it continues to privilege the phallus as a marker of power and normativity.

While earlier chapters in *Freud Upside Down* discuss how black writers throughout the twentieth century have revised psychoanalytic paradigms to account for the black subject and more specifically to encourage certain discourses of interracialism (whether it be through integration or through advancing the United States's potential as a mulatto nation), chapter 6, "Racial Sincerity and the Biracial Body in Danzy Senna's *Caucasia*," argues that Senna's 1998 novel challenges psychological conceptions of identity formation to construct more comprehensive articulations of blackness. Contrary to historical novels of passing, *Caucasia* does not advocate the potential reification of more racial categories, nor does it advance neoliberal notions of colorblindness. My analyses of *Caucasia* brings *Freud Upside Down* full circle in that the novel draws upon tropes of the tragic mulatto and uses them to provide a more nuanced read of the multiracial subject. The chapter diverges from the historicist impulses of the earlier chapters of this book by engaging John Jackson's notion of "racial sincerity" to consider the extent to which race functions as a psychic, and not just bodily or ocular, trope. Though different in methodology from the other chapters, this one performs the important function of gesturing toward a new direction in the dialogue between psychoanalysis and black literature and culture. As psychoanalysis becomes increasingly amorphous within both academic and popular culture, and race becomes a more fluid, malleable, and contested category, we have to conceive new ways of imagining and interpreting the racial and psychoanalytic relation. In one of the novel's early scenes, the young, light-skinned protagonist Birdie Lee describes herself through the lens of her older, dark-skinned sister, Cole: "When I was still too small for mirrors I saw her as the reflection that proved my own existence. Back then, I was content to see only Cole, three years older than me, and imagine that her face—cinnamon-skinned, curly-haired, serious—was my own" (*Caucasia* 5). Such identifications occur throughout *Caucasia,* signaling the ways that the novel's instances of racial becoming function as psychical processes. I also propose that Senna's explicit intertextuality with her mother Fanny Howe's novel, *The Deep North,* provides an opening to examine Senna's psychical narrative of racial identity formation.

This book is not comprehensive nor is it exhaustive. There are any number of texts and authors that could potentially underscore how the resistance to static racial categories, particularly blackness, serves as a primary concern for African American authors at specific moments in black literary history. The writerly investment in Freudian and Freudian-inspired ideas since the 1920s has materialized as a rich space of intellectual inquiry, and for that reason, the focus of this book is restricted to literary and print culture. I have limited my discussion to the authors in this work because they explicitly engage psychological ideas as a way to link questions about race to a larger social context and use the intersection between the social and psychical forces that shape racial identification to disrupt racial boundaries. The authors examined in *Freud Upside Down* draw selectively on the psychoanalytic tradition, and each suggests certain revisions of it. Yet I am certain that there remain a number of black intellectual and social contributions to psychoanalytic culture that have yet to be uncovered. My impetus in writing this book emerges from my disbelief that, given the tremendous popularity of psychoanalytic thought in American popular and intellectual culture, African Americans were largely marginal to these conversations. Yet every major history of American psychoanalysis makes no mention of the black intellectual and literary response to, or influence on, the culture of psychoanalysis in the United States.[4] My desire in *Freud Upside Down* is rather simple: to call attention to a black presence in the cultural life of psychoanalysis, and to underscore the influence of psychoanalytic culture in the shaping of black lives.

1

The Politics and Production of Interiority in the *Messenger* Magazine (1922–23)

The November 1922 issue of the *Messenger* magazine promoted its editorial series, "The Mirrors of Harlem: Psychoanalyzing New York's Colored First Citizens" (after the first column, the subtitle was changed to "Studies in 'Colored' Psychoanalysis"), which was to make its first run in the periodical in the following month. The series, written by the *Messenger*'s assistant editor Floyd J. Calvin, promised in-depth exposés of figures such as James Weldon Johnson, Chandler Owen, and W. E. B Du Bois. The series was advertised as "a most interesting and clever piece of writing" and validated Calvin's lay psychoanalysis by informing the *Messenger*'s audience that Calvin had chosen "here and there bits of conversation, little unconscious actions, impressive displays and show-offs, calm, thoughtful, intelligent approach[es] to any question . . . after two years of close observation of the men about whom he writes" (516; see also fig. 1). Calvin's psychoanalytic essays are noteworthy because they created a new standard for the periodical's editorials and pushed the boundaries of black journalism from mere reportage to an expansive interpretation of the subject. Despite the short run of Calvin's editorials, subsequent contributors to the *Messenger* followed his model by appropriating and reformulating psychoanalytic logic and vocabulary to give further credence to their political claims. Calvin's example is significant in that he radicalized the nature of the editorial through his appropriation of a psychoanalytic model. In doing so, he provided a glimpse not only of the inner lives of his "analysands" but also of the dynamics and dynamism of African American print culture in the 1920s.

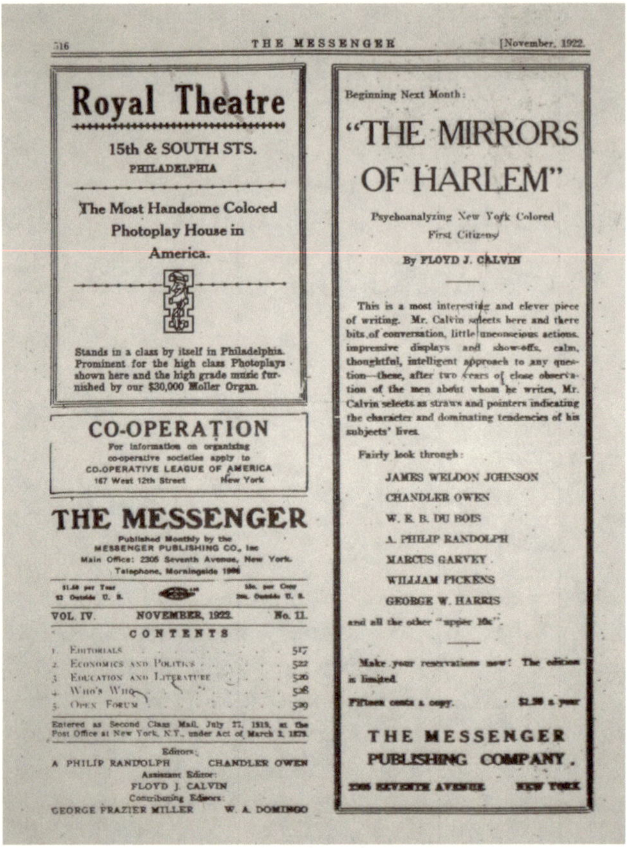
516 THE MESSENGER [November, 1922.

Royal Theatre
15th & SOUTH STS.
PHILADELPHIA
The Most Handsome Colored Photoplay House in America.
Stands in a class by itself in Philadelphia. Prominent for the high class Photoplays shown here and the high grade music furnished by our $30,000 Moller Organ.

CO-OPERATION
For information on organizing co-operative societies apply to
CO-OPERATIVE LEAGUE OF AMERICA
167 West 12th Street New York

THE MESSENGER
Published Monthly by the
MESSENGER PUBLISHING CO., Inc
Main Office: 2305 Seventh Avenue, New York.

VOL. IV. NOVEMBER, 1922. No. 11.

CONTENTS
1. Editorials 517
2. Economics and Politics 522
3. Education and Literature 526
4. Who's Who 528
5. Open Forum 529

Editors:
A. PHILIP RANDOLPH CHANDLER OWEN
Assistant Editor:
FLOYD J. CALVIN
Contributing Editors:
GEORGE FRAZIER MILLER W. A. DOMINGO

Beginning Next Month:
"THE MIRRORS OF HARLEM"
Psychoanalyzing New York Colored First Citizens
By FLOYD J. CALVIN

This is a most interesting and clever piece of writing. Mr. Calvin selects here and there bits of conversation, little unconscious actions, impressive displays and show-offs, calm, thoughtful, intelligent approach to any question—these, after two years of close observation of the men about whom he writes, Mr. Calvin selects as straws and pointers indicating the character and dominating tendencies of his subjects' lives.

Fairly look through:
JAMES WELDON JOHNSON
CHANDLER OWEN
W. E. B. DU BOIS
A. PHILIP RANDOLPH
MARCUS GARVEY
WILLIAM PICKENS
GEORGE W. HARRIS
and all the other "upper 10s".

Make your reservations now! The edition is limited.
Fifteen cents a copy.

THE MESSENGER PUBLISHING COMPANY.
2305 SEVENTH AVENUE NEW YORK

Figure 1. Advertisement for Floyd J. Calvin's series, "The Mirrors of Harlem: Psychoanalyzing New York's Colored First Citizens." (*Messenger*, November 1922)

This chapter examines how African American print culture embraced psychoanalytic models to both revise the racist eugenicist narratives of the period and further the project of "racial amalgamation" (Hutchinson, "Mediating 'Race'" 532) Specifically, I am intrigued by the ways in which the 1922–23 series of articles in the *Messenger* used psychoanalysis to engage the problem of interracialism. George Hutchinson has deftly observed that "one gleans from *The Messenger* the notion that cultural similarities between black and white Americans are hidden by a shared racial discourse, a culturally specific

'American' (that is, U.S.) phenomenon sustaining the widely shared faith in essential racial differences. Moreover, at the heart of the rituals of this faith one finds an ironic deconstruction of it, a flirting with the color line that hides while enacting the 'amalgamation' continually going on beneath the cover of racial reasoning" (532). Hutchinson's interpretation of the *Messenger*'s program of racial amalgamation is structured largely by his reading of the socialist imperatives of the magazine, which *Messenger* founder A. Philip Randolph advocated primarily to promote the integration of U.S. labor unions. But in addition to the *Messenger*'s socialist leanings, its appropriation and revision of Freudian and Freudian-derived psychoanalysis is equally compelling in framing its mission to ally whites and African Americans. Rather than look broadly at the magazine's various engagements with psychoanalysis, I take Robert Bagnall's essays, "A Psychoanalysis of Ku Kluxism" and "The Madness of Marcus Garvey"; William Pickens's "Color and Camouflage: A Psychoanalysis"; and Floyd Calvin's short-lived editorial series, "The Mirrors of Harlem: Studies in Colored Psychoanalysis" as exemplars of the ways in which some contributors to the periodical employed psychoanalytic paradigms to ameliorate the difficult relationship between the races. I draw upon the *Messenger* because its staff and contributors were important arbiters of the Harlem Renaissance era, and its peak circulation of 26,000 monthly, for which two-thirds of the subscribers were African American, indicates that the information and ideas within the magazine were disbursed throughout a literate black populace (Kornweibel 52). The narrative that the *Messenger*'s articles present is that psychoanalytic inquiry functions as a force to radicalize thinking along racial lines because it encourages the individual to free himself from repression, which, in the essays I discuss, emerges as the barrier that disallows intimacy or even understanding between blacks and whites. The *Messenger* contributors I examine in this chapter all assume that more attentiveness to individual psyches can and will yield greater racial tolerance and the eventual obliteration of racial and racist thinking altogether. Though the *Messenger* has been expertly analyzed in terms of its sociopolitical relevance, scholars have yet to contemplate the purpose of its psychoanalytic engagements, especially as part of a larger stratagem to debunk the concept and consequences of race.[1]

While the *Messenger*'s psychoanalytic essays constituted a relatively small component of the magazine's overall content, they nonetheless represent a significant yet overlooked element of African American intellectual history and the history of the United States. A concentrated engagement with psychoanalytic discourses within African American artistic and intellectual communities surfaced during the Renaissance era, roughly between 1916 and 1930, in the form of print media, informal salons, and literary texts. While the presence of Freudian analyses within African American artistic, cultural, and social productions in the early twentieth century has been well documented, the extent to which psychoanalysis was used as evidentiary knowledge meant to complement existing and multivalent projects of racial uplift and inclusion has not. The significance of the *Messenger*'s various treatments of psychoanalysis lies in their potential to disrupt existing historical narratives that, due to their relative exclusion of African Americans, suggest that black intellectual and literary communities were impervious to the pervasive psychoanalytic culture of the 1920s. Perhaps most importantly, the *Messenger*'s brand of "colored psychoanalysis" produced a reconciliation of psychoanalytic and socialist ideologies—a project that was considered nearly inconceivable in public mainstream discourses of the period, which sometimes highlighted competing tensions between Freudian and Marxist thought. As such, the extent of black engagement with psychoanalysis was both dialogic and revisionist in nature.

This chapter demonstrates that African American intellectuals of the Harlem Renaissance era were as anxious about the liberating possibilities of psychoanalysis as their white modernist counterparts, who believed that "the negative and positive advantages of psychoanalysis appealed to the postwar generation: it gave them an apparently justifiable means of 'scoffing scientifically and wisely' at the old standards, and it furnished an opportunity to search for new bases of human conduct" (Hoffman 59). As such, the Renaissance era produced a body of intellectual work that deployed psychoanalysis to explode the boundaries of racial categories. That psychoanalysis would be the methodology of choice to advance an agenda that sought to deconstruct the category of race makes sense, given that psychoanalytic discourses were motivated by their privileging of an inward consciousness. For a community of people who were bound by the politics of the exterior, psychoanalysis served the desire of many African American writers and scholars who sought to promote the psychological depth of the black subject. Much has been made of the racist praxis of psychoanalysis and its contribution to nineteenth- and twentieth-century discourses of primitivity, but less attention has been given to the variant ways in which black subjects used psychoanalysis as a counterdiscursive method to assert a psychologically superior subjectivity. By marshaling the language of psychic depth, the *Messenger* ultimately sought to influence the political and social discourses of interracialism.[2]

Signifyin' Psychoanalysis and the Rhetoric of Interracialism

African American print culture in the 1920s and 1930s, including periodicals, newspapers, and literary texts, was instrumental in constructing and conveying a collective resistance to white hegemony. This period witnessed the emergence of major news journals, most notably the *Crisis* (1910), the *Messenger* (1917), *Opportunity* (1923), and the short-lived *Fire!!* (1926), that provided an African American populace with accounts of racial terrorism, vignettes of black achievement, artistic reviews and notices, new works of poetry and short fiction, and significant international reports on race. The *Messenger*, the conception of socialist and activist A. Philip Randolph, was first and foremost a socialist enterprise. In the magazine's first issue, Randolph wrote that the mission of the publication was "to appeal to reason, to lift our pens above the cringing demagogy of the time, and above the cheap peanut politics of the old reactionary Negro leaders. Patriotism has no appeal to us; justice has. Party has no weight with us; principle has." The first issue of the *Messenger* appeared in the midst of the rising popularity of the periodical. Black folks in the North as well as in the rural South consumed the pages of such publications for news and lifestyle reports that spoke to their political and social concerns. Though the magazine was often on the verge of folding, it maintained an expansive and loyal readership during its seventeen-year existence.

The *Messenger*'s credo distinguishes it from the two other popular periodicals of the time—the NAACP's *Crisis* and the Urban League's *Opportunity*—which were more artistically focused and coincided with the Du Boisian and Lockian beliefs that racial progress could be accomplished through artistic achievement. Sondra K. Wilson has noted that "*The Messenger* called for a brand of socialism that would emancipate the workers of America and institute a just economic system. Randolph and [Chandler] Owen believed that centuries of capitalism had perpetuated the existing system which disenfranchised both black and white workers, and they conceived the idea of using unions as a means to achieving a smooth and painless socialist revolution" (xxii). Randolph and Owen also assumed that by marking the similarities between the black and white working class, other social and cultural bridges could be formed between the races. Hutchinson remarks that "*The Messenger* attributed racial prejudice to capitalism, insisted on the 'Americanness' of African Americans, and continually called for interracial worker solidarity . . . if the United States was to be the site of a new form of 'indigenous' socialism, it also, *The Messenger* suggested, would give birth to a new people and a 'mulatto' national culture" (*Harlem Renaissance* 291). The *Messenger* frequently published cartoons that depicted the parallel social and economic plights of the black and white working classes in order to emphasize the message that there was very little, if any, distinction between the races and that the root cause of racism was U.S. capitalism, which threatened everyone. One illustration depicts a black dog and a white dog chewing on the same bare bone while the abundant fat meat of financial profits are available to the "capital" hound. The image not only is a stark representation of the magazine's socialist impetus, but it also gives a sense of the *Messenger*'s call for interracial solidarity.

The *Messenger*'s emphasis on interracial solidarity for workers remained a consistent theme even when A. Philip Randolph temporarily left to pursue his work with the Brotherhood of Sleeping Car Porters in 1923 and George Schuyler took rein of the magazine. However, the trope of interracialism broadened into a more cultural and intimate context under Schuyler. Even before Schuyler's arrival, the *Messenger*'s ideological focus was more interracial than intraracial, but after Schuyler became editor the magazine began to emphasize its goal of a mulatto nation. Schuyler undoubtedly had a personal investment in establishing and promoting the interracialist cause: his wife, Josephine Cogdell, was white, and he believed his daughter to be representative of the "potential rise of a new or superior American racial type, a mulatto master race of democrats" (J. Ferguson 18). Thus, the currency he afforded to the project of interracialism during his tenure was considerable.

The irony of the *Messenger*'s attempts at an African Americanist psychoanalytic inquiry, specifically in pursuit of a mulatto nation, is that it reinscribes the very notion of race mixing or *Mischling* that Freud desperately and consciously elided in his own analysis. Freud was famously ambivalent about his origins as an Eastern Jew. Bearing witness to the subjugation of Eastern Jews, Freud constructed his own self-image as an acculturated Jew. The increasingly anti-Semitic environment of Central Europe, which was perpetuated by the medical sciences, led to the spawning of creative racial narratives meant to further demonize Jews by aligning them with an even more reviled race, the African. Such began the fiction that, as Sander Gilman notes, "Jews are a 'mongrel' race, who interbred with Africans during the period of the Alexandrian exile." This fiction led to the construction of "the fantasy of the difference of the male genitalia was displaced upward—onto visible parts of the body, onto the face and the hands where it marked the skin with blackness" (*Freud* 21). At its inception, Freudian analysis was overdetermined by an insistent claim of Jewish purity to dissociate it (and Freud himself) from the primitive African. Yet even in its glaring absence from psychoanalytic discourse, blackness figures as a defining category that essentially determined Freud's formation of the white or off-white Jewish subject. According to Gilman, Freud's anxieties about racial purity were heightened in 1911, when he became a member of the International Society for the Protection of Mothers and Sexual Reform, which advised its members to breed selectively. However, Freud's continuous clashes with anti-Semitism marked by his racially infused rift with Carl Jung led him to declare a Jewish nationalism that was distinct from any other racial category, including Aryan. To invoke Freudian and Freudian-derived psychoanalysis to bring together the distinct racial categories that Freud believed eternally dissimilar was a radical reimagining of the uses of psychoanalytic thought. For Freud, blackness signified a space of willful ignorance or unknowability, but for the writers of the *Messenger*, blackness structured the entire framework of the white psyche and the social conditions that those psychical inclinations produced.[3]

The Privileging of "Depth": Floyd Calvin's Psychoanalytic Subjects

The *Messenger*'s first and most explicit engagement with the psychoanalytic culture of the 1920s emerged in Calvin's "Mirrors of Harlem" essays, the first of which coincided with the beginning of George Schuyler's tenure at the *Messenger*.[4] The series signals one of the many substantive and stylistic transformations the magazine was to experience under Schuyler's direction, specifically a greater investment in American popular culture and hence the magazine's interest in psychoanalytic thought. Calvin's column was less concerned with the science behind psychoanalysis and more interested in the liberty it allowed for an uncensored critique of his political and social adversaries. Although Calvin's employment of psychoanalysis was not explicitly an effort to further an interracial ideal, it is appropriate and significant to underscore Calvin's column because it provides substantive clues about the role that psychoanalysis played within black intellectual and cultural spheres that were decidedly dissimilar from white American appropriations of the science. In particular, this section examines the ways in which Calvin's deployment of psychoanalysis was an attempt to distinguish the *Messenger* from other popular magazines of the period, such as the *Crisis* (edited by W. E. B Du Bois), *Opportunity* (edited by Charles Johnson), and the *Negro World* (edited by Marcus Garvey). But Calvin sought to accomplish more than simply point to the ways that the *Messenger* was different from these other publications; he also wanted to discredit other writers by performing disparaging psychoanalytic readings emphasizing, in particular, their lack of depth.

During this period, there was a great deal of competitive jockeying for legitimacy and authority in black magazines. As such, the editorial was arguably the most important feature of the *Messenger,* as it was central to the establishment of the publication as the only ideologically and politically accurate news source for the black populace. At this time, a periodical's editors could dramatically impact the success or failure of the publication. This was certainly the example of the *Crisis,* which witnessed a growth in circulation from 1,000 in 1910 to 94,000 in 1919, paralleling the rise of Du Bois's popularity and influence in intellectual and social circles. Hence the *Messenger*'s banner that claimed it was "the only magazine of scientific radicalism in the world published by Negroes" was an obvious strategy to acquire readers. It also distinguished the magazine from the *Crisis* and *Opportunity* in significant ways. The long-standing campaign against Marcus Garvey was perhaps its most vehement expression of disdain for black nationalism, which the editors equated with Ku Klux Klan ideology. Even the magazine's most seemingly benign news reports were compromised by some element of editorial prose. Calvin's column often made claims about the editorial acumen of other journalists, noting that, for example, "Alderman [George W.] Harris is by far the most intelligent and progressive weekly newspaper editor in Harlem. One has only to compare the publication for proof of this assertion. He has the rare faculty among Negroes to distinguish between his editorial and news columns" (December 1922). The following month, Calvin surmises that "the editor of *The Crisis* has his faults and makes his mistakes, but he is seldom taken to task for them intelligently," at which point he performs a pseudo-psychoanalytic analyses of Du Bois's editorial management, exploring his refusal to publish a potentially incendiary poem written by Archibald H. Grimké (which was eventually published by the *Messenger*). After Calvin recounts and critiques Du Bois's decision, he concludes that "*The Messenger* is the only Negro publication that has fundamentally inquired into Dr. Du Bois's editorial habits and methods. Readers of this journal might recall 'The Crisis of *The Crisis*,' 'Du Bois and *The Crisis*,' 'Mr. Grimké and *The Crisis*,' 'Du Bois Fails as a Theopist,' 'Du Bois on Revolution,' etc., for substantiation of this claim" (January 1923). This fundamental inquiry reflects, to a small degree, how Calvin imagines the signification of psychoanalysis rather than the methodology of the practice as a vehicle that enables him to make visible the hidden character of figures like Du Bois. For Calvin, psychoanalysis or depth functions as a way to animate and elevate the quality of journalistic prose, which enables him to carve a unique critical space for himself within black political discourses. Further, Calvin's inclusion of a psychological dimension to the editorial imbues it with an esoteric and even trendy edge, and in some ways works to complicate black public debates about racial uplift.

The notion of "depth" took on a special significance in the 1920s, as it was (as Joel Pfister notes) "fast becoming a commonsense category that supported the ideological proliferation of 'psychological' identities" ("On Conceptualizing" 18). While the title of Calvin's column, "The Mirrors of Harlem: Studies in 'Colored' Psychoanalysis," certainly suggests that it would perform a revision of Freudian thought tweaked for the black masses, the studies are actually poignant critiques and musings on various social and political figures. The mirror imagery in the title indicates that Calvin will offer, in the most basic terms, a reflection of the various personalities that constitute and inform the Harlem political and cultural scene, and his in-depth attention to personality in the studies promises to reveal an authentic and insightful image of black luminaries of the moment.

William Pickens, field secretary for the NAACP and later frequent contributor to the *Messenger,* is Calvin's subject in the inaugural December 1922 column. The first study consists of the following vignettes:

> My office is two flights up. Of a morning I sat at my desk reading a newspaper. Blam! Blam! Blam! came an unusually loud noise up the first flight. It kept coming nearer and nearer and getting louder and louder until finally three heavy raps came on my door. I opened and greeted Prof. William Pickens.
>
> * * *
>
> I was walking down 8th Avenue at mid-day. Suddenly a colored man passed by running—bareheaded. No one else seemed to be so excited so I quickened my pace to see what might cause him such discomfiture. By craning my neck and straining my eyes I finally saw him stop a man who was walking in the opposite direction, and begin talking earnestly. Evidently the pursuer had forgotten to mention something in a late conversation. I recognized the hatless man as Prof. William Pickens.
>
> * * *
>
> I was crossing 136th Street at 7th Avenue. I had just looked to the left and taken one step forward, looking to the right. Suddenly: *Honk!* and the wind

> of a five-passenger car fanned my face. A glimpse told me that the man at the wheel was Prof. William Pickens.
>
> * * *
>
> "Sure I'll lend you the books. If I'm not there when you call here's a note to my wife; she'll understand." I called about 7:30 p.m. Will Jr. answered the bell. A strong bass voice yelled up from the dining table below: "Give the gentlemen a seat. I'll be up in a minute."
>
> * * *
>
> Writing to Marcus Garvey on July 24, 1922, Prof. William Pickens said: ". . . In that you make a poor deal: for twelve million people you give up everything, and in exchange you get nothing." "Everything" and "nothing" were capitalized.
>
> Again: "I would rather be a plain black American fighting in the ranks against the klan and all its brood than to be the Imperial Wizard of the Ku Klux Klan or the Allied Imperial Blizzard of the U.N.I.A. [Universal Negro Improvement Association]." This whole passage was capitalized with italics.
>
> * * *
>
> William Pickens is probably the most prolific Negro writer not bearing the label of a professional editor. He has a zeal for giving his opinion on current events, and while he touches no dynamic and fundamental depths, his articles are, nevertheless, quite interesting. He exercises great skill in dressing the "surface" of our racial wounds, then speaks of his work so admirably you think has eradicated the evil by purifying the blood! (545)

Initially, Calvin's interpretation of psychoanalysis, in this "analysis" of Pickens, appears to be a common misappropriation of Freudian knowledge. As Hoffman explains: "psychoanalysis was . . . the key by which access could be had to the 'best circles.' Sandor Ferenczi, Hungarian analyst, suggested that in America the interest 'is somewhat superficial and that the deeper side is somewhat neglected.' Psychoanalysis was a delightful excuse for 'talking about oneself.' In this way, the terms of psychoanalysis became 'household words'—repression, fixation, sublimation, complex (*all* behavior patterns or attitudes were 'complexes'), defense mechanism—were badly misused labels attached at almost any time to a sentence, or included in a summary analysis of character" (66). Such was, arguably, the case with Calvin's subsequent articles, in which he poses a series of scenarios to eventually draw such analyses that "Mr. [John E.] Bruce is known to the Garveyites and readers of the

Negro World as 'Sir' John E. Bruce. K.C.O.N., ('Knight Commander of the Order of the Nile') I think. He was awarded this title by Mr. Garvey. (I don't know what for, or I would tell for the edification of the curious.)—Oh yes, I almost forgot: Mr. Bruce is also 'Duke of Uganda'—whatever that means" (December 1922); and "Prof. William H. Ferris represents the consequences of 'rote' learning, without the balancing force of originality" (February 1923). The only obvious potential reference to Freudian analyses comes in Calvin's construction of his coincidental encounters with Pickens as dreamlike apparitions. But Calvin's emphasis on the word *colored,* which appears in quotation marks in the series title, and the form of his critique shows that the column represents a Signification on rather than a misappropriation of psychoanalytic concepts and terminology. Henry Louis Gates theorizes that Signification signals that "a simultaneous, but negated parallel discursive (ontological, political) universe exists within the larger white discursive universe" (49). Hence the "'colored' psychoanalysis" Calvin performs both is drawn from and counters features of psychoanalytic thought as presented in the mainstream American thought. The events that comprise Calvin's estimation of Pickens are fragmented scenes that apparently bear no relation to one another other than the fact that Pickens appears unexpectedly, typically as a spectral image. But close examination of the image Calvin paints reveals that he satirically plays upon Pickens's public and self-image as "impulsive, dynamic, and at times, self-serving" (Avery 10), hence the distinct pictures of Pickens running "bareheaded," driving erratically, and being too busy to meet his expected guest.

Calvin's colorful experimentation with the concept of psychoanalysis as a probing of the mind takes on a particular relevance in that his analysis is not structured nor limited by Freudian terms. He uses the label of psychoanalysis to give an air of intellectual gravity to his own editorial claims and assert an erudition that the term *psychoanalysis* implies. Calvin's depictions form the final analysis that Pickens's response to the political project of racial uplift was a rather frenetic, unfocused affair. Though Calvin credits Pickens for being a prolific writer even though he had never served as an editor, Pickens in fact served as a contributing editor for the Associated Negro Press for twenty-one years between 1919 and 1940. Calvin critiques Pickens on the basis that his writing "touches no dynamic and fundamental depths" and that he skillfully addresses only the "'surface' of our racial wounds." Interestingly, it is not the substance of Pickens's policies that irk Calvin but the alleged lack of psychical interiority and depth in his prose. Underlying Calvin's broad indictment of Pickens is a response to Pickens's controversial texts, *The New*

Negro: His Political, Civil, and Mental Status and *Vengeance of the Gods, and Three Other Stories of Real American Color Line Life,* published in 1916 and 1922, respectively. In *The New Negro,* Pickens creates a tale of origin in which at "the dawn of civilization there were no hard and fast lines among the colors of the human race" (9), alluding to what Marlon Ross interprets as the "naturalness of interracial promiscuity" (Ross 36). However, for Calvin, such tales do little in the way of resolving existing tensions between whites and blacks and ultimately fail in their persuasive power to appeal to inspire resolution on either side of the color line. In Calvin's performance of depth, the disconnected scenes of Pickens in action serve as metaphors for Pickens's unpredictability that Calvin is then able to pattern, structure, and narrate into a coherent logic. By reconstructing this seemingly mundane and dysfunctional set of circumstances, Calvin makes visible the murky dimensions of Pickens's subjectivity that his dynamic public image might obscure.

But Calvin's invocation of psychoanalysis to strengthen his editorial position suggests that, in both his and the other emerging versions of psychoanalysis that appear in the *Messenger,* the language of psychoanalysis structured the debates that were taking place between and within black political, social, and cultural factions, including the NAACP (National Association for the Advancement of Colored People), the UNIA (Universal Negro Improvement Association), and the black press. Essentially, Calvin supplants a Eurocentric psychoanalytic paradigm not to create a counterdiscourse, since there is no direct appropriation of specific conceptual frameworks, but rather to construct a metadiscourse to formulate a broader, more in-depth perspective of black personality. The remaining subjects of Calvin's studies concern the UNIA, the Ku Klux Klan, the *Crisis* magazine, and the *New York News,* and he critiques everyone from Marcus Garvey to W. E. B Du Bois to James Weldon Johnson. Though Calvin's version of psychoanalysis coincides with the mainstream appropriation of Freud, who was frequently misinterpreted and misunderstood, his analyses appear more purposeful than a merely innocent or "superficially enthusiastic" appropriation of Freudian ideas (Hoffman 67). Calvin attempted to reshape editorial and journalistic discourse not by engaging a particular methodology or vocabulary but simply by taking seriously the quality and character of "depth." Calvin was the first to engage psychoanalysis in the *Messenger,* and he did so in order to distinguish the periodical as an authoritarian, intellectual publication that examined the interior of racial dynamics. According to Calvin, the magazine provided its readership with insightful accounts of the persons and institutions that threatened its push for social equality. In Calvin's view, psychoanalysis was analogous to the depth of personality, which is a concept that took Freud as its inspiration rather than as its model.[5]

The Psychoanalysis of Racism: William Pickens and the Racial Unconscious

In July 1923, William Pickens published his own psychoanalytic essay in the *Messenger,* which drew directly on a series of Freudian conceptualizations of repression in order to revise Freud's narrative of primitivity. Pickens's refashioning of the paradigms of repression and primitivity suggested that in the recesses of our historical memory resides a space that recalls intimacy between the races. Pickens's essay opens with the edict that "psychoanalysis explains human behavior by the great Unconscious mind. Individual idiosyncrasies, group psychology, 'race questions' are cleared up by this science" ("Color and Camouflage" 773). The primary argument that Pickens attempts to resolve through psychoanalytic application is that whites maintain natural affections toward African Americans that are repressed within the recesses of the Unconscious as a way for them to preserve and secure a sense of identity within a collective. Pickens describes the "Censor" as a psychic mechanism that keeps "many awful 'taboos'" from "coming out of the Unconscious into the Conscious," and it is because of this Censor that friendly interactions between whites and blacks are effectively locked in a "vast storehouse" that holds "all the experiences and impulses of the individual and perhaps of the ancestral race or races to which he belongs" (773). According to Pickens, whites had repressed their historical memory of amity with blacks, and he insists that they work to free themselves from repression and give themselves over to the kind attitudes toward blacks to which they are "naturally" inclined. Pickens believed that psychoanalysis could explain the psychology of racism, specifically the white repression that encourages racist practices against black Americans. In his formulation, "American white people, through their false and unnatural association with black Americans for so many years have their *Unconscious* stored full of repressed desires and feelings respecting people of color" (773–74). Pickens describes the Unconscious as the space where all of our "forbidden desires and repressed emotions" are kept from the Conscious by a Censor that acts as a barrier between our conscious and unconscious emotions. This Censor, according to Pickens, should act as "a guardian or watch-dog" but does not always function properly because if persons are "half-asleep, very tired, drunk, doped, or otherwise 'off [their] nut'" they then have the potential to become "peculiar, queer, idiotic, [or] crazy—according to the temporary or permanent degree of weakness or of relaxation of the Censor." The crux of Pickens's argument is that because white Americans have despised blacks for such a long period of time, when their Censor breaks down there is sometimes a "'gushing over' toward color, when any thing or situation presents itself which the white individual can consciously (and more or less conscientiously) consider 'good reason' or an 'exception' for breaking away from the soul-enslaving custom" (774). Such analysis of the white psyche is a somewhat strange application of psychoanalysis, but it registers as an early attempt to revise the science of the mind so that it might serve as an explanation for the tense division between the races. His claim that whites have to work consciously to keep their desire, kindness, and natural affections toward blacks repressed within the recesses of the Unconscious provides a provocative, if not somewhat specious, explication of racist practices.

To support his theories, Pickens cites two primary examples: one of a black woman who purchased "a black head of hair, of the Asiatic kind" to wear as a wig and another of a black man who grew his hair long and straightened it like "the hair of the Amerindian" (774). Pickens makes a special point of noting that both persons were very "dark-brown and heavy-featured" but that the artificial means by which they used to distinguish themselves from other black Americans played directly into the "color psychosis" of white Americans. For Pickens, these examples illustrate that "[whites] are willing to accept blacks, providing the situation is sufficiently camouflaged to allow the Censor to feel that the accepted black is not exactly of the black people whom the individual and his ancestors have been for so many years fighting and repressing, in the country and in their Consciousness." But he also explores how whites respond to people of African descent who are not perceptively black: "an African Negro girl, under the guise of being a 'Hindu Princess,' won in London the honor of being voted 'one of the few most beautiful women of the world': colored girls, under Pacific-Ocean-sounding names, are holding jobs as 'Hawaiian beauties' in some of the swell tea gardens of New York City." He concludes with the final question, "How long can this repression of nature be supported?"(774). Pickens surmises that a return to the "Unconscious naturalness" of the past is necessary in order to mend the relationship between the races and especially necessary to end racial violence, particularly lynching.

Pickens's formulation is noteworthy in that it blends the basic paradigmatic structure of Freud's uncanny (*unheimlich*) and theory of repression with hints of Jung's "collective unconscious," yet revises these concepts to create a psychoanalytic collage applicable to the racial politics of the *Messenger*. This mélange of Freud and Jung was not uncommon, particularly in the 1920s, when "to many outsiders Freud was merely the first among equals" and the "'new' psychoanalytic psychology of the 1920s often was an eclectic mix of Adler, Jung, and Freud" (Hale 28). Freud's conception of the uncanny signals the return of the familiar, which manifests as a product of past psychic phases, of our unconscious, or of earlier primitive experiences residing in our historical memory. Freud explains, "It seems as if each one of us has been through a phase of individual development corresponding to this animistic stage in primitive men, that none of us has passed through it without preserving certain residues and traces of it which are still capable of manifesting themselves, and that everything which now strikes us as 'uncanny' fulfils the condition of touching those residues of animistic mental activity within us and bringing them to expression" ("Uncanny" 240–41). Similarly, Pickens's references to the group psychology of whites with respect to their ill treatment of blacks would suggest that he was at least familiar with, if not in dialogue with, Jung's notion of the collective unconscious. In Jung's analysis, archetypal paradigms slumber in our personalities and can emerge at any time and in multiple variations depending on our cultural environments. Drawing on Freud's and Jung's formulations, Pickens intimates that psychologies are precoded, and that one's environment determines the extent to which he or she will repress historical memories. Pickens's essay demonstrates the extent to which African Americans were responding to and reinterpreting Freudian claims about the nature of repression, recapitulating those theories to think about relations between whites and African Americans.

Pickens's analysis, while it is overmotivated by his desire for racial harmony, effectively turns a Freudian paradigm on its head. Freud's 1916 "Resistance and Repression" lecture explains the nature of repression using a spatial analogy:

> Let us therefore compare the system of the unconscious to a large entrance hall, in which the mental impulses jostle one another like separate individuals. Adjoining this entrance hall there is a second, narrower room—a kind of drawing room—in which consciousness, too, resides. But on the threshold between these two rooms a watchman performs his function: he examines the different mental impulses, acts as a *censor*, and will not admit them into the drawing room of they displease him. . . . The impulses in the entrance hall of the unconscious are out of sight of the conscious, which is in the other room; to begin with they must remain unconscious. If they have already pushed their

> way forward to the threshold and have been turned back by the watchman, then they are inadmissible to the consciousness; we speak of them as repressed. . . . We are therefore justified in calling this second room the system of the preconscious. (*Complete Introductory Lectures* 295–96, my emphasis)

I have quoted at length to provide a sense of the extent to which Pickens explicitly draws on Freudian analyses. In Freud's conception, when the watchman happens to turn away from his duties, the final result is either condensation, in which "multiple dream-thoughts are combined and amalgamated into a single element of the manifest dream," or displacement, in which "the affect (emotions) associated with threatening impulses are transferred elsewhere (displaced)" (295–96). For Freud, this displacement generally takes the form of perversion or neurosis. In his July 1923 article Pickens appropriates this model and exchanges Freud's sexualized paradigm with a racialized one. Freud's "watchman" becomes Pickens's "watch-dog." For Freud, our repressed sexual desires manifest while we are in a dream state. For Pickens, more primitive desires emerge, so "we dream of . . . many things which only our cave-ancestors or the hairy ancestors of our cave ancestors would do consciously" (773). The preconscious, in Freudian terms, is revised in Pickens's essay to suggest that "white people are human; and the individuals, or his ancestors, may have deeply desired, from time to time, to have normal relations with various colored individuals whom they met up with: to be kind or affectionate, to talk normally to, or to have more intimate associations with. Custom and caste and fear caused most of these desires to go unexpressed and to be instantly repressed and clapped down by the awful Censor into the sub-cellar of the Unconscious" (774). Pickens effectively racializes Freud's theory of repression to suggest that segregation and racism are, among other things, psychologically damaging to the individual and to the larger culture. Whites have repressed natural inclinations to be "kind or affectionate" toward blacks and thus displaced these sentiments with abnormal behaviors, such as mob violence and lynching.

Building a Mulatto Nation and the Neurosis of Marcus Garvey

Pickens's narrative of repressed racial harmony occupies an important space within the *Messenger*'s discourse of interracialism. The magazine was intent on advancing the project of interracialism and turned to psychoanalytic modes as a way to affirm this mission. In this section I explore the *Messenger*'s explicit call for a mulatto nation by examining a number of the magazine's editorials that advocate intermarriage as a viable solution to the country's racial and social crises. However, the *Messenger* not only promoted interracialism but also criticized political leaders who argued against the call for better social relations between blacks and whites. The magazine led a vicious campaign against Marcus Garvey, who was vehemently against racial intermingling and led the cause for repatriation rather than social reformation. But the magazine did more than critique Garvey's political program; it called into question his psychic stability. As such, I suggest that underlying the *Messenger*'s interracial program and its subsequent vilification of Marcus Garvey was the notion that racial intermixture was inextricably linked to psychological depth, and that those who were less "mixed" possessed a greater propensity for insanity.

Three years prior to the publication of Pickens's essay, the "Editors" published an article titled "The New Negro—Who Is He?" (August 1920). The article appropriates Locke's and Du Bois's conception of the new Negro, refers implicitly to Locke and Du Bois as characteristic of the "petit bourgeoisie," and reformulates this figure within the context of socialist ideology and racial intermarriage: "[The New Negro] insists that a society which is based upon justice can only be a society composed of social equals. He insists upon identity of social treatment. *With respect to intermarriage, he maintains that it is the only logical, sound, and correct aim for the Negro to entertain.* He realizes that the acceptance of laws against intermarriage is tantamount to the acceptance of the stigma of inferiority. Besides, laws against intermarriage expose Negro women to sexual exploitation, and deprive their offspring by white men of the right to inherit the property of their father" (74, my emphasis). The editors of the magazine believed that exploding the boundaries of intimacy between blacks and whites would produce a space of open relations on institutional, economic, and social fronts. Such emphasis on interracial marriage directly opposed Garvey's black separatist movement. It also differed from Du Bois's idealized vision of intraracial breeding among the black elite. As Daylanne English argues, "from 1910 to 1934, the *Crisis* advocated a kind of intraracial family planning. . . . . By cataloging and photographing the accomplishments of African Americans, the *Crisis* documented the nonexceptionality, as well as the expansion, of modern black middle-class urbanity" (45). Contrary to Garvey's and Du Bois's philosophies, the *Messenger*'s program of racial blending would eventuate the gradual dissolution of both the black and white races.

This dissolution is anticipated in Archibald Grimké's essay, "Inter-Mixture and Inter-Marriage," which appeared in the *Messenger*'s August 1924 issue. The essay critiques a ruling by Virginia's General Assembly that made it "unlawful for a white person to marry outside his or her own race—i.e. he or she must marry a person with no trace of any but Caucasian blood, or not with more than one-sixteenth of American Indian blood" (260). Grimké takes issue with the law's distance from the more prevalent social reality, which he defined as "illicit intercourse between the races," specifically the "lust of white men for colored women out of wedlock" (263). For Grimké, intermarriage was not the social ill in need of reform, and like the editors' article concerning the New Negro, marriage was the only way to legitimate existing intimate relations between blacks and whites. To encourage mixed-race unions as a strategy for social equality was a unique argument but one that surfaced in every strain of the magazine's social and political outlook.

Schuyler's most apparent homage to interracialism was the radical transformation of the magazine's cover, which shifted from hostile, vivid images of the range of American injustices (figure 2) to frequent representations of fashionable, racially ambiguous women (figures 3 and 4).[6] The mulatto body served as the icon for the *Messenger*'s interracial desires acting, as Cherene Sherrard-Johnson argues, "as a figure of mediation between the binary opposition of black and white, male and female, privilege and subjugation" (864). These visually stunning women debunked the racial eugenics myth that touted the innate inferiority of interracial persons. The covers of the magazine visually reflected the *Messenger*'s increasingly interracial emphasis and also a sign of its succumbing to the forces of mainstream American popular culture. Given the drastic changes in the publication, it is obvious that the *Messenger* was interested in attracting a larger female readership. In popular white magazines in the 1920s, especially women's periodicals such as the *Ladies Home Journal* and *McClure's,* black women were still portrayed as mammies and domestics. However, that picture did not coincide with the advent of the New Negro Woman, nor did it reflect the desires of a community whose overriding goal was social and economic progress. The decision to place women—particularly multiracial women—on the cover of the *Messenger* is relevant to the magazine's favorable and rather sudden inclusion of psychoanalytic themes on its pages for a number of reasons: "Women—long signified by American culture as bearers of fashion—were deployed during the 1920s to help make psychoanalysis and the class identity and self-preoccupation it represented as 'inner' seem chic" (Pfister 172). The women on the cover reflected the magazine's (and Schuyler's) mission to blur the boundary of the color line, and they also represented an attempt

Figure 2. Peace on earth cover. (*Messenger,* December 1923)

to attract more women to its pages. As such, the magazine would have to feature articles that appealed to a female readership, and the rise of articles about psychoanalysis in the mid-1920s was largely due to the interest it held for women.

Featuring women on the *Messenger* covers may be interpreted as an attempt by the publication to attract an audience interested in the development of what Joel Pfister refers to as a "psychological identity" ("Glamorizing" 167).[7] Tropes of "self help" and female empowerment were dimensions of the "science" of popular psychoanalytic discourses that had a mass appeal to all women but particularly to black women who contested the limits of New

Figure 3. The first *Messenger* cover girl. (*Messenger,* March 1924)

Negro womanhood.[8] The *Messenger* retained its socialist agenda throughout Schuyler's tenure as editor, but his gestures toward the furtherance of black capitalism gave the magazine a schizophrenic character. Nonetheless, with the increased attention to dominant black middle-class concerns—specifically, interest in the New Negro and the New Negro Woman—came a discernable interest in a new psychology.

Schuyler and A. Philip Randolph undoubtedly drew upon, or were at least familiar with, the ways in which mainstream periodicals such as the *Masses* magazine experienced a high degree of success due to their attention to the vogue science of psychoanalysis. The *Masses* was a mainstream socialist

Figure 4. The second *Messenger* cover girl. (*Messenger,* May 1924)

publication that featured notable artists and race leaders, including Sherwood Anderson, Hubert Harrison, Mabel Dodge, Carl Sandburg, and Upton Sinclair. The magazine's influence on the literary and journalistic circles of New York was significant. In addition to establishing and advancing the careers of major writers, the *Masses* was one of the many little magazines of the modernist period responsible for the popularization of psychoanalytic thought in the American public sphere. Psychoanalytic topics were especially prevalent in magazines in 1915, reaching its height of popularity in the early 1920s. One of the major contributors and the later coeditor of the *Masses,* Floyd Dell, was an enthusiastic supporter of psychoanalysis, calling Jung "'the clearest, sanest, and wisest' of all the psychoanalysts" (quoted in

Pfister, "Glamorizing" 62). Dell "seemed explicitly to promote psychoanalytic language as a script for new everyday rituals of middle- and upper-class social interaction and identification" (171). If the interracial imperatives of the *Messenger* were out of line with black popular thought outlined in other major African American periodicals, its engagement with psychoanalysis was certainly in lockstep with popular culture of the 1920s. The *Messenger* and the *Masses* were both driven by socialist ideologies, but the *Messenger*'s initial publication materialized in the waning days of the *Masses* and apparently sought to address that periodical's failure to tackle "problems of ethnic and racial identities within a class-defined movement" (Morrison 169). Though, as Ann Douglas has noted, Freud was insistent that "American versions of psychoanalysis were to the Viennese original what mass culture was to elite art, and he was a bitter enemy of the democratic tendencies endemic in the mass arts that America in general and New York in particular hosted" (127), Freudian ideas were central to emerging formulations of the multivalent, individual self. Individual subjectivity was the hallmark of modernity, and the *Messenger* under Schuyler's leadership gave voice to this modernist moment though the lens of African American experience. But the *Messenger*'s appropriation, vulgarization, or Signification of psychoanalysis was employed in part to disrupt dominant cultural notions of racial purity and also to further distance itself from the black nationalist spirit that was at the heart of the political programs of figures like Marcus Garvey.

Robert Bagnall's scathing critique "The Madness of Marcus Garvey" appeared in the *Messenger*'s February 1923 issue. Bagnall was a frequent contributor to the *Messenger* and served as the NAACP director of branches. His ideology concerning race relations was, like that of his *Messenger* colleagues, ardently integrationist. His increasingly socialist leanings placed him at odds with Du Bois, Walter White, and the staff at the NAACP, with the exception of William Pickens, who served as field secretary of the NAACP at the time. Bagnall's and Pickens's relationship with the NAACP became even more fraught as the organization came to rely heavily on financial support from whites and middle-class blacks while doing little to improve the situations of the lower and working classes. The *Messenger*'s program of racial amalgamation emerged first and foremost in its verbal blasting of racial separatism. The rivalry between Garvey and the editorial staff of the *Messenger* was bitter, and Garvey was undoubtedly singled out by the *Messenger* staff because he was vehemently against the notion of interracialism, at one point referring to Julia P. Coleman, president of Hair-Vim Chemical Company, as "a hair straightener and face bleacher," and claiming that George Harris, editor of the

New York News, "maintained a Blue Vein Society church" (quoted in Avery 70). Although the denigration of Garvey came in many forms, there was a focused attempt to discredit Garvey by attacking his psychical character. An even more compelling rationale for the *Messenger*'s smear campaign against Garvey was that while the *Messenger* reached over twenty thousand readers monthly, Garvey was in the process of orchestrating the largest mass movement in African American history. Unlike the editors of the *Messenger,* who at one point printed that intermarriage was the "only logical, sound, and correct aim" ("New Negro" 74) for Negroes, Garvey's message was quite the opposite: "Unfortunately there is a disposition on the part of a certain element of our people in America, the West Indies and Africa, to hold themselves upon the 'better class' or 'privileged' group on the caste of color" (quoted in Kornweibel 152). Garvey was as intent on condemning those who sought to discredit his plan for black repatriation to Africa as the *Messenger*'s contributors were in discouraging those who might follow him. The *Messenger*'s strategy to disempower Garvey included asserting his complicity with the Ku Klux Klan and, in Bagnall's case, accusing the leader of the UNIA of suffering from "paranoia." Bagnall diagnoses what he perceives as Garvey's madness based upon the "characteristic symptoms of this form of insanity" that he finds in Garvey's character. He explains:

> It is hard to understand many of the man's actions except on the assumption that he is insane—that he is a paranoiac. Let us examine the symptoms of paranoia and see how Garvey manifests them. A paranoiac is afflicted with *Egomania.* His world is interpreted in terms of self. The first person of the personal pronoun is ever on his lips. One hears from him a succession of *I, Me.* The world revolves around *him.* Read the *Negro World.* See how its pages are thick with the words *"I, Marcus Garvey"* in every issue. See the self-laudation and egoism manifested there. Listen to Marcus Garvey as he speaks. Then you will think that the description I gave above of a paranoiac is one of Garvey. No sane man would be so gross in self-laudation as Garvey. A paranoiac has delusions of grandeur. He thinks himself great. ("Madness" 638, original emphasis)

Bagnall identifies various features that characterize a paranoiac and applies them to Garvey, imploring the audience to "examine the symptoms of paranoia and see how Garvey manifests them" (638). While both Bagnall and Calvin were both clearly interested in exploring the limits of psychoanalysis, they also shared a disdain for Marcus Garvey. Bagnall was among eight prominent African Americans, including Chandler Owen, A. Philip Randolph, and Robert Abbott, who petitioned the U.S. attorney general to demand Garvey's deportation. There was no shortage of methods to denounce Garvey's black separatist program, but to do so through the invocation of the psyche was a new twist on an old theme. "Paranoia," in Freudian terms, occurs when the ego exists only for the subject and the subject is unable to distinguish reality from the workings of the imagination. What Bagnall describes as a paranoiac emerges more accurately in Freudian terminology as a narcissist. Comparing Garvey with Don Quixote, Bagnall addresses the lure of the "madman" (638), referring to Freud's analysis of "the impressions left behind by the personalities of great leaders—men of overwhelming force of mind or men in whom one of the human impulsions had found its strongest and purest, and therefore often its most one-sided, expression" (Freud, *Civilization* 141).

An even more striking aspect of Bagnall's analysis comes in his physical description of Garvey as "a Jamaican Negro of unmixed stock, squat, stocky, fat and sleek, with protruding jaws, and heavy jowls, small bright pig-like eyes and rather bull-dog like face" (638). Along with the rather curious racist inscriptions Bagnall employs in his disparagement of Garvey is the condemnation that he is of "unmixed stock" and hence racially "pure." Bagnall links Garvey's psychological inferiority to a question of blood, inverting the racial eugenicist arguments that held that such racial amalgamation would lead to the degeneration of the white race.

During this period, such arguments against racial intermixing were made infamous by Virginia's State Registrar of Vital Statistics W. A. Plecker. Plecker was adamantly opposed to racial intermarriage and presented his case at numerous speaking engagements and in contributions to *Eugenics: A Journal for Race Betterment.* In "Race Mixture and the Next Census," Plecker claims that

> the great American problem is the gradual amalgamation, now in progress, of the various and widely differing races which occupy our land. . . . All who have given any serious consideration to this question, uninfluenced by sentimentality or self-interest, are compelled to admit that the intermixture of races as diverse as the white and the Negro certainly injures or destroys the more specialized qualities of the white race. This is done without passing over to the mongrels' qualities which, when combined with even the best, and the best only, of the Negro, would produce a result to compensate for the loss. . . . With the races in as close contact as they are now, the prevention of extra-marital intermixture is practically impossible. This is rendered more difficult with the present indifference of the general public upon this question,

> together with disregard for individual responsibility. The only hope, therefore, of slowing up the process of amalgamation is to prevent intermarriage, endeavoring at the same time to create a wholesome nation-wide sentiment in the minds of young men as to the seriousness of illegitimate racial mixture of any kind. (3)

By reversing the commonly held historical myth that the mixing of the races led to the decline of civilization, the *Messenger* sought to revise the discourse of eugenics and history. But what is most remarkable in Bagnall's essay is that Garvey's lack of racial intermixture contributes to his failing psychological state. Bagnall's article was the first to use a psychoanalytic concept as a method for advancing an agenda of racial amalgamation.

He continues this line of thought in "Psychoanalysis of Ku Kluxism" in the August 1923 issue. In this article, Bagnall offers a cautionary tale of the Ku Klux Klan's rise as a potential sign of the decline of the nation. Bagnall refers to the Klan's primal urge for aggression, noting that "because man is only a veneered savage this savage spirit will persist in him" (789). The Klansmen's insistence on black, Catholic, and Jewish inferiority, Bagnall argues, is the result of their inability to reconcile themselves with the rapidity of social, cultural, and technological progress. Therefore, they resort to the distortion of "science, history, literature, politics, business, and industry" as a way to maintain the status quo. But the anxiety that results in their failure to do so (or rather their perceived failure) manifests itself in violent acts against groups they label as inferior. Bagnall writes that when a white child becomes an adult, "he commits every kind of intolerance, cruelty, and injustice, indulging in savage orgies of mobbism, burnings at the stake, and lynching" (790). Again, Bagnall links racial separatism, whether in the form of black nationalism or white hegemony, to the decline of civilization, noting that "Fascists, our Black Hundreds, our White Guards, our Right Royal Legion, and our Ku Klux Klan" are "all in one spirit" (789). Bagnall makes no distinction between white supremacist groups and black nationalist organizations. He refers to "the three false gods of civilization" as "race pride or race arrogance," "patriotism or nationalism," and "class pride or caste pride" (789). Not only is racial separatism the mark of decline but it is also, for Bagnall, a historical fantasy: "No pure race exists except in myth. Every race has absorbed the blood of other races. The 70,000 black slaves that disappeared in Rome, absorbed into the Latin race, form no isolated example. South Europeans and South Americans with a tinge of Negro blood, and Negroids who have crossed the line, have so intermingled their blood with

American whites until it is impossible for any number of them to absolutely know that they have no Negro blood. . . . The only real race, as Firot says, is the human race, and race pride, or arrogance, is madness" (790). Bagnall does not refer to a specific psychoanalytic concept to build his personality profile of the Ku Klux Klan, as this article is more concerned with debunking the myth of racial purity. Yet as in his critique of Garvey, Bagnall challenges the mental stability of those involved with the Klan or any separatist or nationalist group. Bagnall insists that it is madness for the Klan or any of the other organizations he mentions to insist upon purity since none has existed in the historical memory of the United States.

The *Messenger*'s program of racial amalgamation and its engagement with psychoanalytic thought to endorse this idea was unique to the cultural and political moment of the Harlem Renaissance, which was generally characterized by its vigorous artistic campaign to exemplify a Negro consciousness, if only to satiate the public appetite for all things black. However, writers like Pickens and Bagnall not only were suspicious of the concept of a Negro consciousness but also had created their own historical narratives in which a distinctively Negro consciousness could never exist. They both found in Freudian ideas of repression a framework in which they could construct an historical lineage of miscegenation dating back to the onset of civilization. Psychoanalytic language gave these writers an authenticated and authoritative platform from which to espouse their beliefs and an effective paradigm that would justify their unwavering commitment to the idea of interracialism. The *Messenger* could easily rationalize its call for interracial worker solidarity, but to suggest more intimate ties between the races necessitated a psychological framework. Its appropriation of Freudian conceptualizations of repression was particularly savvy, given that at the heart of psychoanalytic discourse in the 1920s was the desire to release primal urges and stave off neurosis, which placed whites in a complicated bind: to free themselves from repression and potentially transgress the color line or to maintain a repressed subconscious and potentially suffer the consequences of hysteria. But the underlying narrative of all the *Messenger*'s psychoanalytic engagements is an expressed desire for all people, black and white, to disavow the superficialities of epidermal difference and embrace a deeper psychological essence that was once universal.

2

The Anxiety of Birth in Nella Larsen's *Quicksand*

In November 1934, writer and diarist Anaïs Nin took her therapist and lover, Otto Rank, to Harlem for the first time since his arrival to the United States in 1924. The free-spirited Nin frequently traveled to Harlem, where she witnessed "half white people, half black, beautiful women, well-dressed men, and jazz" (32). The "intoxicating and magnificent" scene was Nin's prescription for Rank, who she thought was in need of time away from "people trapped in tragedies"—his patients (8). She recalls the experience in her diary: "Rank could not forget Harlem. He was eager to return to it. He could hardly wait to come to the end of his hard day's work. He said: 'I am tempted to prescribe it to my patients. Go to Harlem!'" (6).

Though Rank never mentions the black subject in his own work, his response to the Harlem scene intimates that, like Nin, he believed that "negroes are natural and possess the secret of joy. That is why they can endure the suffering inflicted upon them. The world maltreats them, but among themselves they are deeply alive, physically and emotionally" (Nin 37). Though Rank was apparently oblivious to the Harlem scene in the 1920s and 1930s, he appealed to a number of Renaissance artists in the 1920s and 1930s because he theorized that artists were able to find relief from the death drive by immortalizing himself themselves in the creation of their works.[1] In his 1929 Yale lecture, "The Psychological Approach to Personal Problems," Rank underscores his differences with Freud: "With Freud, the driving force, and kind of impulsion in the individual, is biological. He conceives it only biologically, which means even in its highest sense, a kind of *procreative* impulse, but not a real creative driving force, of which I think personality consists." (Rank, *Psychology of*

Difference 241, original emphasis) Among those artists fascinated by Rank's concepts was Nella Larsen. Thadious Davis places Larsen's interest in Rank in context, noting that "suffused throughout [Larsen's novels] are the 'new' ideas about human psychology that Larsen had absorbed from her reading of popularized Sigmund Freud and Otto Rank" (310). Rank was fascinated by artistic personalities because he was interested in "placing the artist in the act of creation at the center of his theories of psychoanalysis [and] called attention to the will to create one's personality as more basic than sexual instinct" (Davis 310). That Larsen would be struck by Rank's theories about the artist was not surprising, given Larsen's knowledge of "then-popular notions of inferiority complexes, doubles, and phallic symbols, as well as of psychological interpretations of childhood and its impact on the adult" (Davis 310). Larsen fully exercises her erudition in psychoanalytic thought in her attention to the concepts of repression, psychological doubles, and anxiety in *Passing*, her 1929 novel. Likewise, in *Quicksand* (1928), she also reveals her investment in the neurotic character. Though Davis references Rank's potential impact on Larsen, his theory of birth trauma—which is constituted by the paradoxical anxiety of desiring both individuality and communal belonging, religious ardor, artistic fulfillment, and the anxiety of reproduction—warrants a detailed examination.

At a pivotal moment in the text, the protagonist Helga Crane, a biracial woman whose father has abandoned the family and whose mother has died early in Helga's life, ponders, "What was the matter with her? Was there, without her knowing it, some peculiar lack in her?" (81). Helga's ruminations on her persistent dissatisfaction are the very questions that have puzzled Larsen's critics. Amid the wealth of *Quicksand* analyses, many have sought to understand the psychoanalytic impulses behind Larsen's text and to discern the root cause of Helga's unidentifiable "lack." This lack has been characterized as a result of "narcissistic personality disorder" (B. Johnson 225), "masochistic self-effacement" as a result of the internalization of her parents' racist attitudes (Tate, *Psychoanalysis* 121), and the "repercussions of a history of primitivist assumptions operating in medical, artistic, and popular discourse that work to turn the black female body into a fetish, a grotesque convergence of pathology and hyperbolic, animalistic sexuality" (Defalco 19).[2]

However, none of these analyses provides a comprehensive rationale for the myriad of psychological inconsistencies suffered by the protagonist, and none considers Rank's conceptual framework of "birth trauma" as instructive to an interpretation of *Quicksand,* despite Rank's popularity among Carl Van Vechten's intellectual circles in the 1920s. Helga Crane follows, in a rather paradigmatic fashion, the various processes that Rank theorizes the subject undergoes in order to relieve himself or herself from the anxiety of birth, specifically "symbolic adaptation," "religious sublimation," "artistic idealization," "sexual gratification," and "neurotic reproduction."[3] This chapter examines how Rank's theories provide compelling answers to many of *Quicksand*'s puzzling questions, specifically that of the nature of Helga Crane's ""peculiar lack," and points to one of the ways in which Larsen may have considered Rank useful in her articulation of the psychological ambivalence of the biracial subject while also complicating his formulations.

Larsen's destabilization of race and sexuality in *Quicksand* coincides with the ways that writers exploited psychoanalytic paradigms to question and challenge restrictive social norms and explain social dynamics. Most importantly, psychoanalysis provided a model for writers like Larsen to destabilize static categories of race and sexuality. Though I do not intend to conflate the author with her protagonist, the autobiographical impulses in *Quicksand* are evident and certainly suggest that literature gave Larsen the space to explore the psychical underpinnings of racialized and gendered dynamics both within and outside a U.S. context as well as her own complex subjectivity.

Quicksand opens with Helga Crane reposing in her room at Naxos, an institution she describes as a "show place in the black belt, exemplification of the white man's magnanimity, refutation of the black man's inefficiency" (4), contemplating her exit strategy. At Naxos, Helga is known as a loner, describing herself as the "despised mulatto" whose longing for "beauty" and "nice things" evoke sentiments of pity and condemnation among her peers (6). Helga's feelings of isolation are not solely the product of her frustration with Naxos but are also the result of her estrangement from her family.[4] Having been deserted by Helga's West Indian father, Helga's white mother married a white man and had additional children, leaving Helga as the sole black child. Helga was apparently forced to endure her family's racism as a child and has ended up at Naxos in an effort to become part of a community with her "own" people. There, Helga invites further disdain by her peers because she refuses to become "naturalized" to the Naxos regime. The intense feelings of loneliness and unhappiness have produced Helga's "lack somewhere," which she had initially believed to be "a lack of understanding on the part of the community." She has come to perceive, however, "that the fault had been partly hers" (7). Naxos reflects, for Helga, the stifled nature of African American power and beauty functioning like a "big knife with cruelly sharp edges ruthlessly cutting all to a pattern, the white man's pattern" (4). Helga confronts the principal, Dr. Anderson, to inform him of her departure and is further enraged at his imploring her to stay based on his erroneous supposition that she maintains "tendencies inherited from good stock" (21). Her departure from Naxos signals the first of a series of journeys Helga embarks upon in order to locate a space of belonging. Helga returns home to Chicago, where she finds that her uncle Peter Nilssen, a white man, has married a white woman who refuses to acknowledge their black niece. After departing Chicago for New York, Helga befriends Anne Grey, only to realize that Anne's insular community of "snobbish black folk," her obsession with the rhetoric of racial uplift, and her almost pathological hatred for whites fail to allow Helga the freedom of experience and personality she desires (46). An unexpected letter from Uncle Peter accompanied by a sizeable check enables Helga to leave New York, where "the mere sight of the serene tan and brown faces about her stung like a personal insult" (53). Taking Uncle Peter's advice, Helga leaves for Copenhagen to visit and perhaps permanently reside with her aunt Katrina Dahl.

Upon her arrival in Denmark, her aunt and uncle begin the process of transforming Helga from a "prim American maiden" into a "queer dark creature" (69). Eventually, Helga fatigues of this latest performance as an exotic primitive and finds herself homesick for Negroes. She decides to return to New York, where she finds Dr. Anderson married to her former friend, Anne Grey. After a failed attempt to have an affair with Dr. Anderson, Helga experiences a psychological break and finds refuge in a church where she is "saved" by the Reverend Pleasant Green. The novel concludes in Alabama, where Helga has married the reverend and given birth to their five children. Such is the quicksand to which she succumbs: over the course of the novel Helga attempts to locate a community to which she can belong, and she will only be satisfied in one that will recognize and validate her interracial identity. However, each social environment she inhabits appears more invested in reifying Helga's blackness than in acknowledging her complex interracial and intercultural subjectivity.[5]

Moreover, the common element in this diverse sets of relations is that they work to instantiate particular assumptions about Helga's race and gender. Though mainstream psychoanalytic culture in the 1920s was not especially mindful of the multiracial subject, it did provide liberating possibilities, as well as a paradigm and vocabulary, for rearticulating the structures by which subjects are confined. Larsen's portrayal of Helga as a capricious body that moves through various social spaces intimates a larger desire to invent a new language that expresses a new way of being. Such a desire is consistent with the motivation of many writers during the 1920s, for whom psychoanalysis provided an innovative approach to articulate their interior selves. The ubiquity of the racial one-drop rule, as well as Helga's perceived rejection by and separation from her white mother, leaves her with little choice but to assume a singular black identity, which drives her instability and unhappiness. Though Helga Crane embarks upon a series of self-defeating journeys in order to locate a racial utopia, she ultimately fails. Helga's desire to fulfill her racial lack is fueled not only by the search for a surrogate father, as some critics have claimed, but also by the need to find relief from the separation she experienced from her mother. George Hutchinson has observed that analyses of *Quicksand* tend to portray "biracial subjectivity . . . [as] inherently neurotic, curable only by purging a 'whiteness' within" ("Subject to Disappearance" 178). Conversely, I read Helga's lack as an attempt to reclaim "whiteness" as embodied by the absent mother and to resolve the anxiety she experiences as the result of her mother's rejection.

This chapter examines Larsen's construction in *Quicksand* of a complexly psychological character, arguing that she does so in dialogue with the multiple discourses of gender, class, race, and sexuality. In recounting the circumstances of her illegitimate birth, Helga Crane realizes that "she had outraged her own pride, and she had terribly wronged her mother by insidious implication. Why? Her thoughts lingered with her mother, long dead. . . . Her daughter hoped she had been happy, happy beyond most human creatures, in the little time it had lasted, the little time before the gay suave scoundrel, Helga's father, had left her" (23). Helga's white mother emerges as the missing element that could quell her anxiety and discontent. Such a reading is not inconsistent with Hutchinson's recent biography of Larsen, whom Helga Crane largely mirrors. Hutchinson claims that although Larsen's mother readily acknowledged her existence to friends and neighbors, her stepfather "had erased Nella from the family, an act of denial indicating both shame about his 'colored' stepdaughter and the expectation that she would never return" (67).

Maternally Fixated: Otto Rank, Freud, and the Trauma of Birth

Otto Rank is perhaps best known as Sigmund Freud's most devoted student, friend, collaborator, and, eventually, dissenter.[6] The divergent paths Rank and Freud would ultimately take may have stemmed from their different educational backgrounds: Freud was primarily a medical scientist and Rank was well versed in philosophy, art, literature, psychology, and history. Although Freud served as Rank's mentor, Freud was also able to draw upon Rank's knowledge of the social and cultural world and integrate it within his psychoanalytic theories. Rank is credited with widening the scope of psychoanalysis from a "narrow medical technique" to a "world philosophy" (Kampf 5), and his burgeoning interest in cultural, social, and artistic spheres led him to experiment with therapeutic practices outside of traditional psychoanalytic thought and to develop a perspective on individual personality that operated outside the context of Freudian psychoanalysis.

Rank's initial visit to the United States was in May 1924, at the time that his book *The Trauma of Birth* began to gain momentum with American audiences. In the preface of that work, Rank wrote that his theories "proceeded from the consistent application of the method created by Freud, and from the doctrine based on the method" (xviii). Using Freudian analysis as the basis for his formulations, Rank attempted to provide "a general and a wider knowledge through a direct comprehension of the unconscious" (xiii). Although he conceived of his project as a complement to Freudian psychoanalysis rather than a departure from it, Rank also revealed his intent to broaden the methods initially put forth by Freud. In a February 15, 1924, letter to Freud, Rank attempted to correct any misinterpretation Freud may have found in his analysis of birth trauma. The letter was also an effort to repair the disintegrating relationship between the two men: "I hope you will not think that I want to present my work as something totally new and independent. On the contrary, I would like to stress that I can boast of a more extensive concordance with your views and an even stronger connection with them. The concept of anxiety at birth takes the first place. As I have said, not only do I find no contradiction, but rather the most perfect harmony with your theory of drives" (quoted in Lieberman 214).

Rank's insistence, however, that "the strongest resistance to the severance of the libido transference at the end of the analysis is expressed in the form of the earliest *infantile fixation on the mother*" led Freud to repudiate the student who had once been like a son (*Trauma* 4, original emphasis). In Freud's conception of the Oedipus complex, the male child enters into competition with the father, ultimately desiring to be the father, and in acting out this role makes the mother the object of his desire. Although male and female children experience the Oedipus complex differently, for both the mother is the first love object. However, Rank understood the role of the mother as the primary source of love *and* anxiety for the child—an ambivalence that commences at birth. Rank believed that the "mother image" was a "phantom of *Angst* and longing, guilt and desire, at once terrifying and thrilling" (Kramer 5, original emphasis).

Rank developed his formulation of birth trauma as a theory of anxiety, in an effort to construct a biological and psychological bridge that would explain neurotic behavior. He asserted that the traumatic experience of entering an environment wholly foreign to the child produces an anxiety that manifests itself in a fixation on the mother's womb or as a desire to return symbolically to the mother. The trauma of birth is experienced universally and is internalized in one of two ways—either in the form of neurosis or of artistic production. Rank's theory of birth trauma led to his conceptualization of psychological birth or "individuation"; he was "fundamentally concerned with individuation as a process which begins with separation from the maternal matrix" (*Trauma* 7). Thus, for the subject to overcome the anxiety of birth, he or she must work to develop an individual personality separate and distinct from that of the mother. Since the subject is unable to return to the womb physically, Rank theorized that "the calming 'therapeutic' effect of the reunion with her" would have to be fulfilled at the level of the symbolic (*Trauma* 12). The source of anxiety stems from the child's experience of having been extracted from a space that represents life. The removal from the mother's womb thus signals the certainty of death. The subject performs various symbolic acts that represent the prolonging of life, hence the artist's superior ability to confront the death drive.

Rank theorized that the trauma of birth initially establishes a pattern of anxiety for the subject and then the subject begins the course of development toward individuation, which he or she both desires and fears. It is here that Rank's formulation veers from the Freudian model, which constructs the neurotic character within a framework of sexual drives and human instinct. Rank could not reconcile himself to the idea that a person would instinctually be led throughout the course of his or her life to "abreact the fear precipitated by the birth experience" (*Trauma* 74), which is why he placed anxiety at the core of his theory of birth trauma. Because the subject is overwhelmed by being thrust into the world, the desire to return to the mother and relive oneness with the womb is crucial and repetitive. In addition, the subject's fear of maternal separation also marks a fear of death: "To be born means to be responsible for one's own separate existence and survival; and in this separateness man experiences his finiteness; he comes to know of death, to fear the loss of his hard won individuality and to perceive the connection between birth and death" (64).

The conflict that exists between birth and death can never be resolved, but it can be ameliorated by "creating something which transcends the self [e.g., giving birth], therapeutically through identification, socially and historically through the creation of culture in all its aspects—myth, art, religion, and social mores" (72). Rank's theories were of particular interest to the New York artistic community precisely because he thought the artistic mind mastered anxiety by inserting the self into a creative product that would long outlive the subject. In this way, the subject's wish for perpetuity is met through the ability to transcend the self through artistic production. Rank's therapy encouraged patients to repeat traumatic situations, "regress to the period of the Oedipal complex," then "endure [the analyst's] own unrequited Oedipal love." The therapist would remove himself as the "mirror" for the patient and, in turn, "the patient would learn to give up for good the satisfaction of his infantile libidinal cravings for new and more realistic satisfactions" (Hale 55–56). For Rank, the neurotic subject would only cease to repeat this pattern when the patient was allowed "to repeat with better success in analysis the separation from the mother. . . . The analysis finally turns out to be a belated accomplishment of the incomplete mastery of birth trauma" (*Trauma* 5).

Rank's formulation of this trauma creates a space in which to understand more fully how the mother actively shapes the ego and identity of the child. In Rank's analysis, the relationship between mother and child is considered relevant and significant outside the context of the father. The mother is constructed as the primary locus of anxiety and neurosis for the child, and the father's role does not emerge until much later in the child's psychological development, leaving the mother as the sole source of the child's primal anxiety. Rank believed that the womb was a protective space, not only from the social world but also from the father. Once the mother gives birth, the child is no longer protected and the act of delivery comes to represent abandonment or, worse, betrayal.

Nonetheless, Rank's theory offers a way to better explain Helga Crane's pattern of self-destructive behavior throughout *Quicksand,* and it provides some insight as to how the peculiar lack she experiences may stem from her fixation on a deceased, lost mother. Rank formulated the trauma of birth (the child's violent separation from the mother) as a "profound philosophical understanding of the human need for belonging—that is, uniting with something or someone larger than the self—or of creating something which transcends the self in order to ensure the perpetuity of the self" (Menaker 135). This interpretation of the mother-child relationship and its enduring consequences further elucidates the nature of Helga's tempestuous relationships with men, the peculiar lack she speaks of throughout the text, and her desire to belong to a social community. "The anxiety implicit in the process of birth itself," Rank argues, "is transformed through the emergence of consciousness from anxiety on a biological level, to psychological anxiety which is induced by all symbols of separation and aloneness. With growing consciousness, the human creature gradually acquires an awareness of time, of growth and maturation, of age, and ultimately of death" (quoted in Menaker 71). Rank concludes that all births are traumatic, to some extent, but in his explanation of neurosis the birth experience emerges as particularly brutal, so much so that the subject is indelibly marked. Helga Crane's volatile episodes, abrupt departures, and turbulent relationships underscore her relative inability to belong to any racial or social community. The fragmented nature of her biracial subjectivity, in that she experiences being born of two disparate racial groups in an era of racial segregation, is yet another relevant and powerful site of psychic dislocation that Rank never considered but that emerges as a particularly crucial challenge to one's identity. Although Rank does not imagine race, or more specifically biracialism, as a feature of the traumatic birth experience, the hostility, alienation, and denigration the mixed-race child would undergo, especially in the early twentieth century, undoubtedly qualifies as a severe experience.[7]

Claudia Tate suggests that Helga's repression and "willful refusal to love the abandoning father" serves as the root cause of her puzzling behavior throughout the text (*Psychoanalysis* 138). However, this focus on the father fails to give credence to the extent to which Helga's deceased mother contributes to her lack, which manifests itself in the form of an unresolved fixation. Helga's inability to escape her mother's image creates a symbiotic but anxiety-producing relationship between mother and daughter, which Rank suggests is only resolved "with freeing of the unconscious mother fixation" (*Psychology of Difference* 71). In this way, Helga's character formation reconciles—albeit imperfectly—Rank's theory of birth trauma with Freud's Oedipal formulation. Helga Crane's relationship (or lack thereof) with her father follows the classical Oedipal narrative, but this model fails to provide an adequate explanation of the formative mother-child role in *Quicksand*:

> That second marriage to a man of her own race, but not of her own kind—so passionately, so instinctively resented by Helga even at the trivial age of six—she now understood as a grievous necessity. Even foolish, desperate women must have food and clothing; even unloved little Negro girls must somehow be provided for. Memory, flown back to those years following the marriage, dealt her torturing stabs. Before her rose the pictures of her mother's careful management to avoid those ugly scarifying quarrels which even at this far-off time caused an uncontrollable shudder, her own childish self-effacement, the savage unkindness of her stepbrothers and sisters, and the jealous, malicious

> hatred of her mother's husband. Summers, winters, years, passing in one long, changeless stretch of aching misery of soul. Her mother's death, when Helga was fifteen. (23)

The maternal rejection Helga suffers but somehow understands fuels her desire to belong, and her repeated attempts to belong to a community contribute to her overwhelming anxiety. As expressed in the previous passage, Helga's feelings toward her mother are ambivalent at best—she is at once sympathetic to her mother's plight and resentful of her mother's rejection after she marries a white man. The extent to which these emotions and behaviors manifest themselves in Helga's subsequent interactions can best be explained in terms of her memory, which Helga claims "dealt her torturing stabs."

In Rankian psychoanalysis, "memory is symbolized in the mind and may reappear with its accompanying emotion, when there is a new reality, because its pattern, which resembles the situation of the original experience, re-evokes it. The new experience is 'real' in its own right, but it is metaphorical in relation to the original experience it resembles" (Menaker 68). Thus, the memory of Helga's maternal rejection manifests itself in all future interactions. Helga's pattern of separation can be read in terms of her attempt to belong to a social group that both recognizes and validates her individuality. Such a desire corresponds with Rank's view of human psychology as the persistent tension to live as an individual yet become part of a broader social and spiritual community.

Although Helga is rejected by her white family at every turn, her interaction with Mrs. Hayes-Rore, a noted "race woman" who employs her during the transition from Chicago to New York, vividly demonstrates the black community's investment in preserving racial boundaries and denying Helga's claims to whiteness. Mrs. Hayes-Rore altogether refuses to acknowledge Helga's white mother, pointing to another dimension of Helga's lack. Helga attempts to evade questions posed by Mrs. Hayes-Rore with regard to her family, but once Helga resigns herself to sharing the "horrid" details of her parents' acts of miscegenation and betrayal, Hayes-Rore abandons the topic, "dealing as it did with race intermingling and possible adultery," since "among black people, as among white people, it is tacitly understood that these things are not mentioned—and therefore they do not exist" (39). Mrs. Hayes-Rore's response to Helga's tale reveals her feelings toward whites and her inability to suffer Helga's company without offering sentiments of pity and denial. She further invalidates Helga's whiteness by recommending to her that she "wouldn't mention that my people were white. . . . Colored people won't understand it. . . . I'll just tell Anne that you're a friend of mine whose mother's dead. That'll place you well enough and it's all true" (41). Mrs. Hayes-Rore's decision to render Helga's mother dead in order to create the illusion of racial homogeneity further fragments Helga's fragile identity and points to the (symbolic) death of her mother as the only recourse for Helga's successful initiation into her new community.

Symbolic Formations: Copenhagen as the Motherland

Rank theorized that one strategic element subjects employ to reproduce the space of the womb is symbolic adaptation. In Rank's view, humans maintain the unique ability to cope with varying social and geographic spaces through the creation of symbols. For example, the construction of material spaces like huts is one of the ways that subjects attempt to replicate maternal space.[8] The formation of such spaces performs the symbolic function of enabling the subject to recapture the gratifying experience of the womb since, he argues, there already exists within us the "powerful tendency to re-establish the pleasurable situation just left" (*Trauma* 187). Further, Rank posits his concept of symbolic adaptation as the potential opening to "new vistas in the understanding in the development of culture: from the nursery, which is only an extension of the kangaroo's pouch . . . to the social-displacement-and-substitute-formations of such concepts as fatherland, nation, and state" (188). As such, Helga's journey to Denmark immediately following her exit from Naxos is an attempt to acquire a similar "'psychical' quality of feeling" that she enjoyed while attached to her mother (*Trauma* 187).

The element of race, especially when the race of the mother and child differs within a sociocultural context, invariably complicates any psychoanalytic formulation of the ego and identification. This is particularly the case when using Rank's analyses to understand the conflicted relationship between mother and child and the child's inability to move beyond a fixation on the mother. In the case of Helga Crane, any woman who would be able to act as a mother figure (Mrs. Nilssen, Mrs. Hayes-Rore, Fru Dahl) and thus make possible the transference necessary to detach symbolically and emotionally from the mother fails to fulfill this need for Helga because any mother figure in the text exposes or reveals some inadequacy or lack in Helga's character. Larsen forecloses the possibility for Helga to adequately establish an emotional, motherlike bond with any of these women, and within these interactions she finds that her peculiar lack is not only internal but also external and shifting. Helga's interracial subjectivity is consistently a matter of conflict and question, and because her blackness is always already assumed, Helga comes to associate the rejection by her mother as a lack. This is not to say that Helga's journey is a search for the whiteness she was denied by her refigured white family; rather, it is fundamentally a search for wholeness that would be made possible in symbolically reclaiming her mother (i.e., through transference). In this light, Larsen constructs Helga's excursion to Denmark as particularly important; it is an attempt to join herself once again to the lost mother by returning to her mother's birthplace, Copenhagen, a symbolic "motherland."

For Helga, Copenhagen brings "pleasant memories of her childhood visits there" (55), and her trip is made even more pleasant when a "man grown old in the service of the Scandinavian America [steamship] line remembered her as the little dark girl who had crossed with her mother years ago" (68). That the only pleasant memories Helga holds of her childhood are of the travel to Copenhagen indicates the extent to which she has romanticized and privileged her mother. These initial sentiments of happiness only exacerbate the stinging rejection she experiences once her mother remarried. In typical fashion, however, Helga's pattern reemerges, and the failure of her Denmark experience symbolizes yet another failed attempt to become one with her mother. Rather than leave Denmark with a renewed affection for her mother, she comes to reject that space and the whiteness it represents. In Copenhagen, Helga also has a brief affair with Axel Olsen, a famous painter. In some critiques Axel Olsen is read as the surrogate for Helga's mother, and by rejecting his marriage offer she may also be read as rejecting her mother for her perceived disloyalty. During his courtship of Helga, Olsen paints a distorted picture of Helga that adds to her growing contempt for him: "The picture—she had never quite, in spite of her deep interest in him, and her desire for his admiration and approval, forgiven Olsen for that portrait. It wasn't, she contended, herself at all, but some disgusting sensual creature with her features. Herr and Fru Dahl had not exactly liked it either, although collections, artists, and critics had been unanimous in their praise and it had been hung on the line at an annual exhibition, where it had attracted much flattering attention and many tempting offers" (89).

Olsen's distorted portrait further objectifies Helga. His misrecognition overwhelms her, especially since the permanence of the painting intensifies her Otherness. The gaze is intended to provide a semblance of wholeness or to promote the fantasy of such unity. But Olsen's gaze is the first visual representation of Helga's fragmentation, making it a product of both the real and the imaginary. Helga's excursion to Copenhagen reads as a failed attempt to recapture her whiteness and thus complete the fantasy of wholeness, which had been stripped from her by her mother, stepfather, and siblings. Kalpana

Sheshadri-Crooks offers the compelling argument that "the fantasy of encountering whiteness would be, for the subject of race, to recover the missing substance of one's being. It would be to coincide, not with a transcendental ideal, some rarefied model of bodily perfection, but with the 'gaze,' that void in the Other, a piece of the Real that could annihilate difference" (*Desiring* 59).

The journey to Denmark affords Helga the possibility of recovering the missing substance of her being, which would both close the distance between her and her biological mother and render her whole. Rather than fill the void of whiteness, however, Helga's experience in Denmark makes her fragmentation more visible. In Olsen's picture, Helga's lack or rather difference is immortalized. Helga's rejection of Olsen, Fru and Herr Dahl, and Copenhagen enacts the process that Rank theorized occurs when the female child attempts to move beyond her maternal fixation by converting "love into hate, which is the characteristic mechanism for the compulsion neurosis." The experience in Denmark produces a shift in Helga's feelings for her mother. Once she departs Denmark, Helga experiences what Rank would describe as "another kind of fixation to the mother to whom one is now bound by hate." Although the common psychoanalytic reading suggests that Helga's troubled life results from an absent father, subjects attempt "to overcome their own longing to return [to the womb] by getting rid of the mother" in Rank's assessment (*Trauma* 58). As such, Helga's mother reemerges as the locus of her anxiety.

Because Helga's mother has already passed, her anxiety has nowhere else to go but inward. After her experience in Denmark, Helga loses the compassion she once held for her mother, a development evidenced by her newfound decision to forgive her father, whom she initially perceived as little more than a "gay suave scoundrel." Helga now repudiates the mother and follows a more Freudian Oedipal impulse by transferring the desire and fulfillment she once attributed to the mother to her father. Kimberly Monda reads Helga's newfound adoration for her father as completing the "repudiation of her white mother, whose cruel withdrawal made it impossible for her to develop a sense of her own agency; it also allows her to replace racist stereotypes about black people with her own definition of what she admires in the African American community. This identification with her father frees Helga from her self-destructive need for recognition from her distant mother, allowing her to gain temporary access to a sense of agency and therefore to her repressed sexuality" (33).

However, this transference of love is also problematic because Helga's hatred for her mother remains at the core of her sympathy with her father, and thereby the fixation on the mother remains, as well. Even though the father becomes more visible toward the conclusion of *Quicksand,* Helga Crane's pressing need for a surrogate is still mediated through her love-hate emotions for her mother. As Rank writes, "the root of the 'death wish' is the desire of the female child to become free of the mother, and it is possible that the 'death wish' is turned upon the subject as the 'most severe self-punishment'" (*Trauma* 59).

Helga's repudiation of her mother after returning from Copenhagen manifests itself in sadomasochistic behavior and quickly begins her downward spiral into depression, anxiety, and death. In Rank's formulation, the essence of the neurotic character is a failure to overcome the anxiety of birth. Rank asserts that in addition to the "life instinct" that drives us toward individuality, competence, and independence, we also possess a death instinct, which drives us to become part of a family or community. The push and pull between the life and death instincts evident in Helga Crane may offer a rationale for her seemingly erratic pattern of behavior—her desire to belong, coupled with her desire to be free and independent. Helga's desire is sadomasochistic, because while she (unconsciously) seeks recognition as an interracial subject, she repudiates those who accept her as such. She experiences the same pattern of rejection and separation that began with her biological parents, and the men and women she subsequently encounters throughout the text emerge as inadequate surrogates for her dead mother and absent father.

The Failure of "Sexual Gratification" and the Religious Sublime

Rank also points to sexual gratification and religious sublimation as processes by which the subject attempts to resolve the attachment to the lost mother. In Helga's case, the failure to enact a sexual relationship with Dr. Anderson (which I discuss below) drives her to a state of religious sublimation. Freud conceptualized sublimation as a way to explain desires that are not necessarily driven by sexual impulses. Rank understands religious sublimation as a critical force in the subject's desire to seek a symbolic womb. When the subject undergoes religious sublimation, he or she attempts to free himself or herself from the binding relationship to the mother, and gives himself or herself over to the father, God. Rank aligns the process of religious conversion with the process of social development. Helga's conversion experience in the church can be interpreted as the giving over of herself to the paternal or Oedipal paradigm, which she has resisted throughout the novel by rejecting various forms of institutional and social power (Naxos, marriage, New

Negro doctrines). Once Helga returns from Copenhagen, she reestablishes her relationship with a masculine figure of authority, the Naxos principal Dr. Anderson.

In her introduction to the 1986 reprint of *Quicksand* and *Passing*, Deborah McDowell describes Helga as "divided psychically between a desire for sexual fulfillment and a longing for social respectability . . . Helga's sexual repression is understandable," McDowell argues, "given her 'illegitimate' origins and her proper upbringing" (xvii). McDowell's interpretation of Helga's repressed sexuality certainly coincides with the shame associated with her parents' union, but within a Rankian context, sexual inhibitions are also "motivated by the libidinal attachment to and the consequent fear of separation from the mother who is experienced as all-powerful, both giving and depriving" (Menaker 52–53). Because the mother acts as such a force in the development of the child's ego and overall psychological development, "the self-inhibition of destructive, sadistic impulses must occur out of fear that were the child to act on them [she] would lose the mother on whom [she] is dependent and to whom [she] is libidinally attached" (Menaker 58–59). Because Helga's biological mother is already dead, the fear of losing the mother is largely symbolic. For Helga, the mother represents the key to wholeness, unity, and the potential satisfaction of desire. By acting out her sexual desire, she risks losing the respectability, good stock, and "formal calm her mother had represented" (92), which she no longer values because she has come to hate the mother and embrace the lost father. But in Rank's view, "sexual love, then, which realizes its climax in that mating of two beings, proves to be the most sublime attempt to re-establish the primal situation between mother and child, which only finds its complete realization in a new embryo" (*Trauma* 43). Helga's decision to leave Copenhagen and to act on her sexual desires is associated with the repudiation of the mother, which emerges when the "strict prohibitions of the mother (who prescribes cleanliness) are met with resentment and rebellion on the part of the child." Helga's need to discharge her new feelings of dissatisfaction toward her mother can be read as the result of incorporating "the strict mother image as part of [her] own ego which demands punishment out of guilt for [her] sadistic impulses" (Menaker 53).

At a cocktail party, Dr. Anderson proposes that he and Helga engage in a sexual affair, and she agrees. Helga attempts to give in to her repressed desires by agreeing to become Anderson's mistress, which, I argue, also signals her desire to break from the maternal. I consider Helga's anticipated affair with Dr. Anderson as the act that would free her from sexual repression and the guilt associated with disappointing her mother, and would ultimately enable her to detach. She resolves to become his mistress and is eager for their "coming consummation," planned for the next evening. However, when they meet again the situation sours when he attributes his sexual overtures to "Tavenor's rotten cocktails," withdraws his proposition, and apologizes for his misguided behavior the previous night (107). Because Helga initially envisions Dr. Anderson's role at Naxos as a paternal one, his sexual rejection operates at the level of the paternal as well. The rejection is particularly damaging for Helga, since her failure to consummate the affair further signals her attachment to the mother but also makes visible her repressed desire for the father.

Dr. Anderson's rejection sends Helga into a tailspin: "For days, for weeks, voluptuous visions had haunted her. Desire had burned in her flesh with uncontrollable violence. The wish to give herself had been so intense that Dr. Anderson's surprising, trivial apology loomed as a direct refusal of the offering" (109). Reeling in sentiments of humiliation and betrayal, Helga ventures out onto the streets on a windy and rainy night, searching for some reprieve from the sadness and anger of her latest rejection. She stumbles into a church service, and the "wailing singing" of the worshippers moves her to experience a range of emotions, culminating in Helga's conversion from a "pore los' Jezebel" to a born-again Christian. Helga thinks that "she had found, she was sure, the intangible thing for which, indefinitely, always she had craved" (120). Finally, Helga unleashes her sexual inhibitions in a religious context, where her conversion "simulates sexual excitement and orgasmic release," as McDowell observes in the introduction (xx). Rank writes that organized religion originated with the individual need to address the "finiteness" of human existence within a social collective. He also understands religion as one of the ways in which individuals deal with the loss of "protection given by the mother (womb)" (*Trauma* 90). Thus, it is significant that Helga's orgasmic release takes place within the confines of the church, which, according to Rank, provides a safe environment in which one can attempt to undergo the transition from libidinal attachment to individuation and release oneself from anxiety.

Helga's entrance into the church signals the impending conclusion of her physical journey; she has traveled within and beyond national borders in search of fulfillment. Her excursion is a final transcendence of space, from the material to the spiritual. Helga's passage from the street, where she is consistently recognized as a sexual body, to the church, where she is transformed into a spiritual or religious body, blurs the boundary between the self and space and enables her to internalize the energies of her environment. The scene in which Helga is "saved" spiritually removes her body from an explicitly racialized, materialist context to a spiritual, ritualized one, which provides her the illusion of unity, individuation, and the satisfaction of being part of a social collective. *Quicksand* initially presents organized religion as a means to salvation and wholeness, but it quickly becomes the institution that binds and suffocates Helga. Rank theorized that organized religion serves the human need for immortality by supporting faith in the existence of a spiritual dimension in life, which manifests itself in the existence of what he calls "a soul" (Rank, *Psychology and the Soul* 11). Rank also understood that the church provides individuals with a community united by a belief in spiritual transcendence and the continuity of the self. The conversion experience momentarily fulfills Helga because she is able to release her repressed sexual desires and move closer to God and thus closer to an inorganic state of being. Helga's conversion experience finds her in the care of the Reverend Pleasant Green, who escorts her back to her room. Not knowing whether to relish or regret their consummation, she marries him.

Artistic Idealization and the Neurosis of Birth

The final scene of the novel takes place in a small Alabama community that reveres Rev. Green and tolerates his bride. Consumed by the rustic appeal of the South and their three children (with a fourth on the way), Helga finds life in Alabama suitable. Her desire to guard against the death drive initiated by the act of birth is overwhelming in the final moments of the narrative. She produces, almost formulaically, most of Rank's phases necessary to overcome the anxiety of birth trauma, including sexual gratification and religious sublimation. In Alabama, she tries to reclaim her "inherent racial need for gorgeousness" by attempting to beautify her home (18), which recalls another Rankian phase, "artistic idealization." In marrying Rev. Green, Helga adopts the "*religious* factor, which in every particular detail, especially in the presentation of the body, is equivalent to a further life in the womb" (Rank, *Trauma* 150, original emphasis). After marrying Green, Helga also attempts to recapture the "*artistic* factor" (150, original emphasis). Rank develops his theory of the relation of the drive to become an artist to the anxiety of birth by analyzing the origins of Greek and Egyptian art. Using Egyptian art as an example, Rank notes that "to *create* a piece of sculpture is, in Egyptian, *to bring to life*; the sculptor's work is designated by the causative form of the word 'to live.' That this is no mere question of assonance but of inner similarity is confirmed by the occurrence of proper names for statues, raising them to the level of individuals" (149, original emphasis). In the same way, Helga attempts to enliven the utter dreariness of her southern surroundings:

> When she worked [in the garden], she felt that life was utterly filled with the glory and the marvel of God. Helga did not reason about this feeling, as she did not at that time reason about anything. It was enough that it was there, coloring all her thoughts and acts. It endowed the four rooms of her ugly brown house with a kindly radiance, obliterating the stark bareness of its white plaster walls and the nakedness of its uncovered painted floors. It even softened the choppy lines of the shiny oak furniture and subdued the awesome horribleness of the religious pictures. And all the other houses and cabins shared in this illumination. And the people. The dark undecorated women unceasingly concerned with the actual business of life, its rounds of births and christenings, of loves and marriages, of deaths and funerals, were to Helga miraculously beautiful. (121)

This passage strikingly articulates the way aesthetics play a crucial role in Helga's subjectivity. Her room at Naxos is attractively decorated, with a "blue Chinese carpet" and "oriental silk," and in Copenhagen her aunt and uncle adorn her in "striking things, exotic things" (1, 68). Such adornments are glaringly absent in her new environment, and Helga's futile attempt to transform the "ugly brown house" and "dark undecorated women" into more aesthetically pleasing objects emerges as a strategy to preserve her vision of immortality. As noted above, the artist plays a significant role in Rank's theory of will because it is the artist who strives for immortality through art and through identification with a collective spiritual or cultural environment. This is precisely why artists above all others can overcome the anxiety of separation and the fear of death that accompanies it. In this way, artists are better equipped to reconcile the material and spiritual duality of life.

But Helga's spiritual revitalization is fleeting and her sense of artistic fulfillment almost impossible to enjoy. She rebels against the "white man's God" and "this childlike trust in full compensation for all woes and deprivations in 'kingdom come'" (133). She views religious rhetoric about the preservation of the soul and the glory of the afterlife as inapplicable to black people who believe so blindly in a spirituality that "blunt[s] the perceptions" and "rob[s] life of its crudest truths" (133). In addition to the loss of religious zeal, Helga's artistic inclinations vanish. The illusion of beauty Helga initially reserves for her new home and community slowly dissipates once she is confronted with the reality of her husband, who is the antithesis of "pleasant."

With her marriage to the Reverend Pleasant Green, Helga makes a final attempt to assume a normalized role within the symbolic order. She bears his children, further signifying her desire to evoke the absent father by idealizing procreation. In Freud's view of the woman's experience of the Oedipal complex, the subject "can find relief from her crippling sense of inadequacy only through a heterosexual, procreative cathexis, and by aligning herself with the qualities of passivity, exhibitionism, and masochism which make her the perfect 'match' for the properly Oedipalized male subject" (Silverman 143). However, Freudian analysis fails to account for what occurs in Helga's marriage to Rev. Green. As Rank's paradigmatic interpretation of the mother's role in the child's neurosis suggests, Helga's anxiety is not rooted in her paternal relationship but in her maternal one. She uses the relationships she develops with men to mediate her conflicted love-hate fixation on her mother.

This use of men as mediators for Helga's maternal fixation is apparent earlier in the novel, when Helga confronts Dr. Anderson regarding her intent to leave Naxos. Barbara Johnson describes the scene in Dr. Anderson's office as a moment in which Helga is initially "drawn toward the appeal of the omnipotent selfobject [Dr. Anderson], the merger with the idealized other" (259). But his reference to her as a lady metaphorically breaks the mirror by showing her that "he is not omnipotent (since he does not really know anything about her) but also that what he wants to value in her is something she thinks she does not and cannot possess" (B. Johnson 260). In addition to fulfilling the role as a potential "selfobject," Dr. Anderson also serves an Oedipal function. He attempts to convince Helga to remain at Naxos because the institution needs more people with Helga's sense of values and aesthetics. He tells her, "'You're a lady.' 'You have dignity and breeding.'" Anderson continues to "praise" her by noting that she has qualities "inherited from good stock" (*Quicksand* 23), implying that he envisions Helga as part of his bourgeois project of racial uplift. However, she "corrects" Dr. Anderson by noting not only that she is from a "Chicago slum" (21), but also that she is the illegitimate product of a possibly adulterous union between a white woman and a black man—an immigrant and a gambler, respectively. In referring to Helga's womanhood and breeding, Dr. Anderson envisions Helga in the role of "New Negro Mother," an identity supported by W. E. B Du Bois, who believed that the survival of the race was dependent upon black women (particularly middle-class black women) fulfilling their maternal role. Larsen makes a direct reference to this concept in a later scene with Helga and her former fiancé, James Vayle, who informs Helga that she must have children because "the *others* will still have [children] . . . the race is sterile at the top" (103). We can read Dr. Anderson's plea for Helga to continue her tenure at Naxos as an offer to place her in a mothering role where her "social role, like her reproductive role, would support an emerging pan-African nationalism, explicitly defined as male" (Berg 109). Helga initially contemplates remaining at Naxos not in the name of service but "for this man who was talking so earnestly of his work, his plans, his hopes. An insistent need to be a part of them sprang upon her" (*Quick-*

sand 20). At the outset, Helga is not offended by Dr. Anderson's suggestion to enter his own symbolic order and appears pleased to contribute to the mock familial structure he conceives at Naxos. However when he exposes her void (her lack of good "stock"), Helga's maternal feelings become feelings of inadequacy. Her overwhelming lack does not render her capable of mothering the race or consummating this vision with Dr. Anderson. At this juncture in the narrative, Helga's refusal to enact a mothering role among the students at Naxos reads as a refusal to reconcile the familial rift. The reader is privy to Helga's unconscious at work as she momentarily contemplates joining Dr. Anderson's familial vision, and the narrator notes a "compunction tweaking in her heart for even having entertained the notion of deserting him" (20). In Rank's framework, the subject desires to "reproduce the complete return . . . sometimes by means of the defence mechanism of identification in neurotic symptoms, instead of attaining this through the consummation of the sexual act, and through the creation of a new living being with whom they can identify themselves" (*Trauma* 189). This is the scene that concretizes Helga's infertility, thereby spawning her series of departures in search of a geographic space that will allow her a full expression of individuality and protect her from a sense of decline.

At the novel's conclusion, Helga enacts Rank's repetition of the primal situation, as she prepares to give birth to her fifth child. This ending suggests that Helga, who has been largely constituted by her freedom of mobility, has now sunk into the quicksand of her marriage and motherhood, and that her imminent death marks the final release from her present psychical and physical confinement. In Rank's formulation of birth trauma, women are able to overcome anxiety more successfully than their male counterparts because they can physically repeat the birthing process by bearing children. For Rank, "here lies . . . the fundamental difference in the whole psychical development of man and woman. The woman is in the position, through a complete reproduction of the primal situation, namely through actual repetition of pregnancy and parturition, to procure for herself the most far-reaching approach to the primal gratification" (*Trauma* 189). Rank admits that birth anxiety has a stronger influence on some than on others. In these instances, the subject's desire for children becomes more intense, and the anxiety continues to find its release through reproduction.

While Helga's shifting lack is the source of her unhappiness because she cannot be "whole," racially or otherwise, in a context that is defined by its racial and gendered stratification, the drive to fulfill a sense of completion through repetition keeps her alive but fixated on a damaging tie to the mother.

Helga puts an end to her sadomasochistic impulses successively through her sexuality (childbirth) and death. After her first three children, Helga no longer finds pleasure in sex or in childbirth, yet she continues both at her own peril. Hutchinson reasons that Helga's final decision to remain in Alabama with her children, and specifically her belief that, if she left, "through the rest of her lifetime she would be hearing their cry of 'Mummy, Mummy, Mummy,' through sleepless nights" derives from Helga's own "crying for the Danish mother whom 'race' in America has stolen from her" (*Search* 238). Hence "the reason Helga Crane cannot save herself in this conclusion . . . has everything to do with American society's suppression of the color line" (238). Rev. Green's insistence that she fulfill her maternal duty traps her in a repetitive cycle of sex and reproduction, from which death is the only reprieve. However, her death could also be read as an act that can facilitate the successful individuation of her own children.

Rank believed that the trauma of birth would never be fully relieved, but a mark of one's successful individuation would emerge once one learned "to live with his split, his conflict, his ambivalence, which no therapy could take away, for if it could, it would take with it the actual spring of life" (*Psychology of Difference* 47). Perhaps Larsen found Rank's call for the subject to simply learn to exist with his ambivalence both an affirmation and a model for the expression of her unique racial composition and her then-progressive notions of a woman's role. In many respects, Rank's model successfully captured the psychic split that Larsen articulated through Helga's struggle to locate a distinct subjectivity against racial and gendered limitations. Helga's dilemma is indicative of the internal conflict that, in Rank's version of psychoanalysis, defines most subjects in the modern world: the push to assert a unique identity or individuality yet at the same time "become part of some meaningful, communal expression" (*Trauma* 4). Helga's excursions are the physical manifestation of an interior striving for definition, and through Rank's model of birth trauma Larsen makes that interiority legible. Though Larsen may have drawn upon and found comfort in Rank's explanatory paradigm, the elements of race and gender complicate his formulation, which makes no claims about the influence of racial difference within the familial matrix. Like many writers of the 1920s, Larsen found within psychoanalysis, and with Rank's model in particular, a way to explain the complex processes of interiority. But even with Rank's neat paradigm, Larsen could not reconcile the predicament of her interracial female subject.

3

Art's Imperfect End

Race and Gurdjieff in Jean Toomer's "Transatlantic"

Interracialism emerged as a pervasive theme in the 1920s and 1930s, as evidenced by the wealth of literary and popular texts that vividly detailed the politics of mixed-race subjectivity. But underlying these narratives of racial intermixture was a broader concern with the subject's desire to belong to a community while maintaining some semblance of particularity. Perhaps this is why Otto Rank's recognition that all persons maintain a simultaneous desire to exist as individuals yet belong to a communal structure struck a particular chord with writers of the period. Jean Toomer probed the ambivalence of individualism and belonging, and concluded that this reconciliation could only materialize through the transcendence of race—a concept that Toomer consistently stressed was both divisive and fictive. Toomer struggled with the desire to exist as an individual subject yet also to be recognized as a part of the larger "American" race. After the 1923 publication of *Cane,* Toomer began work on another novel in which the consciousness of his new protagonist was "tortured for synthesis" (Hutchinson, "Jean Toomer" 382). Hortense Spillers articulates the extent to which individual subjectivity has been an undervalued concept in many African American cultural communities. According to Spillers, "what is missing in African American cultural analysis is a concept of the 'one.' . . . Though there is a hidden allegiance to the idea of the 'superstar'/hero . . . it is widely believed that black people cannot afford to be individualistic" (394). Both Larsen and Toomer engage aspects of psychoanalytic thought in their literary works as a way to imagine a way out of the paradox of race by privileging the interior or psychological self. While Larsen's protagonists ultimately fail in their projects to disregard social pressures to conform to a singular racial identity, Toomer more explicitly constructs the dialectic of the self and the group—an inherently psychoanalytic concept—as the only viable vehicle that would allow for racial transcendence.

Ironically enough, in recent years Jean Toomer's decision to eschew the issue of race has garnered as much critical and scholarly attention as his best-known literary accomplishment, *Cane*. Toomer's stance against race is largely attributed to his adherence to the psycho-religious philosophies of the mystic Georges Gurdjieff.[1] His doctrine centered on the concept of "self-observation" and the belief that we are all in a waking sleep, which we can transcend through practiced meditation and group therapy.

The early years of Georges Ivanovitch Gurdjieff's life remain as mysterious as his elusive persona. Biographers of Gurdjieff believe he was born sometime around 1866 in Alexandropol, in the southern Transcaucasian part of Russia. As a child, Gurdjieff was considered extremely precocious and began to receive training for the priesthood and medicine. Though religious spirituality permeated Gurdjieff's later teachings, his travels throughout the Middle East and Asia also informed the tenets of his analysis. As such, Gurdjieff's key concepts are influenced by the beliefs of Orthodox Christianity, Islam, Hinduism, Buddhism, and Judaism. But the underlying principle of Gurdjieff's doctrines stems from the belief that most people lead "mechanical" lives, lacking the capacity to comprehend and experience their interior selves fully. The process of awakening oneself requires a rigorous and simultaneous project of introspection, group therapy and physical exercise. Gurdjieff considered all of these activities equally important in the development of consciousness. In 1922, Gurdjieff created the Institute for the Harmonious Development of Man in Fontainebleau-sur-Avon, France. After Gurdjieff was nearly killed in a car accident in 1924, he broadened the scope of his teachings and focused less on the physical element of "the Work"—his description of the teachings—and more on the oral and written components of his therapy. The new written work Gurdjieff produced was imbued with the modernist sensibilities of the time and echoed Freudian and Jungian psychoanalysis.

Gurdjieff maintained that consciousness, for most individuals, is only an illusion, which is consistent with Freudian psychoanalysis. For Gurdjieff, consciousness emerges in four distinct phases. In the first state an individual encounters glimpses of the subconscious in the form of dreams. The second phase, the phase in which persons are typically located, is waking sleep. In this state individuals do not and cannot exercise full control of their thoughts, actions, nor emotions. Self-remembering is the third phase, in which individuals have the potential to recognize when they have fallen into mechanicality and to maintain a sense of awareness that would allow them to awaken. The final stage is "objective consciousness," in which one develops an acute sense of the world and can experience it emotively and intellectually rather than mechanically.[2]

It was largely due to the influence of Gurdjieff's teachings that Toomer became less interested in concretizing racial categories and more dedicated to transcending the fixation on external differences between the so-called races. Although a number of scholars have attributed Toomer's break from the Renaissance discourse of racial uplift to his eventual acceptance of Gurdjieffian precepts, there has been little acknowledgment of the specific ways in which Toomer imagined the obliteration of racial thinking through Gurdjieff's models of self-knowledge.[3] As such, Toomer's literary career is articulated in fairly binary terms, with *Cane* standing as a symbol of his affection for and affiliation with African American culture—"my growing need for artistic expression has pulled me deeper and deeper into the Negro group" (quoted in Kerman and Eldridge 96)—and his association with Gurdjieff signifying his disavowal from any and all racial belonging:

> What then am I?
> I am at once no one of the races and I am all of them.
> I belong to no one of them and I belong to all.
> I am, in a strict racial sense, a member of a new race. (quoted in Kerman and Eldridge 341)

Yet Toomer's engagement with U.S. race relations and the Gurdjieff Institute was far more nuanced in that he wanted to craft a Gurdjieffian approach to the acute problems of U.S. racism in the 1920s, even though such an interpretation of Gurdjieffian methods was a severe transgression of Gurdjieff's philosophy of individuation.[4] Toomer's disruption of Gurdjieffian methods to address the problem of race in the United States worked against Gurdjieff's ideal of "individualization," a "process of self-creation" which Toomer considered "the most significant personal, social, or political concept imaginable" (Whalan 598). But Toomer's troubling of Gurdjieffian mysticism points to the ambivalence he faced in attempting to exist simply as part of the American or human race and signals his inability to divorce himself completely from the racialized politics of the United States. While Toomer certainly believed that racial mixing in America produced a new race of which he was a product, he also recognized that the project of transcending race would be gradual. Toomer was convinced that his studies with Gurdjieff could further that ambition. Gurdjieff's influence enabled Toomer to consider himself and others in terms other than race, yet he was also keenly aware of the embeddedness of racial determinism, particularly among Americans, and thus imagined the application of Gurdjieffian philosophies as a prescription for the dissolution of racial categorization and prejudice. Toomer's work after *Cane* intimates that he was not dismissive of the concept of race, nor did he completely reject the persistence of racial identifications. This is not to suggest, of course, that Toomer was not dedicated to the project of antiracialism but rather to propose that he had to engage strategically the very racial discourses he wished to avoid in order to make Gurdjieff's message palatable to a U.S. populace consumed with racial determinism.

A critical look at the unpublished story "Transatlantic" offers compelling insight on his vision of the eradication of racial thinking through the employment of Gurdjieffian thought, demonstrating the value of such psychoreligious methods in the deconstruction of racial paradigms. "Transatlantic" illustrates Toomer's rendering of Gurdjieff's philosophies as a methodology that would enable the transcendence of racialized thought and allow individuals to form relationships and bonds based on more authentic, human emotions rather than on racial or cultural particularities. The story features an unnamed narrator whose persona is overtly similar to Toomer's. He is a debonair, racially ambiguous figure who appears well versed in theories of psychology and social discourse, and he uses his intellectual superiority and charisma to transform the characters of the people around him. The narrator voyages by sea from the United States to Europe en route to a commune much like Gurdjieff's institute in France. During his journey he makes a number of acquaintances, mostly women, whom he engages in casual banter. Each conversation is marked by a revelation of the interlocutor's prejudice and insecurity, and each dialogue concludes with the narrator's successful interpretation and resolution of the problem through the application of Gurdjieffian precepts. Consistent with Gurdjieffian logic, the narrator does not offer advice, nor does he preach against the ills of the characters' various intolerances. Instead of instructing those he encounters as to how they might resolve their various dilemmas, he merely suggests to them the life-altering possibilities that await them should they achieve individualization.

The narrator's air of superiority emerges not only because he believes himself to be the sole person on board who is not living a mechanical life, but also because he is the only racially ambiguous person within the group. In their biography of Toomer, Cynthia Earl Kerman and Richard Eldridge surmise that "as 'a member of a new race, produced from a blending of bloods which existed in recognized races,' this character's attraction for others, the secret of his power, is that he cannot be typed" (188). Further, Diana Williams has argued that while Toomer's works "suggest a yearning for racelessness, they also imply . . . that this raceless transcendence can only be attained by people of mixed race descent" (191). "Transatlantic" does not necessarily demonstrate a yearning for racelessness but rather a yearning for something other than race to serve as a window into the self. The narrator appears to privilege his multiraciality, viewing it as a "third eye" that broadens his sense of perception and introspection. The narrator's observations at the beginning of the story and his interactions with other characters throughout would suggest that all people, not merely those who possess a mixed-race heritage, can move beyond their racialized beliefs to lead individualized lives free of outside influences. One can speculate that while Toomer was not interested in usurping Gurdjieff's authority and may not even have thought it possible to do so, his violation of Gurdjieffian logic to address the question of race was Toomer's clear demarcation of a territory from which Gurdjieff could not and would not speak. Clearly, the narrator attributes his ability to move seamlessly among the ship's various "types" to his multiracial, multiethnic subjectivity. The multivalent insight attributed to the multiracial subject is not uncharacteristic of the literary tradition from which Toomer emerged. His Harlem Renaissance counterparts Nella Larsen, James Weldon Johnson, and Jessie Fauset had each created protagonists who navigated various geographic and social spaces with a critical eye. The observer positionality of Larsen's Helga Crane, Johnson's ex-colored man, and Fauset's Angela Murray is made possible by their intimate knowledge of the races on both sides of the color line. Such knowledge enables them to judge, critique, manipulate, and objectify the various persons they encounter and spaces they inhabit, as Toomer's narrator extends his unique perspective to guide others toward an individualized mode of awareness.

Life After *Cane*

The increasingly predominant narrative of Toomer's literary demise is that after *Cane* the "issue of race virtually disappears from Toomer's work" (Rauve 68), and that Toomer's goal to raise "mankind to a higher level of being and awareness . . . would have been better served if he had confined himself to writing essays or, still better, if he had continued to write books like *Cane*" (Byrd 123). Rudolph Byrd observes that "Transatlantic" and Toomer's other post-*Cane* text, "The Gallonwerps," are not "novels in the sense that we would like them to be; they are not masterful prose works in which an author seeks to reorder reality through the filter of his own inspired imagination" (122). The relative absence of any extended critical interpretation of "Transatlantic" to some extent confirms the mediocrity of the work. But in disregarding "Transatlantic" we have perhaps overlooked a significant transitional phase in Toomer's personal and literary existence after *Cane*. The blandness of Toomer's "objective" stories has historically repelled critics and readers.[5] But in order to gain a more comprehensive appreciation of Toomer's negotiations with race even as he denounced the concept, we must bypass the formal and stylistic failures of "Transatlantic" in order to appreciate more fully the content of Toomer's "objective" works. Given Toomer's enduring dedication to the project of racial transcendence, his objective works were in one sense the most meaningful works he ever produced; after *Cane* he dedicated his literary career to the personal and social mission of advancing Gurdjieff's philosophical models. I would like to suggest that the relevance of "Transatlantic" lies in its very mundaneness. In the story, Toomer constructs a microcosmic portrait of a society that can shift organically, albeit slowly, from its obsession with race to a state of psychological liberation through the practical application of Gurdjieffian thought. Byrd notes that "Transatlantic" was singular in that it "was the novel in which [Toomer] attempted to give the most extensive treatment of his theme of human development, and it represents his most self-conscious rendering of Gurdjieff's teachings" (108). In an odd but perhaps effective comparison, Toomer and Paul Gilroy share a similar ideology with respect to the project of erasing race. Each recognizes the extent to which racialized persons have been the victims of "race-thinking," but for whites the "alchemical magic of racial mastery" has "distorted and delimited their experiences in other ways," hence divesting them of "their individuality, their humanity" (Gilroy 15). Both Gilroy's "planetary humanism" and Toomer's objective art involve the obliteration of existing values, particularly the reified conceptualization of race, in order to further the humanity of blacks and whites alike.[6]

The political climate of the United States in the late 1920s and 1930s almost necessitated that Toomer think more strategically about the relationship between the racial politics of the era and Gurdjieffian philosophies, especially if he desired to attract more persons to Gurdjieff's mission. Toomer wrote "Transatlantic" in 1931—the year of the Scottsboro trial.[7] Langston Hughes, a friend of Toomer's and an advocate for the Scottsboro Nine, appealed to Toomer, thereby forcing him to respond to one of the most racially charged and divisive moments in U.S. history. Hughes writes to Toomer: "I am a writer also. I know what it means to receive continually by mail requests and appeals for aid. So, believe me, I would not write you now were it not of the utmost urgency. The nine Scottsboro boys are still under sentence of death in Alabama. The new trials come up this November. There is a great and immediate need for funds to see that their defense is carried through adequately and that, if necessary, further appeals be taken to the State and United States Supreme Court in order that lynch laws may not triumph, and that these boys, in spite of pronounced evidence of their innocence, are not again sentenced to death." In addition to making a monetary request, Hughes implores Toomer "to express in words what you feel about the plight of these young Negroes in a Birmingham jail, (and I hope you will be so moved), send me a short statement that we may release to the press of America. Any comment from you would be of inestimable value in arousing public opinion against hasty and unfair trials for Negroes, and in securing a fair hearing for these young black boys under the shadow of death in Alabama. This letter is being sent to those American writers who have based their inspiration (or a portion of it) on the life of the Negro peoples."[8]

Though Toomer had long ceased to write books like *Cane,* to which Hughes undoubtedly refers when he describes those writers who have "based their inspiration . . . on the life of the Negro peoples," he responded affirmatively to Hughes's request. Toomer's response, while less than moving, illustrates the awkward marriage between race and Gurdjieff that he attempted to construct after *Cane.* He contextualizes the Scottsboro boys' struggle within a Gurdjieffian model, asserting that "those who have been caught in a machine will sympathize with the plight of the Scottsboro boys. Those who have freed themselves will realize how much they owe to the help of others. So let us help these boys in every way we can, for surely their suffering is greater than our own. Justice aids life; law often takes it. That we need less law and more justice has never been so true as it is today. It would be an amazing thing for the world at large and for the nine S[cottsboro] boys in particular to have justice prevail in their case. Those who have been caught in a machine, who have gotten free, realize how much they owe to the help of others." Although he would attempt to live a racially free existence, the shadow of his former life would not allow him to forget the insidiousness of U.S. racial prejudice. Yet Toomer firmly held that Gurdjieffian principles could bring about self-awareness and hence amicable relations between the races. Hughes's letter illustrates one among many of the challenges Toomer faced in his attempt to adhere to Gurdjieff's teachings while at the same time redefining his position as a non-racialized subject. Such a process would necessitate his involvement in racial discourses of the time, but Toomer's stance on social activism emerged from Gurdjieff's position that individuals need not and should not engage in sociopolitical affairs.

The generic tone and deracialized context of Toomer's response to Hughes articulates Toomer's allegiance to Gurdjieff's nonracial philosophy. Gurdjieff reasoned that man "has a tremendous responsibility to the universe, but none to social systems," and if he succeeds in transforming himself, "energies are released that have cosmic consequences" (Kerman and Eldridge 266). One has to wonder about the nature of the "machine" Toomer references, which seems related not only to law but also to the notion of being bound within a racial system; the predicament of the Scottsboro boys has as much, if not more, to do with the racial or racist order as the legal system. This machine simply reproduces the problem of race, and its consequences, especially for black Americans, remain eerily constant. The insistence on the transformation of the individual self has been historically a rather problematic concept in black communities, but it is consistent with Toomer's choice to embrace Gurdjieff's personalized practice. But this rationale would undoubtedly pose a problem for African American subjects, particularly in the 1920s and 1930s, who were not only living under the thumb of social and institutional racism but who were also producing and promoting a black aesthetic that emerged from what they understood to be a distinct racial consciousness. Toomer imagined the refashioning of individual subjectivity as potentially more effective than short-lived and often competing social programs and practices.

Toomer clearly struggled with a crisis of individuality that, despite his nonracial philosophy, located him squarely within a generation of black intellectualism. According to Robert Reid-Pharr, "black American intellectualism might be understood simply as that incessant mapping of the conflict between personal and communal desire" (28), a desire that shapes the psychical dilemma of Larsen's protagonist, as I argue in the previous chapter. While writers like Wright, Ellison, and Baldwin took on the project of rearticulating the terms of "blackness" as a way to address this conflict, Toomer envisioned Gurdjieffian methods as the most effective bridge between the self and the group. Like Larsen, Toomer turned to a pseudopsychoanalytic model to articulate the psychic predicament of the racialized subject who desired to exist outside of the confines of race and more crucially, as Ross Posnock argues, outside dominant notions of racial authenticity.[9]

By the time Toomer was eighteen, he had already begun to feel alienated from both his family and his community. Interestingly, these sentiments did not produce within Toomer a sense of inferiority but rather one of exceptionalism. At a fairly young age, Toomer's experience of isolation endowed him with substantial respect for the individual subject. This attention to individual subjectivity was an anomalous position in Harlem in the 1920s and 1930s and, as Rebecca Rauve suggests, "Gurdjieff taught pupils to look for the '*real* I' among the multiple, mechanical *Is* that directed their lives" (original emphasis). It was perhaps "this emphasis on strengthening the self rather than subjugating it that attracted certain writers and artists" (58). Years after Toomer would leave Gurdjieff and take up Jungian analysis, he would continue to celebrate the faculties of the individual.[10] "Transatlantic" further articulates Toomer's emphasis on individual character and the degree to which each person has the capacity for development and change. Gurdjieff stressed the importance of individuality, which he understood in a "cosmic context" as the "definite fulfillment of oneself as one was always intended to be, the spiritual fleshing-out of what, untrained, tends to remain emaciated" (Shirley 49). Toomer's interest in psychological approaches would manifest throughout his life, as evidenced by his participation with Gurdjieff, Jungian analysis, and even his attempt to incorporate Jungian analyses with the religious philosophy he was to adopt later in life, Quakerism.

Toomer's response to the Scottsboro case also reveals the extent to which he believed the concept of race to be both a social construction and a psychological condition. In an unpublished review of Eugene O'Neill's *The Emperor Jones,* Toomer notes that it

> is obvious of course that a distinct racial flavor is created by having a Negro set the part of Brutus Jones. But this has to do with presentation, and not with the actual construction of the drama. In this construction, Mr. O'Neill first establishes fear by means of suggestion and association. This original feeling is increased by physical circumstances: a forest, and the beating of a tom-tom. And then, as fear intensifies to the point where it overpowers Jones, it successively unlocks chambers of the Emperor's unconscious. Now the contents of the unconscious not only vary with individuals; they are differentiated because of race, by social conditions due to race. And, in fact, Brutus Jones lives through sections of an unconscious which is peculiar to the Negro. . . . And the Emperor Jones is therefore a section of Negro psychology presented in significant dramatic form.

According to Toomer, his review of *The Emperor Jones* was written after the play "had already been explained, criticized, and accepted as an achievement in experimental dramatic form. Likewise, its significances for the Negro have been recognized." But Toomer's review attempts to fill a lacuna in the body of criticism of the play by pointing to its psychological qualities. *The Emperor Jones* dramatizes, for Toomer, a racial unconscious that finds its expression through the social conditions due to race, which assumes that raced subjects experience a unique and specific relationship to their social environment that produce in them a racially inflected psyche. There is something unseemly about Toomer's reference to the awakening of a racial unconscious made possible through fear, a "forest," and the "beating of a tom-tom," precisely because it harkens back to more Jungian formulations of blackness, specifically the idea that black subjectivity is largely formed and informed by white racism. More significantly, however, by linking racial identification to the psychical state of the "unconscious," Toomer imagines the transcendence of this identification through psycho-religious paradigms.

What Toomer finds fascinating about *The Emperor Jones* is its depiction of a distinctly "Negro psychology." While he acknowledges the presence of such a psychology, he also identifies the extent to which it is socially produced. Toomer references this notion of a racial unconscious or "racial memory" in a 1933 version of his autobiography, in which he writes that

> [we] have reason to believe that [racial memory] exists and persists in our subconscious as a deposit of experiences which antedate by centuries the life of the given individual. So it may be that we have a memory even deeper than this, a quintessence of experiences which articulate the life of man on earth. So it may be that some cells of our being recall a world not of this earth which we inhabited [aeons?] ago, a world profoundly right for us except that it lacked supreme difficulties. So we left that world for this—and thereafter have existed with nostalgia as the undercurrent of our emotions. But here, not only do we lack that sense of profound rightness, but the difficulties we came for, though plentiful enough, are too often petty or futile.[11]

Toomer's suggestion that there exists a memory that antedates our racial memory ("a memory even deeper than this") and which points to the possibility to tap even further into the recesses of the unconscious to locate such a repressed or forgotten psychical space. Such interpretations of the unconscious were part and parcel of African American appropriations of psychoanalysis in the 1920s. This articulation of "race memory" or "race consciousness" points to the idea that there is a "memory" that existed before "race," which could also explain why Toomer was wedded to the idea that the eradication of race would have to begin with the eradication of racial thought.

Gurdjieff in Harlem

Though Toomer did not wish to maintain a singular black identity, he did not desire to dissolve completely the relationships he had formed with African American writers and intellectuals during the Renaissance era. Toomer began to think about the relationship between Gurdjieff's philosophies and race once A. R. Orage asked him to form a group of black intellectuals in Harlem. Toomer's and Orage's mission was to "convince those in [Toomer's] former literary life that a nonracial philosophy was preferable" (Kerman and Eldridge 143). Among those who attended Toomer's Harlem group were Aaron Douglas, Dorothy Peterson, Nella Larsen, and Wallace Thurman. In Jon Woodson's "textual blueprint" of the Harlem Gurdjieff group, one of the main features of Gurdjieffian "race texts" is that the works "perform an 'attack on race,'" meaning that the "mimetic level of the text[s] will take the form of a satire in which every form of racialism, color consciousness, and race consciousness is ridiculed. The thesis presented in the text is that racialism can only be combated by fostering in each individual a sense of internal freedom from external influences" (27). As such, "Transatlantic" is a classic model of Gurdjieff's race texts as the narrator applies the principles of Gurdjieff to his various interactions with those on the ship.

"Transatlantic" opens with the narrator's observations of the passengers on the S.S. *Burgundy* as they prepare to sail from New York to Europe. He examines them as they load the ship and notices that

> the Paquebot Burgundy usually attracted people of a certain stamp. They were urbane, rather cosmopolitan, often talented, a bit smart, and all ready for a good time. As [he] gazed, [he] was surprised to see no one who interested me. Everyone looked amiable enough but rather ordinary. Had the Burgundy failed to draw her class this time? Or perhaps my [his] eyes were at fault. They were tired, having suffered considerable strain the week before. . . . All this would pass after the first day out; each person, released by the sea and a free environment, would begin to show his and her own peculiar kind of blooming. Now, however, the life [he] viewed was cramped, contracted, hectic. The bodies of these people twitched and jerked with land-rhythms, land-lack rhythms—taxis, subways, all the rush and bang of a big city.

The spaciousness of the vessel offers an obvious respite for its passengers, who are generally burdened by the stresses and excesses of urban life, and it is because of the ocean's liberating effects that Toomer's narrator wisely imagines it as an idyllic space for the transformation of consciousness and the release of inhibitions and prejudices. The ship emerges as an appropriate space to test and practice Gurdjieff's principles because, though informed by Freudian psychoanalysis, Gurdjieffian processes of psychical transformation do not occur in the intimate and isolated context of the analyst's office. Similar to Freud's protégé Otto Rank, Gurdjieff attempted to address the need for individual expression and the somewhat contradictory desire for communal belonging. Moreover, Gurdjieff recognized that the process of individualization involved interaction with others and thus must be experienced while fully integrated in the social world. Those who followed Gurdjieff were encouraged to practice their teachings outside of their respective "Work" groups. Gurdjieff implored his students to "carry out self-observation in everyday life; in our rooms we cannot develop a master" (quoted in Wellbeloved 87). Consistent with Gurdjieffian principles, "Transatlantic" is a novel that concerns itself "with the concrete situation of our immediate existence and what we make of it" (Bennett, *Is There* 77). Thus the space of the ship fosters a certain dynamic between its passengers. They are confined enough to allow for some form of interaction yet maintain sufficient mobility to mediate that interaction. In addition, the very placelessness and mobility of the ship acts as a metaphor for the indeterminacy and fluidity of identity.

In his essay "Three Psychological Classes," Toomer theorizes that most individuals belong to the "mass of people" who "more or less unconsciously form and constitute the collective life; whose behavior is that known as collective behavior." Toomer generalizes that this class is one of followers and conformists: "Whatever in general is being done in their social melieu [sic], these people do. Whatever is being felt, these people feel. Whatever is being thought, these people think. Their interests, aims, purposes, ambitions, desires, points of view, opinions—in short, their entire reactions are of the kind which are generally prevalent in their place, class, and time. This mass-group includes all unindividualized people, to whatever social class—lower, middle, or upper class—they may belong."

The narrator of "Transatlantic" believes that the ship's passengers fall into this category, yet he optimistically envisions, as Toomer explains in "Three Psychological Classes," that the group will morph into the "very small class of human beings who have been able by some means to achieve a state of being, a condition of existence, such that their manifestations namely, their actions, feelings, and thoughts, are not mass-directed, but self-directed and individualized. In time, they think, feel, and act for themselves, having risen superior to collective influences." These initial observations introduce the narrator's simultaneous project and desire for his fellow passengers.

Like Toomer, the "Transatlantic" narrator undertakes the journey across the Atlantic as an opportunity to create an environment in which racial thinking gives way to conceptualizing oneself and others outside the context of categories and hierarchies. As such, the narrator intends to expose some of the ship's passengers to their psychological potential. At the outset of the story, the narrator deems himself superior to the other passengers. He scrutinizes their movements and expressions and inserts himself into their lives to assist them with what he perceives as their various dilemmas. His position as observer, watching people make "their first adjustments to ship-life, trying their chairs, leaning against the rail, eyeing each other at a distance . . . not yet available for the forming of this eight-day world" (15), allows him the critical distance necessary to shape his encounters with them through the course of his journey. The narrator remains in an objective position, outside and above the other passengers on board, and looks upon them as subjects of study: "It was a fascinating study, this social behavior of people on the sea. Evidently it was governed by definite specific factors and general laws. Also, I had no doubt but that it would take a very plastic person or one strongly individualized to be a law unto himself in these conditions. Would we have a week of Blue Sundays? Or, at the opposite pole, would we have one of those rare and thrilling experiences to be had when the entire ship comes together, when each person is quickened with the sense that he is vividly participating in the total life of a human world?" (52–53). The narrator sees the ship's passengers as a microcosm of U.S. cultural dynamics, and he also identifies the difficulty one faces in extracting oneself from the collective identity of the group. Setting himself apart from the other passengers, he invariably understands his role as the strongly individualized person. The final line of the passage reflects the narrator's desire that the passengers begin to imagine themselves as part of a larger, global community. Such is Toomer's and Gurdjieff's desire for the larger social world: that communal life may be formed through individual expression.

The draft cover of "Transatlantic" introduces the reader to the narrator's positioning of himself in relation to the other passengers (see fig. 5). The cover illustration is enigmatic at best but closely resembles the Enneagram, a diagram frequently used by Gurdjieff, which he inherited from the "Nagshbandi Sufis, one of the most profoundly mystical schools of Sufism" (Shirley 107). Gurdjieff developed the modern use of the Enneagram, which he claimed was a "universal symbol, 'the fundamental hieroglyph of a universal language which has as many different meanings as there are levels of men'" (Wellbeloved 66). He used the Enneagram to illustrate the various phases and possibilities of human development. More recent applications of the Enneagram have used the diagram as a method to map one's personality type, much like the signs of the zodiac. This, however, is not what Gurdjieff had in mind: "Gurdjieff said nothing about using the enneagram as a personality

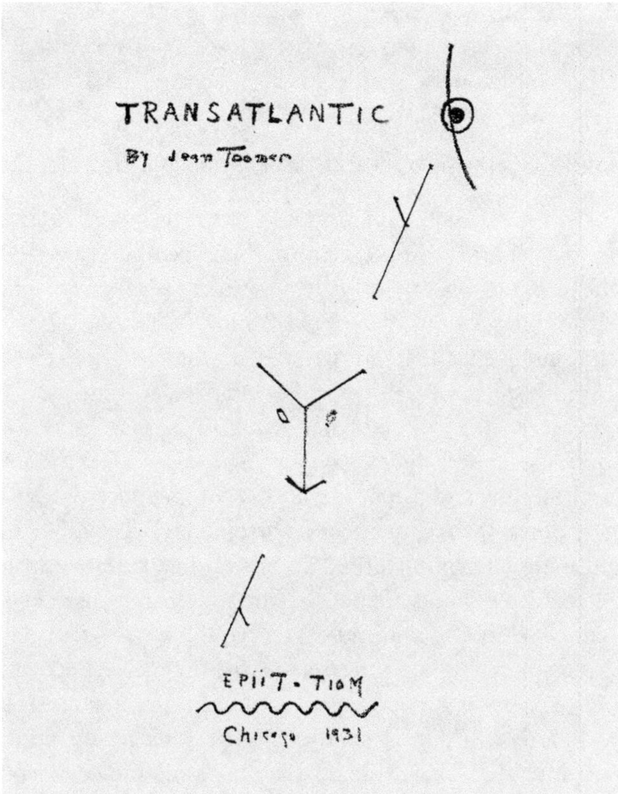

Figure 5. Mock-up cover for Jean Toomer's "Transatlantic." (Image courtesy of Beinecke Rare Book and Manuscript Library, Yale University)

assessment device, or for 'readings.' Everything in the universe has a place on a scale. . . . The nine-pointed figure of the enneagram is . . . a schematic for the transformation of energy within man and in the cosmos" (Shirley 164). Toomer's appropriation of the Enneagram as a potential cover design for his book indicates the extent to which he, or rather the narrator, assumes the role of guide throughout the journey. Only "trained" individuals can properly access the full meaning of the Enneagram, and those who are able to do so, like many mystics, are supposedly endowed with special powers. The mystery of the Enneagram functions on two levels in "Transatlantic": the narrator emerges as the resident mystic who can assist the passengers with realizing their own psychic potential, and Toomer as author positions himself as a teacher from whom readers can learn the same lessons and values of Gurdjieffian therapy.

Transgressing Boundaries and Inspiring Individuation

Inasmuch as Toomer imagined Gurdjieff's precepts as instructive for the dismantling of categories and hierarchies, the issue of class in the text undermines the extent to which Gurdjieff's brand of universalism was, in fact, universal. From his previous experience on the *Burgundy,* the narrator of "Transatlantic" notes that it "stands to other ships as . . . New York stands to the rest of America, or as Washington Square district stands to New York, or as the *New Yorker* stands to the other magazines. It is well-bred, a bit stylish, up-to-date, clever, intelligent, gay, sophisticated, and, at the same time, rather natural, simple, and direct" (25). This commentary on the ship and its passengers points to Toomer's (and Gurdjieff's) belief that "those who were most likely to become absorbed in the Gurdjieffian philosophy would be educated, relatively successful people who were seeking a remedy for the 'incompleteness'" (Kerman and Eldridge 114). If Toomer was interested in spreading his psycho-religious doctrines across the racial spectrum, he was not as concerned with its appeal across economic lines. In fact, as the narrator attempts to provide categories for various persons he encounters on the *Burgundy,* he finds that "there was no drunk, and no buffoon. Not a single person had been consistently in his cups. No one continuously made an ass of himself. Nor, by the way, was there a gold-digger" (149). However, the text does insinuate that the narrator evokes the label of "gold-digger" from the other passengers. The narrator reveals to a friend that "[Marsh] calls me, you know, Adolphe Menjou. She thinks, or pretends to think, I am a suave student of love-affairs, a professional philanderer" (165). Toomer himself has frequently been regarded as a gold digger because of his proclivity for befriending and becoming intimate with wealthy women. He was known for surrounding himself with wealthy persons who could advance his own social position and contribute greatly to the Institute for the Harmonious Development of Man, which was constantly in need of money.[12] Adolphe Menjou was best known for his lead role in Charlie Chaplin's *A Woman of Paris* (1923), which established his reputation as a debonair ladies' man. Perhaps the best-known victim of overzealous typecasting, Menjou played this role in more than a hundred films, including *The Sheik* (1921). Siobhan Somerville refers to Toomer's construction of the sheik figure in Toomer's unfinished work "Sheik and Anti-Sheik," noting that "'queer' figures such as the 'sheik' appear repeatedly in Toomer's texts, whether autobiographical or not, to throw into question normative categories of race and masculinity" (156). Toomer's charisma, particularly his appeal to women, was considered instrumental to his role as a potential leader and "recruiter" for Gurdjieff's groups. His allusion to Adolphe Menjou points to yet another dimension of his "exceptionalism," particularly the ability of the sheik figure to challenge and transgress seemingly fixed boundaries.

The narrator of "Transatlantic" convincingly disrupts the racial logic operative on the ship, and there is one instance in which the boundaries of sexuality are tested as well. In a brief scene, the narrator tries to predict the sexual dynamics between the passengers. He figures that "all the women [will] fall in love with the young man and envy the girl. All the men [will] fall in love with the girl and are jealous of the man. . . . I had, by the way, already picked out my handsome young man" (49). The turn is startling. Thus far, the narrator's dealings had all been with various women aboard the boat. But his description of the young man who catches his eye is the most colorful in the narrative: "He had all the marks, and, so far as I could judge, deserved to have them. He was sitting across the way with a group of men much less vivid than himself. I watched him. He had spirit. It was clear, vivid, direct, cast in the mould of the best American youth. His features were fine, with humorous bold blue eyes and mobile lips. He was easy and sure of himself, without assertion and without conceit. He had probably petted too much to fall very hard for any casual acquaintance on the boat. But there he was, waiting for the girl to catch his eye" (49). The final line of the passage reads rather disappointingly. The narrator suspects that he is too old to "catch his eye" and instead figures that "my old duck was a candidate for the elderly kind" (49). Such moments point to the narrator's fluidity, which serve as a driving force in the story. By weaving through various social circles, he is able to produce an aura of unpredictability, ambiguity and adaptability that simultaneously disarms and fascinates the other passengers.

The narrator recognizes how important the system of classification is for most Americans, and it is this insistence on categorizing others that he challenges on the ship. He notices that there is one young woman in particular, Marsh, who desires to figure him out before she can decide whether or not she could potentially enjoy him as a "steady ship-companion" (10). According to the narrator: "It was still an open question, and it seemed to be of some importance to her. I could guess the reason. . . . It found expression in questions as to my nationality. It seemed that I looked different from anyone she had ever seen. And, as she was the kind of person—a direct physical type—who particularly notices the body first and is curious about its marks and descent, she could not help but be interested in the, to her, strange provocative figure sitting at the table next to her. Her curiosity was so obvious, insistent, and direct that it stimulated me" (10).

Marsh seems to be the prototypical candidate who could benefit positively from the influence of Gurdjieff. Her need to classify the narrator places limitations on any genuine interaction they could have with each other, but the narrator seeks to move Marsh beyond the need to categorize by informing her that he is "Dutch, Spanish, French, Welsh, Scotch, German, omitting Indian and Negro because, knowing the emotions often associated with these latter names, I did not wish just then to chance arousing them" (13). Though the narrator intends to befuddle Marsh further by overwhelming her with his racial composition, his exclusion of the categories Negro and Indian is noteworthy. His omission implies that exposure of his full racial genealogy would preclude his ability to traverse the racial divide symbolically and would trouble a potential companionship or intimate relationship between himself and Marsh. To divulge his racial inheritance fully would immediately limit any interaction between him and the others of the ship. Despite Toomer's willingness to participate thoroughly in Gurdjieffian esoterics, his status as a raced subject was ultimately in conflict with this mode of thought. According to Woodson, Toomer dealt with the incompatibility of Gurdjieff and the race issue through a "paradoxical" insistence that "African-Americans had to disidentify themselves as African-Americans, yet remain conscious that they were African-Americans" (33). Toomer's integration of race within and through Gurdjieffian logic was quite strategic in that it undermined a core element of Gurdjieffian thought, the tenet of "non-identification." Gurdjieff believed identification to be the result of the fear to exist as an individual subject within the world. The tendency toward identification, Gurdjieff affirmed, inhibits the process of self-development and self-awareness. This scene affirms Woodson's interpretation of the distinction between disidentification and consciousness, because the reader is made aware of the narrator's full racial and ethnic status while Marsh is not.

Though the narrator is eventually outed by a friend who is aware of the "Indian and the Negro" components of his racial makeup, the issue of the narrator's race does not resurface. But this initial elision of the narrator's blackness undermines what at the outset appears to be his unrelenting faith in the potentiality of human development. Even though the narrator of "Transatlantic" strongly advocates a nonracial philosophy, perhaps "this fantasy of disembodied citizenship [is] one that belies Toomer's own internalized notions of the racialized male body as the spectacularized site of pleasure and fear," as Siobhan Somerville has commented (163). Though Toomer's writing post-*Cane* is not governed by racial themes, the issue of race is inescapable for Toomer and clearly emerges as a mediating factor in the narrator's social identity. The narrator reads Marsh's caution as indicative of her indoctrination as a white subject but also signals the possibility that she is a subject willing to change. He recognizes through his observations and intimate knowledge of American perceptions of race that Marsh's simultaneous interest in and aversion to him is the result of her natural curiosity (and perhaps attraction to him) coupled with the collective influence of white racism and prejudice. The issue of race in "Transatlantic" registers as a reality that is not fixed which the narrator (and Toomer) must confront.

The narrator again confronts the issue of race when he meets "two girls perched on a piece of deck-machinery." He notes that the "lady in blue was reserved, but the younger girl was quite talkative and ran on giving items about herself" (35). During the course of their conversation, she asks the narrator whether or not he had seen "those niggers on board." The narrator merely nods and she adds, "I didn't think they allowed niggers on these boats. At least not in first-class. One of them has a chair next to a white woman. Did you see the one with white paint on his face? I think he looks awful. Why do you suppose they do that. . . . It doesn't make them look white. It makes them look awful" (36). Despite the woman's obvious racial prejudice, the narrator does not counter her with scorn, nor does he reveal that he is, at least in part, a "nigger" too. The woman's comments reveal her expectation that the boat would be segregated, and her attention to the position of the black man's chair next to the white woman makes her disdain for interracial interaction even more explicit. Additionally, the woman references "white paint" on the man's face, which is an indication of his desire to model European features. Though the precise nature of the white paint is not clear, the woman could be referring to the use of skin lighteners by a number of darker-complexioned African Americans, as frequently advertised in black periodicals from the turn of the century through the 1930s. Though many of these publications exalted the notion of racial pride, they contradictorily featured advertisements that "promised to 'remove black skin' and to 'turn the skin of a black or brown person four or five shades lighter'" (Lake 56).

After listening patiently to the younger girl's commentary, the narrator offers a critical response: "People tend to take the color of their environment. . . . In the matter of looks, of personal appearance, the mass of people try to conform to the dominant preferences and prejudices. Especially so if, as in the present case, the dominant color is different from their own. The dominant color in America is white. If the darker races are not brought into sharp contrast or conflict with it, it doesn't affect them much. Thus with the Indian who lives off by himself. But if a dark race is brought into contrast, as the Negro is, this race is likely to be compelled to wish to change its skin" (37). The narrator's response, noticeably free of emotion, is a rational, almost sociological explanation of the black man's masquerading. Strategically, the narrator reserves judgment of the woman and the black man, who are trapped in a racial logic that appears to be psychically damaging to both. The narrator implies that it is precisely because of the racial perceptions of the lady in blue that the black man strives for lighter skin. The black man desires to identify with the dominant group, and the lady in blue has conformed and contributed to the prejudices of that same group. Here again, Toomer subtly expresses the dangers of both racial perspectives and group identification. The lady in blue reflects, "Race prejudice is a strange thing . . . I wonder if we can overcome it?" At this point, the narrator simply replies, "An individualized person is no longer subject to it" (37). He then informs the woman that an "individualized person" is "one who, by effort, has risen superior to the influence which conditioned him" (38). The narrator's response that an individualized person is no longer subject to racism is an interesting turn of phrase. By not revealing his Indian and Negro stock, the narrator is passing in this scene. Therefore, the statement could refer to the fact that raced persons who have achieved individualization are no longer affected by racial prejudice. Of course, this would belie the fact that most African Americans are unable to conceal their blackness so easily. The narrator's position also does not consider that his lighter color may make him more palatable to whites who are aware of his multiracial identity. On the other hand, he implies that those who would be guilty of racism are no longer subject to such sentiments. The narrator's implication, then, is that the process of individualization effectively frees both blacks and whites from the psychologically damaging effects of race.

Given the particular historical and cultural moment in which this novel was produced, the narrator's answers to Marsh and the women on deck are cunning and subversive yet equally troubling. It is the narrator's strategy to draw attention away from the minor yet distinctive epidermal disparity between himself and the other passengers with whom he chooses to socialize by unabashedly exercising his psychological superiority. I emphasize the word *chooses* because the "nigger on the boat" only figures into the story as part of the woman on deck's racist comment, which is interesting given the multitude of careful observations the reader is made to suffer through throughout the text. However, by acting as the confidante and lay analyst for others aboard the ship, the narrator theoretically levels the playing field by establishing himself as an exceptional Other. By carving out an emotional and intellectual space that he can master, the narrator successfully manipulates the other passengers aboard the ship.

In style and content, "Transatlantic" is as far removed from *Cane* as one could imagine. A lingering thread of Toomer's former "black" life, however, is his construction of the narrator, who resembles more than any other Toomer character Lewis from "Kabnis." Somerville has identified the presence of a Lewis-like figure in many of Toomer's stories, noting that "Toomer's 'queer,' racially ambiguous male characters are in fact idealized figures, godlike rather than tragic" (164). In "Kabnis," Lewis functions as the story's "'queer,' racially ambiguous" character who "disrupts the familiar routines and alliances in the town, eliciting suspicion from white and black townspeople alike" (140). The narrator in "Transatlantic" operates to a different end in that his interactions are intended to ally individuals even though he intentionally destabilizes their existing values and beliefs. Indeed, the narrator imagines the dismantling of boundaries among all of the passengers on the *Burgundy*.

Shortly after the narrator's encounter with two women on deck, he makes the acquaintance of another young woman, Edith, who involves him in a number of debates on topics ranging from the level of protection America should provide to its citizens abroad to whether or not the American disdain for the English is innate. Despite the narrator's powerful skills of persuasion with the other passengers, Edith presents a challenge: "I could neither change her feelings nor make contact with her mind. Our forms and processes seemed to be entirely different. Her mind went one direction working on its own, to me, peculiar way. I could not overtake it. I could not make it conform to mine; nor could I shape my thoughts so that she could grasp them. We were at sixes and sevens" (93). However, when the subject of prejudice arises (when Edith reveals her bias against the British), the narrator is finally able to influence her perceptions. He explains to her that "both scientific thought and common sense pointed to the conclusion that national and racial prejudices were matters of environmental conditioning. Give the same person a different environment—and he or she would have an entirely different set of prejudices and preferences" (97). The narrator finally convinces Edith that this is the explanation for her bigoted feelings and he is "surprised to find that our minds, of a sudden, had contacted" (97–98). He then suggests how she might begin to overcome her prejudices: "The importance of this view . . . lies in this: that we can recondition, re-educate people. Insofar as it is a matter of their experience, we can change them, or better, they can change themselves" (98). Once Edith acknowledges that the dissipation of her prejudice is possible, "a weight seemed to lift from her. Over-tenseness gave way to a smiling relief. Our talk went easier" (99).

Later, pondering his conversation with Edith, the narrator questions the roots of her prejudice: "I could give her ideas. She could present to me the challenge of a human being who is trying intelligently to solve a difficult problem. What was this problem? Had her relations with someone she loved been twisted by an Irish-English prejudice? Or by a Catholic-Protestant prejudice? Edith was Catholic. Or, what was equally probable, had some painful experience made her bitter, and then, had this bitterness aroused and found vent through race prejudice?" (102). The scene with Edith further abstracts the issue of prejudice from a black-white binary and shores up the narrator's analysis of the very constructedness of bias, racial or otherwise. In this passage, Toomer implies that while the racialized body brings racial prejudice into fuller relief, intolerance exists even in the absence of the racialized body. Collectively, these episodes point to Toomer's evolved perspectives on both the psychology of race and the ambivalent nature of human interaction.

While the narrator makes no effort to probe the subconscious minds of the passengers aboard the *Burgundy,* his method of destabilizing their core beliefs allows them to shift their perspectives independently. The narrator merely plants the seeds for change and enables them to take whatever form they might. His artistic vision to "understand [how] life . . . of right beginnings and perfect endings, can be lived" is informed by the knowledge that "all things existing in the universe exist for something. This includes you, myself, man, earth, all life and all experience. All that happens has meaning in relation to this something. It, a vast One, and also an infinite multiplicity, is intelligible. It is our task to understand. But for us, for now, this one truth is enough. It is an art to end perfectly" (239). Unfortunately, Jean Toomer's own "art" met a rather imperfect ending. He never completely reconciled his allegiance to Gurdjieff and his ties with his former black life, nor was he able to find an aesthetically compelling way to incorporate Gurdjieff's philosophies within his literary form. In the fictional world of "Transatlantic," the savvy narrator can embody the enlightened self of which Toomer dreamed. But even in the idyllic "eight-day world" that Toomer portrays in "Transatlantic," racial prejudice is inexorable, even if coolly confronted. In a letter to his friend, Paul, Toomer writes about his disengagement from Gurdjieff with the simple explanation, "for some reasons known to me, and some unknown, I am, for better or worse, out of it—and I want to remain out, quite out—until such a time, if and when that time comes, that I again move towards it by impulses arising within myself. As you know, some drinks mix; some don't."[13] After Gurdjieff, Toomer experimented with Jungian analysis and Quakerism but later admitted that he had been disappointed by all of these systems of belief. Even though Toomer had explicitly denounced any allegiance to a particular racial group, the presence of race in "Transatlantic" reveals the ambivalent nature of Toomer's refusal. Toomer's engagement with Gurdjieffian principles did not obliterate his desire to exist as a racial subject; rather, Toomer's appropriation of Gurdjieff complicated his notion of race in that he recognized, as John L. Jackson Jr. notes, that "people are not simply racial objects (to be verified from without) but racial subjects with an interiority that is never completely and unquestionably clear" (18). Toomer's "objective art" could more accurately be read not as an imitation of Gurdjieffian techniques, but as a messy negotiation of the past and present. The expression of this ambivalence could only find its form in an imperfect end.

4

"A genuine cooperation"

Richard Wright's and Ralph Ellison's Psychoanalytic Conversations

On January 6, 1953, three months after the publication of *Black Skin, White Masks,* psychiatrist Frantz Fanon wrote what could best be considered a fan letter to Richard Wright.[1] In it, Fanon informs Wright that he has read *Native Son, Black Boy,* and *Twelve Million Black Voices* but would like to read more of Wright's texts to complete a study of "la portèe humaine," or the psychological impact, of Wright's oeuvre. By 1953, Wright was well established as a literary giant and critic and Fanon was but an emerging analyst. Yet Fanon tells Wright that their interest in black and white relations, globally, is mutual. Fanon acknowledges that while his name must be unknown to Wright ("Mon nom doit vous être inconnu"), he is equally concerned with the "systematic misconceptions" between blacks and whites ("où je me proposais montrer les méconnaissances systématiques des Blancs et des Noirs"), which also serve as the central focus of his recent and only text. The letter from Fanon to Wright reveals the influence of Wright's articulations of African American experience on Fanon's own thinking about colonized subjectivities. In addition, Fanon's letter allows for a reshaping of the dominant circumscription of Wright as an "urban realist" or "naturalist" and points to the psychical import of his work to analysts themselves. But more generally, the letter signals an important shift in the way black writers after the period of the Harlem Renaissance began to think about psychoanalysis as more than a theoretical space merely to be appropriated for literary use or as political ends to a discourse in which they could actively participate and potentially reshape.

Richard Wright and Ralph Ellison are perhaps the best exemplars of the evolution of the relationship between African American literary and psychoanalytic communities from the Harlem Renaissance to the World War II era.

What we begin to witness in the middle of the twentieth century, and what Fanon's letter to Wright suggests, is an emerging and unprecedented dialogue, a symbiosis, between black writers and practicing analysts. The result of such an interaction is that, for the first time, black writers and psychoanalysts were able to meld their mutual interests to extend the boundaries of literary analysis and psychoanalytic therapy, creating opportunities to materially change the lives of African Americans through psychoanalytic processes. The 1940s and 1950s witnessed the rise of social psychiatry, which meant that analysts and their patients were no longer isolated within the realm of the privileged few. Within this historical moment, psychoanalytic psychiatry increasingly linked the nature of one's social environment to his or her psychological state, and as a result the discourse of psychoanalysis diverged into two separate entities: the more "traditional" analysts who continued to privilege the role of the family in the shaping of individual subjectivities, and those analysts who deviated from Freudian-inspired paradigms to investigate the impact of society on the subject. The result, as Dan Blazer notes, was that social psychiatry became a form of "social activism," in that it served as a "movement to change society (and to study society) to lessen emotional suffering" (69). In this way, postwar psychoanalysis was imagined as an "emancipatory therapy" that could effectively articulate and respond to the psychological crisis of African American experience.[2] It was during this same period that Ellison and Wright became active and integral parts of the discursive formation of American psychoanalysis. However, it is also significant to note that Ellison and Wright diverged greatly from the then popular and accepted idea that psychoanalysis could effectively "cure" psychological problems that emerged as the result of social conditions. Their belief was that flaws in U.S. democracy ran so deep that until the United States became a free and equal state, African Americans would suffer from socially induced neurosis. While mainstream America began to regard psychoanalysis as a way to resolve problems facing both the individual and society, Wright and Ellison were less convinced that it might have such curative affects on African Americans who were the unfortunate victims of an uneven U.S. democracy. Still, they believed that psychoanalysis was the most effective methodology available to interpret and explain the prevalence of mental illness and social deviance within black communities. They maintained enough faith in the science to offer their energies and resources to establish, with analyst and friend Dr. Frederic Wertham, Harlem's first psychiatric facility, the Lafargue Mental Hygiene Clinic.

This chapter examines Wright's and Ellison's interventions within World War II–era psychoanalytic discourses, specifically marking the way that black literary insights became intrinsic to extending the scope of psychoanalytic thought by challenging it to contend with the racial politics of the time. Though in the 1940s the idea that psychoanalysis could influence the social world of the American masses was largely an accepted one, Ellison's and Wright's notion that psychoanalysis could also empower African Americans to confront the issues of urbanization, displacement, and racism was visionary and contributed greatly to the emerging field of social psychiatry. Both writers were encouraged by the relative success of this burgeoning science, but they were also aware of the limitations of a psychoanalytic approach to the multitude of problems plaguing African Americans. As such, the conversations between Wright, Ellison, and the psychoanalytic communities of which they aimed to be a part reveal the sometimes contradictory and problematic nature of deploying a psychoanalytic model to address material problems within marginalized, specifically black, communities and further define the contours of both writers' ambitions to inform, rather than merely draw upon, psychoanalytic discourses.

While Ellison and Wright identified uneven social conditions as the source of psychical instability, the deployment of a psychoanalytic paradigm to address these concerns proved inherently problematic. Their advocacy of psychoanalytic therapy to address the psychological malaise experienced by black subjects intimates some complicity with the conservative impulses of psychoanalysis in the years during and immediately following World War II. For example, Wright referred to the work of the Lafargue clinic as "the extension of the very concept of psychiatry into a new realm, the application of psychiatry to the masses, the turning of Freud upside down" (R. Wright, "Psychiatry"), which suggests that the clinic would perform a radical revisioning of Freudian logic to address the specificity of black American experience. Even though Ellison and Wright imagined themselves contributing to the subversive reframing of racialized subjectivity, their efforts were largely undermined by the governing framework of postwar psychoanalysis that was defined by its normalizing imperatives. In the 1940s and 1950s, psychoanalysis emerged as a dominant social force that effectively influenced cultural attitudes and perceptions, severely marking the limits of what might be considered "normal" and "deviant" behaviors. At the same time that analysts created the terms of pathological conduct, many advanced new theories about ways that psychoanalytic psychiatry could properly "assimilate" blacks, "cure" homosexuals, and further "domesticate" women.

Put simply, methodology matters. The term *mental hygiene,* which was defined in the nineteenth century by Dr. Isaac Ray as the "management of the bodily powers in regard to exercise, rest, food, clothing and climate, the laws of breeding, the government of the passions, the sympathy with current emotions and opinions, [and] the discipline of the intellect" (quoted in Besley 128) and emerged as an entire movement during World War II, emphasizes the psychoanalytic imperative to ensure that the individual performs in accordance with the governing laws and norms of his or her social environment.[3] While Ellison and Wright were certainly invested, to a large degree, in the power of psychoanalytic psychiatry to give African Americans "insight into the relation between his problems and his environment" (Ellison, "Harlem Is Nowhere" 327), there was also an investment in making certain that African Americans were read as "normative" subjects in the larger public sphere.

In what follows, I examine the interanimating dialogue among Wright, Ellison, and popular analysts of the period, specifically Dr. Benjamin Karpman, Dr. Frederic Wertham, and Dr. Harry Stack Sullivan. Collectively, these exchanges articulate the precariousness of crafting an emancipatory psychoanalytic model that would address the deleterious psychical effects of racism and prejudice within the context of a repressive social sphere that contributed to notions of black inferiority. From these conversations, Wright and Ellison crystallized their formulations about the possibilities that could emerge from the application of psychoanalytic psychiatry to black social and psychical crises, which I argue emerged more forcefully in their publicity essays for the Lafargue clinic, Wright's "Psychiatry Comes to Harlem" and Ellison's "Harlem Is Nowhere." I also consider how these essays further articulate the way both authors implicated an inequitable American democracy as the source of psychological dysfunction among marginalized citizens. Finally, I conclude the chapter with an investigation of the Golden Day scene in Ellison's *Invisible Man,* which provides a relevant literary example of the tenuous relation between Freudian thought, psychoanalytic therapy, and black subjectivity. This scene precisely demonstrates the way that the psychoanalytic preoccupation with modes of normativity during and immediately after World War II were intertwined with a larger civil rights agenda, particularly Ellison's vision of black inclusion within the fabric of American cultural, social, and political life.

Wright and Dr. Benjamin Karpman

In the postwar period, a confluence of factors, most notably the mass publication of lay texts by U.S. analysts, the emigration of a host of European analysts to the United States following the onset of World War II, and the pervasiveness of "shell shock" among U.S. veterans, contributed to the popularity of psychoanalytic discourse among mainstream audiences. Nathan Hale Jr.'s *The Rise and Crisis of Psychoanalysis in the United States* notes that the breadth of social and familial experiences, including "dreams and the unconscious, childhood and sexuality, family relationships, love, aggression, and death" that psychoanalysis claimed to address "were reflected in the growing publicity about psychoanalysis which attracted new patients who, in turn, provided a market for yet more information" (76). By 1940, psychoanalysis had extended its reach beyond the professional and upper classes and become accessible to a broad middle-class clientele. The media's interest in psychoanalytic thought engendered an unprecedented popularity among mainstream audiences and, as a result, made the most famous analysts public figures and household names. It was during this time that Wright began to consider more ambitiously potential collaborations with prominent analysts who might be willing to broaden psychoanalytic therapy to treat those within marginalized communities. In October 1942, Wright and Dr. Benjamin Karpman began a correspondence that reveals the desire of both writer and analyst to join forces in the interest of crafting a more substantive relationship between black subjectivity and psychoanalytic thought. It is significant that this correspondence began a mere three months after Wright's withdrawal from the Communist Party on the basis that, as Michael Fabre points out, "the socialism practiced by the American Communist Party did not give enough attention to the fight against racism and the development of the individual" (231). Given this rationale, it is appropriate that Wright would turn to psychoanalysis as a model that would help him to fulfill his mission as a writer and social critic. Karpman expresses his long-standing interest in African American experience to Wright, specifically noting that a "psychoanalytic volume on the subject of black-white relations," a suggestion of Wright's, was an idea he had "been carrying in [his] mind for over twenty years."[4] Karpman's close friendship with philosopher Alain Locke, an architect and an arbiter of the Harlem Renaissance, would have certainly made him privy to the range of social, political, and economic factors that posed varying psychical consequences for African Americans. Though the correspondence between Wright and Karpman lasted only approximately two years, their interaction is significant in that it crystallizes the collaborative efforts between psychoanalytic and black literary communities during the 1940s and 1950s, and perhaps more importantly demonstrates why such efforts were difficult to establish.

Wright's international celebrity after the 1940 publication of *Native Son* made him as attractive to psychoanalysts as they were to him. In an April 1943 letter, Karpman suggests that Wright produce an article for *Harper's Magazine* that "might deal with such a topic as 'The Blind Inability of the White Man to Understand the Psychology of the Negro,' which blindness is a defense barrier put up by him, while the negro too, when dealing with white people, is also on the defensive." Karpman informs Wright that the article would reach a larger audience given Wright's notoriety, since Karpman's "name [was] not well known and carries little weight" yet Wright's "position [was] different."[5] Such a request may partially explain why Karpman entertained an alliance with Wright. At the time, American analysts were enjoying a popularity similar to that of celebrities. Jonathan Freedman notes that not only were analysts employed as "consultants" on Hollywood films, but they also served as analysts for a number of celebrities and Hollywood producers.[6] Even in Michael Fabre's lengthy biography of Wright, Karpman's name surfaces only twice, and both instances briefly reference Karpman in association with Wright's attempt to use his personal contacts at the Marshall Field Foundation to support Karpman's "collected material on the psychopathology of the Negro American" (286). Because Wright was well-known in mainstream literary circles, coauthoring with him would greatly advance Karpman's professional ambitions. However, one might well speculate that Karpman's request would raise an eyebrow for Wright, given that he had written an entire novel (*Native Son*) in which the theme of blindness, particularly as it relates to the relationship between Bigger Thomas and the Dalton family, plays a central role. This request sets the tone for the difficulty Karpman and Wright would experience in attempting to collaborate on any mutual projects, since Karpman was intent on providing the substance that Wright was expected to animate.

Karpman's appeal was one of many instances in which the nature of the collaboration Karpman imagined between himself and Wright would be that of merely analyst and fiction writer. There appears, especially on Karpman's end, a sense of frustration about where the work of the analyst ends and the work of the writer begins. The undertone of his letters suggests that, while Karpman admires Wright's accomplishments as a fiction writer, he is less inclined to allow him to bring his own psychological insights to any collaborative project. When Wright suggests that they work on the two-volume project on black-white relations, Karpman's immediate response is that such a project is "hardly realizable." He informs Wright that he could assist him but that "for this work [Karpman would] need as assistants men and women who [were] trained to present the material in a scientific manner." Karpman's vision of a working relationship with Wright entailed both his providing the material and analyses from his various case studies and Wright employing his skill as a writer to "novelize" these studies. He explains to Wright that "fiction writers and dramatists have often used psychiatric material by just reading available literature, so again psychiatry has got nothing out of it. It seems to me, though, that such utilization of the material does not give the fiction writer the best that Psychiatry is able to give. Psychiatrists are in possession of a far deeper and more profound material dealing with human emotions that rarely if ever finds its way into print. . . . When the new Fiction Writer will drop some of his megalomania, give some credit to the psychiatrist, a genuine cooperation will be possible."[7] In this particular letter, Karpman emphasizes the value that he brings to a potential partnership with Wright, which is first-hand experience with a range of case studies. By having direct access to a working psychoanalyst, Wright would be able to extend the scope of his literary endeavors. In Karpman's view, the fact that writers appropriate psychoanalytic studies primarily from published texts severely limits their literary potential, so "a genuine cooperation" between the two would work to both expose the fiction writer to a broader range of material and popularize scientific studies produced by analysts. However, it becomes apparent that Wright's vision of "a genuine cooperation" would allow him to contribute his own psychological insights to any mutual projects. As such, Wright's push to engage psychoanalysis was not merely for the entertainment of a reading audience but a step in the process of "healing" disenfranchised citizens so that they could address their inequitable condition. In other words, Wright was not necessarily interested in merely fictionalizing Karpman's studies but felt compelled to craft his own psychological insights on the lives of marginalized persons. Perhaps what Karpman considers Wright's "megalomania" is in fact Wright's compulsion to erect a bridge between psychoanalysis and African American experience in an effort to effect material change within black communities.

In addition to his correspondence with Karpman and his burgeoning friendship with analyst Dr. Frederic Wertham, with whom he would later collaborate to establish Harlem's first mental health facility, Wright assiduously studied major psychological and sociological texts.[8] From Wright's lay studies in psychoanalysis came the belief that psychoanalytic therapy could materially improve the lives of African Americans. Claudia Tate acknowledges that Wright "invested more than intellectual curiosity in psychoanalysis" and that "for him, psychoanalysis was a principal source of his inspiration and a genuine reflection of his faith in the power of 'scientific, rational inquiry' to probe 'into the nature of things'" (*Psychoanalysis* 93–94). Given Wright's ambition to employ psychoanalytic thought to address the psychical impact of urban life on black subjects, Karpman's reduction of him as merely a fiction writer was entirely out of sync with the way Wright imagined himself as both an intellectual and a critic. In fact, according to Fabre, Wright considered his "mission as a writer 'to create a new life by intensifying the sensibilities and to work towards world understanding by improving living conditions'" (Fabre 203). Both Fabre and Tate point to Wright's "field work," particularly his visits to educational institutions and correctional facilities as well as his personal experiences, which provided him with invaluable insight on the psychological effects of racism, urbanization, and disenfranchisement.

Yet Wright's potential as an authority on such matters was lost on Karpman, who considered himself "a specialist in minorities." Karpman explains to Wright that he is "sincerely convinced" that he can provide an "interpretation of the negro problem such as has never been attempted by anyone before and it is doubtful that it will ever be done by somebody else." Among Karpman's "special qualifications" for pursuing his "psychogenetic study on the problems of the negro" is "an intimate contact with the people for the past twenty five years, which [he] doubts that many white people have had an opportunity to have"—a contact that he "sought," "nourished," "cultivated," and "gave all the sunshine [he] could." In his final words to Wright, Karpman emphasizes that he "had met among [his] students Bigger Thomas long before [Wright] ever thought of writing about them."[9] The general content of Karpman's letters reveals that while he was certainly sympathetic to the host of concerns bearing on African American subjectivity in the early 1940s, his self-declaration as a "specialist in minorities" (a group that, for him, included criminals and homosexuals) highlights Karpman's tendency and the tendency of psychoanalysis in general to pathologize so-called minority behaviors.

For postwar psychoanalysts the relationship between criminality and aberrant or deviant sexuality was largely inextricable.[10] Freud was the first analyst to broach the topic of criminality and link it explicitly to psychosexual conflicts.[11] Postwar psychoanalysts furthered this analytic relation to include social influences on deviant behaviors.[12] Because analysts had begun to consider deviant sexuality as the underlying force of criminality, the psychoanalytic impulse was to engender normative sexual relations and, in the process of doing so, quell criminal behaviors. By the time Karpman and Wright began their correspondence, Karpman had already established himself as an eminent analyst and was exploring the relationship between law and criminal psychopathology, which included in particular juvenile delinquency and sexual crimes.[13]

Wright maintained a similar concern with respect to the psychical sources of criminality. In his biography of Richard Wright, Michael Fabre notes that in 1944 Wright began to work on his novella "The Jackal," in which he "planned to study the pathological behavior resulting from fear and anger" due to his "desire to help juvenile delinquents and combat nervous disorders in the ghetto" (271). Their shared interest in deploying psychoanalysis to address these issues within minority and marginalized communities necessarily implicates both Wright and Karpman within the normalizing and reductive framework of psychoanalysis. Karpman explains to Wright that he has always maintained an interest in minorities: "I probably would not have gone into Psychiatry were it not for my feeling that neurotics and psychotics are a greatly misunderstood minority. Similarly, the criminal has been misunderstood and abused as well. I found the same situation existing with respect to homosexuals."[14] The easy slippage from "neurotics and psychotics" to "the criminal" and "homosexuals" points to what was considered the inextricable nature of criminality and nonnormative sexuality and the extent to which both have been pathologized within psychoanalytic discourses. Without suggesting that Wright's intent to address juvenile delinquency and nervous disorders within black communities is problematic, I want to emphasize the implications of his choice to engage a psychoanalytic approach to do so, especially given the overwhelming conservatism of psychoanalysis during the Cold War.

In the absence of Wright's letters to Karpman, it is difficult to ascertain Wright's precise sentiments about Karpman's unproblematic collapsing of the black subject, the criminal subject, and the homosexual. However, Fabre states clearly that "Wright had a terror of homosexuality, associating it with the term hermaphrodite; he had a vague memory of wandering through the streets of Memphis, drunk or maybe drugged, imagining that he had become a hermaphrodite, a kind of devil without a tail" (13–14). Wright's own dangerous collapsing of the homosexual and the hermaphrodite sends a clear signal about his investment in the treatment of homosexuality, which was interpreted not only by American analysts but also the U.S. government as a sign of mental instability.[15] Together, Wright's and Karpman's minority rehabilitation projects raise concerns about methodology. In the process of advocating psychoanalysis as a way to address deviance in black communities, Wright was ultimately complicit in constructing what Roderick Ferguson refers to as a "canonical formation[s]," which "outline trajectories for ethical subject formation; they specify what it means to be a human, a citizen, and a moral being. As champions of normativity, these formations can only be consummated through the regulation of nonheteronormative difference" (66). As such, the imperatives of psychoanalytic therapy were not necessarily to provide mental health services but an attempt to indoctrinate a set of values or norms deemed proper by the larger social order. Even psychoanalytic psychiatry's designation for its therapeutic processes as "mental hygiene" makes explicit its tremendous concern with the sanitization of immoral, improper, and unethical behaviors.

In his 1956 "Psychoanalysis and the Negro Problem," Charles I. Glicksberg poses the question, "Does not the democratic process in America offer the most effective refutation of the theory of immutable, self-contained racial character-entities . . . ? Why should the Negro, because he possesses a different pigmentation, be an exception?" (42). Such inclinations to ascribe some brand of pathological behavior onto black subjects was largely an effect of the role American psychoanalysis played in the World War II period in terms of producing a hegemonic framework of heteronormative conduct. The fact that most blacks were relegated to the social, political, and economic margins was viewed by certain sectors of the psychoanalytic community as a consequence of their natural inferiority. The notion that black folks were "crazy anyway" was a measured defense for the continued exclusion of African Americans from mental health services.[16] Karpman's desire to "cure" black, as well as criminal and homosexual, subjects exposes a fundamental tendency of conservative postwar psychoanalysis to fault the individual or the family, rather than his or her social environment, as the source of psychological problems.

The tone of Karpman's letters and the fact that he and Wright never collaborated on any project show that neither could agree on the terms under which a project could materialize. Yet the significance of Wright and Karpman's relatively brief exchange lies in the imaginative attempt of both men to construct a bridge between African American and psychoanalytic communities, especially at a time when the idea of deploying psychoanalysis to attend to the social and psychical problems experienced by African Americans was considered both unorthodox and implausible. Wright's investment in psychoanalysis as a methodology that might explain the multitude of psychological issues among blacks would not allow him simply to play the role of fiction writer. Karpman's firm belief that analysis was best left to the analyst foreclosed the possibility of any genuine cooperation, especially given his own disciplinary boundaries and Wright's psychoanalytic ambitions.

Wertham's Influence

Though Wright was unable to forge an intellectual collaboration with Karpman, his relationship with Wertham would prove more successful in actualizing his desire to contribute to psychoanalytic discourses. A year prior to his correspondence with Karpman, Wright was led to think more intently about the psychological impetus of criminality after his experience with the Clinton Brewer case. According to Fabre, Wright was deeply disappointed by the outcome of the Brewer case and befriended Wertham after contacting him to help explain "which factors, motives, or psychological abnormality" had prompted Brewer, a prisoner for whom Wright was an advocate, to commit another murder two months after his release (Fabre 236). Their common belief that Brewer's murder had little to do with his actual victims but was caused by a "pathological obsession" developed early in his life served as the impetus of Wright and Wertham's mutual admiration and friendship (236). The dialogue between Wright and Wertham was significant in that it allowed Wright greater insight into the realm of psychoanalytic thought, and eventually led Wertham to try his hand at literary analysis.

In June 1944, Wertham presented "An Unconscious Determinant in *Native Son*" at the annual meeting of the American Psychopathological Association. In his speech, Wertham acknowledged that even though "psychoanalytic studies of works of literature have been undertaken," his project with Wright was unique since "no psychoanalytic study of a literary creation based on analytic study of its author [had] even been undertaken" (321). What is perhaps most noteworthy in Wertham's reading of *Native Son* is that he uses autobiographical elements of Richard Wright's life—hence he analyzes Wright—in an effort to draw "definite conclusions about the psychology of the process of literary creation" (322). Wertham actually privileges his study because of his immediate access to the author, and notes that "psychoanalytic studies of works of literature in which the author was not available may also in many instances have been such rationalizations based mainly on theory" (325). He uses his analysis of Shakespeare's *Hamlet* as one such example in which the analyst could only speculate as to authorial motivation. Wertham excuses the brevity of his study of *Native Son,* explaining that because Wright is such a public figure he does not "feel free to reveal too much personal data. . . . While [he] is handicapped in [his] study of *Hamlet* by the fact that Shakespeare was dead, [he is] handicapped in writing openly about *Native Son* by the fact that Richard Wright is alive" (322). Wertham's analysis of *Native Son* highlights the intensity of the dialogue between Wright and Wertham and demonstrates the kind of "genuine cooperation" Wright had once imagined between himself and Karpman. Further, it is clear that Wright trusted Wertham enough to allow himself to be the subject of analysis, a fact that seemingly drove a wedge between him and Karpman.[17] In as much as both men were interested in the analytic possibilities that would emerge from the convergence of literature and psychoanalysis, they were equally invested in the material possibilities that could arise from using psychoanalysis as a lens to examine and "treat" psychological problems among marginalized persons. Wertham's reading of Wright's *Native Son* began as part of an experiment performed by Wertham and Wright to unearth the psychoanalytic underpinnings of the novel. In *Outsider Citizens: The Remaking of Postwar Identity in Wright, Beauvoir, and Baldwin,* Sarah Relyea comments that "Wright's collaboration with Wertham documents the influence of psychoanalytic concepts on the construction of black masculinity in the 1940s and 1950s" (37). While this is certainly the case, their collaboration more importantly constitutes one of the most important alliances between black literary and psychoanalytic communities; their interaction produced material results in the form of texts, notably Wright's essay "Psychiatry Comes to Harlem"; his novel *Savage Holiday,* which he dedicated to Wertham; and the Lafargue Mental Hygiene Clinic, which served the Harlem community for thirteen years.

Black Subjectivity and the Promise of Psychoanalytic Psychiatry

The front page of the *New York Amsterdam News* on April 27, 1946, ran the headline "Mental Hospitals Bar Negroes." The article claimed that despite the fact that the "taxes of every citizen of New York state" supported the Psychiatric Institute, which was primarily responsible for the mental health services of those residing in New York City, the institute "had been charged with the complete exclusion of Negro patients, both children and adults, from the hospital, and giving inadequate psychotherapy to those few who [were] treated in the out-patient clinic" (1). In response to the relative dearth of psychological health facilities willing to service black patients, the Lafargue Mental Hygiene Clinic opened its doors to a primarily African American clientele in Harlem in March 1946. The clinic's inauguration was considered nothing short of a miracle given that the privilege of psychological therapy was largely the exclusive domain of white patients. Wertham, along with the dedicated assistance of Wright and Ralph Ellison, conceived of the Lafargue clinic as a response to the prevalence of juvenile delinquency in Harlem. Ellison and Wright's investment in this endeavor was substantial in that they were responsible for securing the clinic's location, writing its publicity materials, and recruiting its clientele.

In his September 1946 publicity essay for the clinic, "Psychiatry Comes to Harlem," Wright criticizes the medical profession for pathologizing African Americans and for failing to recognize the true source of psychological conditions affecting blacks—the social order. The inability, or rather the unwillingness, of psychoanalytic communities to acknowledge the role that institutional racism, urbanization, and poverty play in negatively constituting African American subjectivity, for Wright, serves as psychoanalysis's blind spot. The article projects psychological therapy as a viable solution to social problems while remaining critical of psychoanalysis' historical inattention to matters of race and racism. "Psychiatry Comes to Harlem" is one example of the many iterations of "mass cultural American transformations of psychoanalytic theory" (Freedman 95), in that Wright implicates American racism and white hegemony as the root cause of mental illness among black subjects.

Wright's ambition for the Lafargue clinic to revolutionize Freudian psychoanalysis assumes that, as Harold J. Elam argues, the method for addressing the specific forms of psychical trauma experienced by African Americans is not readily "framed in Freudian psychoanalysis or one that fits neatly into white racist notions of black deviance but rather a social psychoanalytic approach professing that change within the social environment can and will affect the black psyche" (614). Elam observes that the sociological and psychological treatments for what he describes as "racial madness" had historically "become intricately intertwined with the so-called Negro problem in America. While white supremacists believed that black inferiority made black people inherently insane, more leftist-minded racial critics, both white and black, argued that conditions of oppression, racism, and restrictive prejudicial practices impressed on blacks a particular type of cultural neurosis" (614). As Wright points out, psychological discourses were largely responsible for assumptions that the mainstream held with respect to the mental condition of African Americans, specifically that "despite the endless flow of black mental patients to our state and city hospitals, doubt is expressed that need for a clinic in Harlem is acute, for it is traditionally assumed that Negroes would naturally account for a large proportion of the mentally ill" (R. Wright, "Psychiatry"). Wright continues to note that the very discourse of psychology has contributed to racist notions that color black people as "'pleasure-loving,' 'lazy,' 'shiftless,' naturally inclined toward crime, slow of comprehension, and irresponsible." The prevalence of violence, juvenile delinquency, and "deviant" sexuality in Harlem is, as Wright explains, the effect of "psychologically repressed need," which "goes underground, gropes for an unguarded outlet in the dark and, once finding it, sneaks out, experimentally tasting the new freedom, then at last gushing forth in a wild torrent, frantic lest a new taboo deprive it of the right to exist." The clinic's location in the basement of St. Philip's Episcopal Church provided Wright the inspiration to imagine the clinic both literally and figuratively as an "underground" institution. Wright's reference to the unleashing of "repressed need" intimates that neurotic behaviors expressed by African Americans are, in part, inspired by the restriction of social freedoms through segregation and discrimination. He reiterates this concern, noting that "the powerful personality conflicts engendered in Negroes by the consistent sabotage of their democratic aspirations in housing, jobs, education, and social mobility creates an environment of anxiety and tension which easily tips the normal emotional scales toward neurosis." Here Wright's formulation of a socially produced neurosis anticipates Deleuze and Guattari's conception of neurosis as a perfectly logical, even normative, response to a capitalist (and racist) social order.[18] By fostering the claim that neurosis is not intrinsic to African American character but an ethically justifiable response to systematic forms of oppression, Wright also acknowledges the inherent limitations of a psychoanalytic method. Yet he nonetheless advocates social psychiatry as the most efficacious path toward the reconciliation of black subjects and the state.

Wright and Ellison, like Wertham, were heavily invested in the democratization of psychoanalytic psychiatry. The dialogue between Wright, Ellison, and psychoanalytic discourses appears to center on the idea of democracy, particularly democracy as a structure that defines and gives meaning to U.S. life. Ellison's democratic idealism, more than Wright's, is firm—so much so that he consistently links an unstable democracy to an unstable psyche. Wright uses the word *democracy* repeatedly in "Psychiatry Comes to Harlem," and Ellison gives it special weight in his publicity essay for the Lafargue clinic, "Harlem Is Nowhere," referring to the clinic as "an underground extension of democracy." Shelly Eversley articulates the relationship between democracy and psychoanalysis that Ellison once imagined, noting that the "unresolved tension between segregation and democracy inadvertently produces a new alliance between psychiatry and art" ("Lunatic's Fancy" 447). Harlem in the 1940s reflected all of the social and economic consequences spurred by the Great Depression; Harlem's population grew dramatically between 1910 and 1950, as did crime, infant mortality, disease, youth delinquency rates, and the volume of low-income housing (Capeci 38). Such was the reality for thousands of black migrants who left the South for the promise of opportunity in the North. "Harlem Is Nowhere," in which he identified white racism as detrimental to the social and psychological world of black Americans, would be Ellison's most poignant critique of Harlem's social conditions.

The black Harlem Ellison portrays is not at all reminiscent of the space that provided the inspiration for so many writers of the Harlem Renaissance. A mere two decades after the Renaissance moment, Ellison describes Harlem in "Harlem Is Nowhere" as "a ruin—many of its ordinary aspects (its crimes, its casual violence, its crumbling buildings with littered area-ways, ill-smelling halls and vermin-invaded rooms) are indistinguishable from the distorted images that appear in dreams, and which, like muggers haunting a lonely hall, quiver in the waking mind with hidden and threatening significance" (321). In "Harlem Is Nowhere," Ellison identifies the clinic as a space whose "importance transcends even its great value as a center for psychotherapy; it represents an underground extension of democracy" (320). The democratic nature of the clinic clarifies the inextricable relation Ellison repeatedly draws between a sound democracy and a sound psyche, and his resolute faith in U.S. democracy extends beyond desegregation and freedom to include a "most dramatic form of social organization." For Ellison, the American plays a particular role within that drama by "asserting his own and his group's values and traditions against those of his fellow citizens" ("Going" 599). The democracy Ellison describes is, in fact, a constant negotiation of cultural values and assumptions that seek reconciliation through political means. The clinic emerges as a refuge within Harlem in which the dynamic between patients and doctors constitutes the idyllic image of a realized democracy and in which competing values are able to be resolved. Ellison describes those in Harlem as inhabiting a social, geographic, and psychological no-man's-land, where they "feel alienated and their whole lives have become a search for answers to the questions, Who am I, What am I, Why am I, and Where? Significantly, in Harlem the reply to the greeting 'How are you?' is often, 'Oh man, I'm nowhere'—a phrase so revealing an attitude so common that is has been reduced to a gesture, a seemingly trivial word" ("Harlem Is Nowhere" 323). Even the invisible narrator acknowledges the integral relationship between psychical well-being and space, noting that "perhaps to lose a sense of where you are implies the danger of losing a sense of who you are" (*Invisible Man* 436). Ellison explains that "the phrase 'I'm nowhere' expresses the feeling borne in upon many Negroes that they have no stable, recognized place in society. One's identity drifts in a capricious reality in which even the most commonly held assumptions are questionable. One 'is' literally, but one is nowhere; one wanders dazed in a ghetto maze, a 'displaced person' of American democracy" (325). To be displaced from or marginal to the processes of democracy creates, for Ellison, the conditions of psychical dis-ease. Ellison's critique of U.S. democracy is as clear as his faith in democratic institutions, which maintain an obligation, as well as a "*psychological function* . . . to protect the citizen against the irrational, incalculable forces that hover about the edges of human life" (324, my emphasis). The irony is that at the same time that democratic institutions are charged with safeguarding its citizens, these very same institutions are responsible for black Americans' continued elision from democratic processes. In the same way that democratic institutions are responsible for the social and economic life of American citizens, so too are they to be held accountable for their psychological well-being. The failure of democratic institutions to provide citizens protection and support can, in Ellison's words, "leave the most balanced Negro open to anxiety" (325).

Similarly to Wright, Ellison performs a transgressive upending of the logic of psychoanalytic thought, indicating that the sickness stems from the social order, not the individual subject. The result of this collapse is that Americans are consistently "yearning and thirsting for a rational social order, and being forced as human beings to live in what [they] like to identify as the 'present,' [they] go on struggling against the built-in conditions which comprise the pathology of American democracy" ("Harlem Is Nowhere" 598). The conditions to which Ellison refers are, undoubtedly, America's racial and racist legacy. The efforts of the Lafargue clinic, then, were meant to both enable blacks to cope with the reality of their alienation from the American mainstream and to establish their presence on the national scene as their sense of pathological dislocation announces the relative failure of U.S. democracy. For Ellison, the clinic, like the novel, enacts an important function of U.S. democracy and serves as a proper model for it as well.

While Ellison primarily argues that uneven social conditions produce various types of mental instability, he also identifies the "collapse of traditional values" and the corruption of a southern-born value system as central to the psychological malaise pervasive among Harlem's population. Echoing E. Franklin Frazier's analysis of the oft-overlooked psychological implications of black migration, Ellison describes the psychical transformation of urban migrants:

> Intelligence tests have measured the quick rise in intellect which takes place in Southern Negroes after moving north, but little attention has been paid to

> the mutations effected in their sensibilities. However, the two go hand in hand. . . . The movement north affects more than the Negro's wage scale; it affects his entire psychosomatic structure. The rapidity of Negro intellectual growth in the North is due partially to objective factors present in their environment, to influences of the industrial city and to a greater political freedom. But there are also changes within the "inner world." In the North energies are released and given *intellectual* channelization—energies which in most Negroes in the South have been forced to take either a *physical* form or, as with potentially intellectual types like Wright, to be expressed as nervous tension, anxiety, and hysteria. . . . And what is called hysteria is suppressed intellectual energy expressed physically. ("Richard Wright's Blues" 138, original emphasis)

Like Frazier, who determined that "contacts and competition with whites in the North had caused [blacks] to lose the provincial community and religious consciousness that had enveloped them in the South and quickened in them a racial consciousness that they had never known" (Frazier 297), Ellison connects one's sense of geographical dislocation to psychic confusion. In Freud's view, hysteria emerges when "the libido which has been liberated from the pathogenic material by repression is not converted . . . but is set free in the shape of anxiety" (Laplanche and Pontalis 38).

By rearticulating Freud's interpretation of hysteria within a racialized context, Ellison reframes the classical psychoanalytic interpretation of hysteria to suggest that perceived psychological disorders among African Americans mask deeper intellectual energies that are repressed due to southern law. In other words, the black southerner who possesses a keen insight into the illogical nature of his inferior position expresses what appears to be, in the psychological sense, hysteria. Ellison reiterates this conclusion in a September 1944 letter to Wright: "I did hear the rumour that you were neurotic again; first it was Bigger and now you. 'If you can't control a nigger, call him crazy,' you know the technique."[19] Hysteria, as a mask or false expression of bridled intellectualism, emerges in an oft-overlooked moment in *Invisible Man* in which a "short, pock-marked man appeared and took Mr. Norton's head between his hands, tilting it at arm's length and then, pinching the chin gently like a barber about to apply a razor, gave a sharp, swift movement" (61). The pock-marked man is one of the patients at the hospital or asylum who, while spending a day of therapy at the Golden Day, takes advantage of the shocked state of Mr. Norton, the white benefactor from the College. After punching Mr. Norton, the pock-marked man diagnoses his act as "a case of *hysteria* . . . [a] mere mild case of *hysteria*" (79) and simply walks away. Within the context of Ellison's earlier reformulation of "hysteria," the pock-marked man identifies Mr. Norton, at least symbolically, as the force responsible for his institutionalization. The scene further speaks to the inadequacy of a classical psychoanalytic approach to account for the specificity of African American experience, particularly as it pertains to the complex dynamics of American racism. That the pock-marked man self-diagnoses his abuse of Mr. Norton as a "mere mild case of hysteria" reveals the patients' awareness that the promise of U.S. progressivism, symbolized by Mr. Norton's misguided altruism, only benefits those, like the invisible narrator, who are blind to its contradictions. If hysteria is suppressed intellectual energy expressed physically, then the pock-marked man's punch to Mr. Norton complicates the idea that the patients lack awareness of their condition and reveals "wisdom" underlying a deeper façade of madness.

Ellison's concern that urbanization has material and psychological effects, both positive and negative, structures his argument for the efficacy of the Lafargue clinic in Harlem.[20] The notion that racially specific experiences—particularly racism, discrimination, segregation, and migration—lie at the heart of the psychological illnesses found among Harlem's citizens informs Ellison's argument in "Harlem Is Nowhere." Ellison asserts that these problems can be addressed or potentially cured through the careful revision of Freudian and Freudian-inspired analyses. The change that the black southerner undergoes upon experiencing life in an urban environment reads as one of both trauma and transformation: "His family disintegrates, his church splinters, his folk wisdom is discarded in the mistaken notion that it in no way applies to urban living, and his formal education (never really his own) provides him with neither scientific description nor rounded philosophical interpretation of the profound forces that are transforming his total being" ("Harlem Is Nowhere" 325). The process of translating southern mores into urban sensibilities proves to be one of the most striking failures of black migration. The virtual loss of a social and religious ethic, for Ellison, creates a class of migrants who experience a splintering of the self, and consequently, lapse into various forms of mental decline. The migrant's head-on collision with urbanity simultaneously expresses the promise and prevarication of the American Dream. Ellison consequently affirms psychoanalysis as a form of therapy that not only liberates the individual from the shackles of a degraded social position but also enables a reconciliation of folk sensibilities with modern urban life. The urban world of the migrant encompasses a host of social ills (high crime, unemployment, and slum dwellings) that inevitably have psychological consequences.

Ellison maintains that "Harlem Is Nowhere" is not about the Lafargue clinic but is more about pressing questions like "who is this total Negro whom the clinic seeks to know; what is the psychological character of the scene in which he dwells; how describe the past which he drags into this scene; and what is the future toward which he stumbles and becomes?" (321). Ellison's reference to the "total Negro" assumes that there has been a failure to articulate adequately the complexity of African American subjectivity, and that the total Negro remains a stranger among us. By delving into the present ("the scene in which he dwells"), the past, and the future of the total Negro, whom America represents as one-dimensional, Ellison creates a picture of African Americans as both legitimate citizens and modern subjects through a psychoanalytic approach. In this moment, Ellison maps the psychological terrain that analysts must endeavor, which is the commingling of a folk past with the technologies of the modern present. Ellison's imperative is not only to argue for the acceptance of African Americans as national citizens but also to construct an image of black people as integral to the discursive formation of modernity. For Ellison, the project of the Lafargue clinic "may be said to concern itself with any possible variations between the three basic social factors shaping an American Negro's personality: he is viewed as a member of a racial and cultural minority, as an American citizen caught in certain political and economic relationships, and as a modern man living in a revolutionary world" (320). The third factor is Ellison's imagining of a radical black subjectivity that mainstream society and the psychoanalytic community have yet to acknowledge and that further contextualizes black folks within the project of modernity. Elsewhere in the essay, Ellison refers to urbanization as "a vast process of change that has swept them from slavery to the conditions of industrial man in a space of time so telescoped (a bare eighty-five years) that it is literally possible for them to step from feudalism into the vortex of industrialism simply by moving across the Mason-Dixon line" (321). Racist discourses of the period, aptly illustrated in Wright's *Native Son,* consistently held to the dictum that black people were completely inassimilable to the modern world, and therefore not only outside of the nation-state but also outside of history.[21] However, a comprehensive psychological portrait of African Americans would reveal that blacks were integral to the formation of this revolutionary world rather than antithetical to it.

As Ellison convincingly argues, the psychological problems of migrants exist because they experience "the tension of the modern man but [are] regarded as primitives" (322). Thus, the failure to recognize them as intrinsic not only to the framing of democracy but also to the processes of modernity inevitably presents a psychological crisis. For Ellison, "Negroes are not unaware that the conditions of their lives demand new definitions of terms like *primitive* and *modern, ethical* and *unethical . . . tragedy* and *comedy, sanity* and *insanity*" (323). The inconsistencies of U.S. democracy read like a version of *Alice in Wonderland* in which conventional logic is upended and linguistic meaning consistently shifts. But as Ellison writes, "the true subject of democracy is not simply material well-being, but the extension of the democratic process in the direction of perfecting itself" (586). In "Harlem Is Nowhere," Ellison reads the successful inclusion of black migrants into the urban sphere as a sign and symbol of a viable American democracy.

Ellison's own geographic hopscotching would have given him firsthand insight into the intricate processes of urbanization, yet his precision in articulating its psychic impact on black migrants was also informed by his first employer in New York City, Dr. Harry Stack Sullivan. Sullivan had already established himself as one of the country's foremost psychoanalysts by the time Ralph Ellison began to work in his office upon his arrival from Tuskegee. But it is important to include here Sullivan's contributions to the field of social psychiatry: he was one of the first U.S. analysts to cross disciplinary borders and work directly with black sociologists, Charles Johnson and E. Franklin Frazier, to offer a psychoanalytic dimension to their sociological projects. Although it is well-known that Ellison worked in Sullivan's office, Sullivan's influence on Ellison's psychical framing of black migrant subjectivity has yet to be examined. Sullivan emerged as one of the leaders of the "eclectic psychodynamic style" of therapy (Hale 174). Psychoanalysts who subscribed to this particular method of treatment borrowed from Freudian theories, particularly those relating to the Oedipus complex and dream interpretation, but were sharply distinguished by their belief that psychosis was largely due to demographic and socioeconomic factors. While Sullivan subscribed to the notion that "dreams linked the psychotic and the normal," he departed from classical psychoanalysis because of its tendency to "overgeneralize" (Hale 175). According to Hale, "the dogmaticism of some who were filled with the 'holy light' of their own personal analyses, the theory that mental disorder resulted from fixations at past stages, and what he [Sullivan] regarded as the projection into infancy and childhood of sexual elements taken from the initial developments of adolescence" (175). Perhaps Sullivan's greatest contribution to Ellison was his formulation that "psychosis was a total 'psychobiological' reaction to a life situation" and his notion that "psychobiological processes were expressed through symbols, of which language was the most developed" (175). Sullivan was one of the most significant psychiatrists in the United States in the years immediately preceding the social psychiatry movement.

Sullivan's theory that schizophrenia could be based upon the extent to which one deviated from common cultural or group norms put forth a "whole new direction in American social psychiatry that placed social factors at the heart of the causation of mental disorders and linked social science and psychiatry" (Hale 176). The relationship between sociology and psychoanalysis that Sullivan worked to foster undoubtedly influenced Ellison, who admitted that throughout his intellectual life he remained "curious as to how one could put Freud and Marx together" (*Going* 206).

In 1937, Sullivan discussed his work interviewing black youths in the rural South in an appendix to Charles Johnson's *Growing Up in the Black Belt* titled "Memorandum on a Psychiatric Reconnaissance." Johnson encouraged Sullivan to pursue his investigations of southern black personality, though Sullivan admits that an "intensive psychiatric study of a few American Negroes of northern urban habitat inspired [in him] an intense interest in the possibilities of obtaining significant data on interpersonal relations . . . [he] was persuaded to undertake a visit of exploration in the deep South" (89–90). The interviews provided Sullivan with a keener sense of "American Negro personality" than prevailing "all-inclusive generalizations about the Negro group," and he concluded his study by noting that "psychiatry as the study of interpersonal relations has a difficult but a most rewarding field in the American Negro, that the Negro of the deep South seems in many respects the most promising for a beginning, and that he and his social situation, with its chronologically well-separated variations from the influx of new elements, constitute one of the most significant social science research fields" (89, 95).

Though most of Sullivan's patients were white, wealthy New Yorkers, his work with Johnson and Frazier allowed him greater psychical insight into African Americans—a group that, as I have suggested, the psychoanalytic community had deemed all but irrelevant. Sullivan was one of the first major analysts to take seriously the formation of black subjectivity, particularly in his treatment of the role geography plays in the construction of one's psychological life. Further, his explicit engagement with black subjects in the South introduced new modes of inquiry, since the study of blacks was virtually uncharted territory in the psychoanalytic profession. In writing about the contributions of Sullivan, Johnson notes that: "the psychiatrist's contribution to the sociologist is that of enough psychiatric sophistication to be aware of likely distortions of communication that will affect seriously the reliability of his data. . . . The explorations, or as he called it 'psychiatric reconnaissance,' into the race system of the Southern states were further evidence of the convictions regarding the relationship of the individual and the group, and of the importance of cultural factors in the definition of personality" (212–13). "Psychiatric reconnaissance" is the phrase Sullivan used to describe the process of deploying psychoanalytic thought to sow the rather uncultivated terrain of racial relations in the United States and identify the potential transformation of the psychological disciplines.

Black Resistance and Black Deviance

While Johnson, Frazier, and Sullivan were optimistic about the possibilities that could transpire from the convergence of psychoanalytic psychiatry and sociology, Ellison admits that America's racial problems are so complex that "a thousand Lafargue clinics could not dispel the sense of unreality that haunts Harlem" ("Harlem Is Nowhere" 327). Even Wertham expressed some skepticism about the value of the clinic, as indicated in a 1953 letter to Richard Wright in which he admitted that "maybe the history of the Clinic is a more important experiment than the Clinic itself."[22] Both Ellison and Wertham recognized that the curative possibilities of psychoanalytic therapy would only emerge once America resolved its ethical schizophrenia. But Ellison's recognition that the patients of the clinic are not passive victims of an inequitable society is of equal significance. Ellison acknowledges that black deviance, in the form of psychical instability, criminality, excessive sexuality, and homosexuality, results from the experience of social dislocation and disenfranchisement, which is in effect the consequence of resistance to the status quo. Ellison makes it clear that the ubiquitous feeling (and reality) of alienation emerges as a result of those in Harlem "rejecting the second-class status assigned them" ("Harlem Is Nowhere" 322). In writing about black deviance as a method of resistance, Cathy Cohen has persuasively argued that "individuals, with relatively little access to dominant power, not only counter or challenge the presiding normative order with regard to family, sex, and desire, but also create new or counter-normative frameworks by which to judge behavior" (30). Ellison's rearticulation of black deviance in "Harlem Is Nowhere" situates Harlem as a community of resistance; however, the rebellion of Harlem residents further distances them from the social world in which they are already alienated. Cohen's argument places Ellison's articulations about deviance in context, showing that while the patients suffer from the inequities fostered by racism and prejudice, they simultaneously reject the dominant order that rejects them (even when their rejection works to their own detriment). The intersections Ellison crafts between black deviance, particularly aberrant sexuality, and black social and political inclusion underscores his revisionary impulse to disrupt the historical logic that reads psychical instability as a natural or inherent element of black character.[23] Ellison introduces the relation between deviance, resistance, and psychical stability in "Harlem Is Nowhere," in a reference to "a boy's participation in the rape-robbery of his mother; a man beating his wife in a park uses boxing 'science' and observ[ing] Marquis of Queensberry rules . . . ; two men hold[ing] a third while a lesbian slashes him to death with a razor blade" as examples of the "surreal fantasies," all notably sexual in nature, that are "acted out upon the streets of Harlem" ("Harlem Is Nowhere" 322). However, this delicate matrix reaches its apex in the Golden Day scene from Ellison's *Invisible Man.*

Of particular interest in the Golden Day scene is the way Ellison extends his thesis about the ethical schizophrenia of American democracy and structures this contradiction within psychoanalytic discourses' preoccupation with normative sexuality. Ellison takes part in the postwar period narrative that treats social deviance as an effect of sexual dysfunction. After an unfortunate encounter leaves Mr. Norton, the white college benefactor, "shocked," the invisible narrator warily takes him to the Golden Day, a local bar and brothel, thinking that whiskey will help him regain his faculties. However, the narrator quickly realizes that patients from the asylum are visiting the Golden Day as well. Ellison describes the patients as "former doctors, lawyers, teachers, Civil Service workers; there were several cooks, a preacher, a politician, and an artist" (*Invisible Man* 74). The narrator harbors ambivalent feelings toward the patients, noting that "they were supposed to be members of the professions toward which at various times I vaguely aspired myself, and even though they never seemed to see me I could never believe that they were really patients" (74). That these former professionals have been relegated to an insane asylum supports Ellison's contention that those who are labeled by mainstream society as crazy are imbricated within an historical logic that undermines black resistance by reframing it as a sign of mental inferiority. The patients have clearly attempted to gain recognition and acceptance from the mainstream through legitimate professional and educational means. Therefore, before they were patients they were models of black middle-class respectability, and as such, it is significant that their expressions take the form of excessive sexuality. While deviant behaviors may not be made with "with explicitly political motives," individuals are willing to "face negative consequences in pursuit of goals important to them, often basic human goals such as pleasure, desire, recognition, and respect" (Cohen 30). The terms *pleasure* and *desire* emerge as complex significations, particularly in the civil rights era when black respectability was coterminous with political and social inclusion.

In "The Color of Discipline: Civil Rights and Black Sexuality," Thaddeus Russell notes that advocates of same-sex marriage and civil rights share the belief that "in order to gain acceptance as full citizens, their constituents adopt the norms of what they believe to be the idealized American citizen—productivity, selflessness, responsibility, sexual restraint" (101). As such, there is an interesting push-pull between the political implications of giving up one's personal desire and practicing sexual restraint to uphold bourgeois standards of respectability. According to one patient, "a short, fat, intelligent-looking man," the hospital sends the patients to the Golden Day to benefit from a day of sexual therapy, but it also "send[s] along an attendant, a kind of censor, to see that the therapy fails" (81). The patients, who seek pleasure from the prostitutes at the Golden Day, are unable to act out their desires due to the supervision of the hospital attendant, aptly named Supercargo. The Golden Day acts as a metonym for U.S. society because it promises freedom and enjoyment, yet one's attempts at achieving either is generally thwarted or only partially achieved. The invocation of Freud's "superego" in the name Supercargo demonstrates Ellison's awareness of the position of psychoanalytic institutions with respect to sexual excessiveness. In Freud's formulation "conscience, self-observation, and the formation of ideals" are all functions of the superego, which serves as a censor of sexual desire (Laplanche and Pontalis 435). According to Sander Gilman, psychoanalytic tropes suggested that Jews were prone to demonstrate a greater degree of sexual excess than whites: "The consistency of character, with its deviant sexual nature, led to the disease that marked the Jew: hysteric. . . . Jews (especially male Jews) are sexually different; they [were] hysterical and their gaze reveal[ed] it" (123). Even though the superego "is grounded on the renunciation of loving and hostile Oedipal wishes, it is subsequently refined, according to Freud, by the contributions of social and cultural requirements (education, religion, morality)" (Laplanche and Pontalis 437). The framework of black bourgeois respectability created yet another mode of subjugation in that black subjects were largely unable to act on their sexual desires for fear of confirming white racism.

Now here's the rub: Supercargo (superego) cannot control his own sexual desires. At one point during the Golden Day fiasco, the invisible narrator barely recognizes Supercargo because he has removed his "hard-starched white uniform" to enjoy sexual relations with one of the prostitutes. Without the uniform and the "strait jacket which he always carried over his arm," the patients are able to overtake him (82). Supercargo's sexual transgression emphasizes Ellison's critique and destabilization of Freud, since the superego, which is supposed to function as a stabilizing factor, entirely loses its force. Consequently, we can read this moment as demonstrating the relative incompatibility between black subjects and psychoanalytic theories. The superego is rendered ineffective within the context of the Golden Day. Further, the scene expresses the tension between notions of black respectability and the freedom to act on one's desire; black folks are so socially and morally restricted that simple acts of pleasure take the form of social and political resistance. It is significant to note that once Supercargo is incapacitated, the patients use the opportunity not to escape but to make "hostile speeches at the top of their voices against the hospital, the state, and the universe" (85). This expression of rage against the supposedly democratic institutions that are meant to protect them signals the patients' acute awareness of the source of their condition. After pummeling Supercargo, the patients rail against the institutions that have rendered them politically invalid, at the level of the state and beyond. The scene also reveals that while on the surface, Supercargo's function was to subdue their sexual desires, his undoing actually allows for the expression of their political wants; their anger toward the universe highlights their expansive feeling of disenfranchisement. The explicit sexual dynamics at the Golden Day veil a delicate political balance that, once disrupted, results in chaos. The consequence of the patients taking over the asylum is that the vet and the invisible narrator are punished for their transgressions, both sexual (socializing with prostitutes at the Golden Day) and racial (assaulting Mr. Norton, the white benefactor), and are involuntarily exiled from the South. The irony of democracy rears its ugly head, showing that one's resistance to the limits of democratic freedoms merely results in further subjugation.

As the Golden Day scene and the scenarios of sexual deviance in "Harlem Is Nowhere" demonstrate, the failure to subscribe to mainstream norms further contributed to black folks' continued exclusion from U.S. democracy. Ellison only had to look as far as Wertham to grasp the extent to which black subjects' failure to adhere to sexual norms would further relegate them to the political margins. Both men believed that deviance, whether sexual or criminal, stemmed from social conditions, and Wertham's mission in particular was to assist individuals in overcoming their afflictions so that they could reorient themselves to the social world. In his 1954 *Seduction of the Innocent,* Wertham notes that: "all human beings have to learn a rationale of controlling, disciplining, and if you will, sublimating sexual impulses. Only a decent social orientation can lead to a decent sex life, for practically all psychological sex problems are ethical problems. . . . Education for a happy life must take into account that sexual irregularities in one way or another may spell great unhappiness and suffering" (175). To consider "psychological sex problems" as problems of ethics imbricates deviant sexuality, including homosexuality, within a system of morality. To act unethically or, as Wertham's formulation suggests, to consciously move outside the bounds of what might be considered normal by disobeying established rules of social conduct naturally puts one at risk for social exclusion. While Ellison's forays into the realm of psychoanalytic thought are generally aligned with Wertham's project of social psychiatry, his reading of sexual deviance, contrary to Wertham's, does not stem from individual subjects but rather from outside forces acting on them. In his notes for "Harlem Is Nowhere," Ellison writes that anxiety that exists "as part of ghetto psychology" as well as "the possible outbreak of a new war" typically "dramatizes itself through some psychosomatic sexual problem."[24] Deviant sexuality emerges in Ellison's writings as a response to social inequity rather than a question of ethical behavior.

Yet Wertham's work literalizes the relationship between blackness and sexuality. While serving as director of the Lafargue clinic, he also headed the Quaker State Emergency Readjustment Center for Homosexuals. The Quaker State Center, which opened three years after the Lafargue clinic, appeared to perform a function similar to that of Lafargue: treating homosexuals or sexual deviants. A 1949 *New York Times* article described the Quaker Center as "the only clinic in the city—and possibly the entire country—that was opened especially to give free psychiatric treatment to persons who committed sexual offenses or showed marked sexual abnormalities" (Greenburg 8). It is instructive to consider that Wertham's method of counteracting violence, which was the driving motivation of his psychological work, was to open a mental health clinic in Harlem to service a poor African American population and then, three years later, to establish another clinic aimed specifically at the treatment of homosexuals. Bart Beaty notes that these "clinics were symptomatic of Wertham's desire to bring psychiatry into the community to counteract the threat of violence and exemplify Wertham's involvement of grassroots organizations" (89). As in Karpman's work, the entanglement of violence, blackness, and sexual deviance that emerges in Wertham's writing raises questions about the extent to which Wertham contributed to the pathologizing of minority subjects. Wertham was a strong advocate of the burgeoning civil rights movement, which was later confirmed by his arguments given to the U.S. Supreme Court in defense of desegregation, yet his work also indicates that the refusal to conform to social codes of normativity forecloses the possibility for social and political inclusion.[25]

The relationship between psychoanalytic psychiatry's promotion of sexual normativity and black social mobility was, in many senses, inextricable. Thaddeus Russell describes an exchange between a young man and Dr. Martin Luther King Jr. in which the young man admits that he has homosexual feelings. King advises him to "'see a good psychiatrist' in order to 'solve'" his problem (117). This exchange takes on a larger significance when considered in the light of the convergence of discourses of psychoanalysis, sexuality, and civil rights in Wright's and Ellison's psychoanalytic investigations. For Ellison and Wright, it is not enough for psychoanalytic psychiatry to work to better the mental lives of black people; it needs to simultaneously engender sociopolitical gains. That King, the reigning and reified symbol of the civil rights movement, looked to psychoanalysis (rather than to God?) to resolve one's "aberrant" sexuality affirms the centrality of psychoanalytic methods to the project of furthering black inclusion within the U.S. mainstream. Russell notes: "The civil rights ideology of the black middle class rose in tandem with a new racial liberalism among white elites that was born out of the discourse of ethnic and racial 'tolerance' during World War II. This emergent ideology made explicit that the price of admission to American society for African Americans would be a surrender to heterosexual norms" (112). Civil rights advocates, including Ellison, perceived that black deviance would be used by racist whites to legitimize racism, and therefore it was equally important to confront the issue of black deviance as it was to condemn U.S. racism. The resistance to the social order through expressions of deviance ultimately undermines the project of integration.

The disciplining of gender and sexual differences proved exigent for raced subjects whose second-class citizenry was a social and legal fact. As Roderick Ferguson persuasively articulates, "American institutions . . . work to discipline the gendered and sexual differences of U.S. minorities in an effort to make those groups conform to national ideals" (58). The deployment of psychoanalysis to enable such processes of national conformity confirmed Ellison and Wright's conviction in psychoanalytic institutions to empower black subjects to cope successfully with their relative alienation from the processes of U.S. democracy. While Ellison's and Wright's participation within psychoanalytic discourses emerges from a larger desire to underscore the radical nature of black interiority, the rehabilitation of the black-criminal-sexual deviant subject also implicates them within a rather problematic agenda to re-form black-criminal-sexually deviant bodies to conform to stringent moral and social codes as a requisite for semilegitimate citizenship. Their interventions within the discourse of postwar psychoanalysis reveal a larger problem of working within the framework of a paradigm that had already dedicated a century to proving the inherent psychical and intellectual inferiority of raced subjects. Despite Ellison's and Wright's efforts to offer an emancipatory psychoanalytic model in which the "total Negro" would, finally, be understood, the normalizing impulses of postwar psychoanalysis all but foreclosed the possibility of "turning Freud upside down" and instead recast cultural perceptions of the black, the criminal, and the sexual deviant as an inextricable, and ultimately incurable, relation.

5

Maternal Anxieties and Political Desires in Adrienne Kennedy's *Dramatic Circle*

In the section titled "Marriage and Motherhood" in Adrienne Kennedy's postmodern autobiography *People Who Led to My Plays,* she writes that "by now many of our friends were 'seeing analysts.' We enjoyed talking about our depressions, the movie *Breathless,* Eve Delphy, Charles Mingus, and Miles Davis. The magazines were filled with photographs of the new Kennedy babies and the perfect life they all led. And one of America's most famous writers married Marilyn Monroe. We talked about that a lot. We talked about James Baldwin and Norman Mailer" (*People* 93). One does not have to look to the journal entry to affirm Kennedy's obsession with the psyche; her Obie-winning drama *Funnyhouse of a Negro* (1964) provides ample evidence for such an argument. But the relevance of this entry to this project's larger concern with African Americanist revisions of psychoanalytic thought lies in the connections it draws among psychoanalysis, popular culture, and the political sphere. Regardless of its apparent lack of associative links, the note confirms that though Freudian psychoanalysis in U.S. popular culture was on the decline during the 1950s and 1960s, the broader realm of psychology was becoming increasingly accessible to a more economically and racially diverse population—so much so that, as Kennedy's diary account attests, discussions concerning the psyche occupied an easy conversational space alongside the latest films, celebrity gossip, and jazz. The rise of psychoanalysis and the decline of psychiatry at this moment signals a shift away from Freudian logic, which had long been considered apolitical in its deft attention to familial structures rather than social systems, and toward a more radical conceptualization of psychology that sought to reconcile the relationship between individual subjectivity and the social world. Indeed, in the late 1950s and 1960s, the lexicon and paradigms of psychological thought served, as Eli Zaretsky explains, "as an inspiration to the student movements of the sixties [and] its ideas reached the highest point of influence in their history," yet at the same time "the psychoanalytic profession collapsed, at least in its classical or Freudian form" (308). At this time, psychoanalysis also served as a focal point of critique, particularly for feminists, who understood the Freudian view to be that psychic structures were grounded in anatomical differences, thereby reducing women to emotional and static subjects. Further, African American writers were skeptical of psychoanalysis's relevance to the social and political lives of marginalized people. Amiri Baraka's passing reference in *The Slave* to the "psychological novel" as "the worst thing that ever happened to the West" (70) and Eldridge Cleaver's disappointing experimentation with psychoanalysis read as insightful expressions of its failure to resonate among a larger African American populace during the era of Black Power.[1]

Given the less-than-favorable reception of psychoanalysis among feminist and African American communities in the 1960s, the centrality of psychoanalytic thought in the work of Adrienne Kennedy marks a singular moment in the intersection of feminism, black power politics, and psychoanalysis. Kennedy's dramas, *Funnyhouse of a Negro* (1964), *The Owl Answers* (1965), and *A Movie Star Has to Star in Black and White* (1976) have each explored the variant ways in which the layered subjugation of black womanhood offers ample material for explorations of the psychical implications of racism and sexism. Though Kennedy's dramas from the Black Arts era were, arguably, her most self-conscious explorations of the psyche, her most explicit foray into the culture of psychoanalysis would emerge almost forty years later in her play *Dramatic Circle* (1992), in which the specters of Sigmund Freud and Frantz Fanon materialize in the life of the drama's protagonist, Suzanne Alexander. Kennedy's engagement with these two figures in *Dramatic Circle* certainly confirms her interest and even investment in discourses of psychoanalysis, but more importantly it highlights the notion that, for Kennedy, the past is always present. In attempting to answer the obvious question as to why, in one of her most contemporary pieces, Kennedy brings Freud and Fanon into play (no pun intended), I would suggest that these figures speak to the ways in which the dual "problems" of race and gender within psychoanalytic and political discourses remain unresolved. By drawing upon Freud and Fanon as symbols of the psychoanalytic and black power movements, respectively, Kennedy's drama actually allows for a rethinking of both discourses, which historically have been largely inattentive to women of color, and demonstrates the extent to which racial and social politics are enmeshed. Although *Dramatic Circle* was published in 1992, the play's racial and gendered dynamics resonate with concerns voiced by black and feminist communities thirty years prior, which is particularly evident in the way that Kennedy collapses the "personal" and the "political" spheres—a defining feature of feminist and psychological discourses of the 1960s. *Dramatic Circle* exemplifies what Elin Diamond describes as an "invitation to political self-consciousness" by placing the most unlikely characters within a tangled web of colonialism and witnessing their formation as political subjects ("Rethinking Identification" 87).[2] Despite its brevity, *Dramatic Circle* presents Suzanne's struggle to reconcile an array of competing identities as soon-to-be mother, wife, artist, and political subject. *Dramatic Circle* maintains a critical relationship to debates in psychoanalysis, as well as to a broader social and political history that engages both second-wave feminism and discourses of black power, thereby exposing the multivalent ways that history informs Kennedy's literary negotiation with psychoanalytic thought and forging an agential space for psychoanalysis's excluded Other.

The presence of Freud and Fanon in *Dramatic Circle* reads ironically, especially since Fanon himself was skeptical about the relevance of Freudian analysis with respect to the experience of raced subjects, noting that "one should investigate the extent to which the conclusions of Freud or of Adler can be applied to the effort to understand the man of color's view of the world" (*Black Skin* 141). Yet both analysts have suffered common criticisms for their interpretations (or lack thereof) of black female subjectivity. Though Fanon provides one of the most salient analyses of black male subjectivity in the history of psychoanalytic thought, his interpretation of black female subjectivity is at best dismissive, and at worst disparaging. With the exception of his narrative assault on writer Mayotte Capecia, Fanon has little to say about the black women, admitting in his influential text *Black Skin, White Masks* that "those who grant our conclusions on the psychosexuality of the white woman may ask what we have to say about the woman of color. I know nothing about her" (179–80). Though Fanon specifically refers to his ignorance of her "psychosexuality," he ultimately fails to consider the ways in which colonialist subjugation operates along racial and gendered lines. Gwen Bergner writes extensively about Fanon's indictment of Mayotte Capecia, underscoring that "Fanon overlooks the ways in which colonial society perpetuates racial inequality through structures of sexual difference. . . . Ironically, such a decontextualized analysis of black femininity re-creates the structure of the colonialist discourse Fanon successfully deconstructs in much of *Black Skin, White Masks*" (13).

But Fanon does more than render black women invisible in the context of colonialism. In the case of Mayotte Capecia, Fanon implicates mixed-race women in the colonial enterprise. While he acknowledges that the psychological life of black men is largely structured around an unattainable desire for whiteness, the mulatto woman's fate as colonialist subject is resolved through the love of a white man: "Something remarkable must have happened on the day when the white man declared his love to the mulatto. . . . From one day to the next, the mulatto went from the class of slaves to that of masters" (58). Fanon either implies that women of color operate in collusion with the colonialist project or he does not fully address the specificity of their subjugation under colonialism. These issues lurk underneath the surface of *Dramatic Circle,* insisting on a critical interrogation of the figures of Freud and Fanon. While Fanon does not appear as an actual character in *Dramatic Circle,* he lingers as a commanding presence whose revolutionary project frames the life of the protagonist, Suzanne Alexander, and indirectly contributes to her psychological break.

Fanon's presence in *Dramatic Circle* illustrates how the political subjectivity of women of color goes unrecognized, and further begs the question, "how do women figure within the discourse of revolutionary masculinism?" (93).[3] More precisely, I am interested in Kennedy's approach to psychoanalysis via Freud and Fanon as the governing framework through which political desires are imagined and produced. For Kennedy, the shaping of political desire by way of psychoanalytic imaginings is even more complex for black female subjects who have either been marginalized or rendered invisible within psychoanalytic circles. The notion of "political desire" emerges as the underlying impetus of Kennedy's domestic drama. The staging of political desire has been expertly crafted in Claudia Tate's seminal text, *Domestic Allegories of Political Desire,* in which she argues that post-Reconstruction domestic novels by African American women were employed to gain "access to social and political events from which 'they as black women were' . . . largely excluded" (5). For Tate, "the social equation between personal and political or private and public works in two directions: not only do public and political social constitutions shape the details of intimate lives; those personal details also form comprehensive social practices and institutions" (9). Though black women may have historically been rendered invisible within political and revolutionary spheres (and continue to be rendered invisible), the personal and the political dialectic as explained by Tate suggests that a black political sphere would not even be possible without the influence of black women.

In fact, I would take this notion a step further and argue that in Kennedy's work the failure to recognize black female subjectivity as integral to the project of black nationalism accounts for the relative failure of the movement, as the play concludes with the death of Fanon, signaling the death of a major era of black political activism. Within *Dramatic Circle,* Kennedy constructs the spaces of psychoanalysis and revolutionary politics as potentially emancipatory sites where raced and gendered subjects can imagine psychological and political freedom. A significant moment in the text arises when Dr. Freudenberger remarks that he "knows" Fanon's book, *Black Skin, White Masks*—a curious admission considering that Fanon's text was published thirteen years after the death of Sigmund Freud. Given that individual psychology was at the center of Freud's analytical method, it is notable that Freudenberger proposes a form of group therapy for Suzanne. As Ann Pellegrini points out, "Fanon's sociogenetic approach makes group identity the leading rather than the trailing edge of analysis and thereby subtly shifts the terms of Freud's distinction between individual and group psychology" (94). But in *Dramatic Circle* individual psychology is replaced with Dr. Freudenberger's application of a method made prevalent by Fanon. The application of such a method also partially explains why Kennedy places Freud and Fanon in dialogue and points to the significance of Freudenberger's familiarity with *Black Skin, White Masks.* For Freudenberger to express familiarity with *Black Skin, White Masks* marks Kennedy's desire to reconcile and critique both theorists. Rather than posing Freudenberger and Fanon as oppositional figures within the text, Kennedy writes them as complementary—in both purpose and method.

Yet as Kennedy demonstrates, both discourses undermine their liberatory potential by failing to consider black women as central to their projects. Indeed, black male political subjectivity has been largely constructed by and through the subjugation of African American women. Michelle Wright maintains a similar thesis with respect to the formation of black male political identities, noting that "Fanon's . . . (re)constitution of a gendered agency in nationalist discourse disabled the possibility of a black female subject at the same time that it enabled the Black male subject who . . . comes into being through the denial of another's subjectivity—in this case, black women" (132). Such was the primary rationale for feminist resistance to the psychoanalytic movement. Kennedy addresses this lack of recognition by exposing the critical gap in Freudian and Fanonian analyses and their relative failure to imagine black women as political subjects. Kennedy attempts to resituate black women within the schema of a radical psychoanalytic politic by calling into question its very limitations and engaging a psychoanalytic discourse to frame the predicament of her characters. While Kennedy treats Fanon sympathetically, and one might even argue venerably, within the play, we also get the sense that she sets out to critique the very man who, as Michelle Wright points out, served as "the central influence and inspiration of the Black Arts Movement" yet "offers no more than a compliant, silent, and veiled woman as a model for female activism" (131). Indeed, what is perhaps most notable about *Dramatic Circle* is Kennedy's clever obfuscation of gender troubles that remain hidden behind the guise of a romantic love story.

Kennedy's invocation of psychoanalytic figures and practices animates the discourse's failure to properly account for the complex subjectivities of black women who appear to fall through the cracks; the play reads as an attempt to inscribe black women into such discourses as critical subjects. Kennedy's convergence of Freud and Fanon speaks to a larger concern about the ways in which, as Anthony Bogues points out, "relationships between the imagination, ways of life, and desire are central to any consideration of the political" (153). Bogues's primary thesis is that desire is central to the ways in which people imagine themselves as political subjects. This desire largely rests upon the need for recognition and is motivated by imagining oneself within a given sociopolitical role. Bogues argues that the machinations of colonial and imperialist power attempt to control and subvert the desire and imagination of marginalized subjects by "capturing" them both to create "a certain kind of species" (156). Bogues's essay is instructive here in terms of the way that it addresses the imagination as a legitimate form of invention that allows a political subjectivity to those who are generally depoliticized by imperialist powers. Similarly, Kennedy recognizes the power of imagination as a vehicle for invention and intervention within exclusionary discourses.

In *Dramatic Circle*, a pregnant Suzanne Alexander anxiously awaits the arrival of her husband, David, who is in Algeria attempting to unearth a conspiracy against Fanon. While waiting in London, Suzanne experiences symptoms of trauma similar to those of the Algerian soldiers. Worried about Suzanne's declining mental health, her sister-in-law Alice seeks psychiatric care for her. Alice explains that "in the past my brother had written me when he had been traveling with Frantz Fanon, the famous psychiatrist and revolutionary from Martinique. He'd written about the psychiatric cases they had encountered in Algeria. I realized now some of the symptoms of Fanon's patients were like Suzanne's symptoms." A nearby chemist recommends that Suzanne receive treatment from Dr. Freudenberger, a popular analyst who "actually went to school in America for a while" (183). Dr. Freudenberger involves Alice and Suzanne in his ongoing "dramatic circle," in which the group is reading Bram Stoker's *Dracula.* He assigns Suzanne the role of Lucy and Alice the role of Mina. According to Freudenberger, the women's participation in the group should help alleviate Suzanne's symptoms. On the surface, *Dramatic Circle* reads as a traditional maternal and matrimonial narrative through which gender roles are left unchallenged and undisturbed and a woman's impending psychological break abates with the arrival of her husband.[4] Such a deceptively simple plotline may explain the relative dearth of critical analyses of the text. Of course, Kennedy does little to stimulate such investigations, as she indicates that in creating many of her characters she is simply "playing around" (Barnett, "Evasion" 164).[5] Despite Kennedy's dismissal of her own literary complexity, *Dramatic Circle* is embedded with a deeper meaning that suggests Suzanne's longing for her husband camouflages the expression of a larger political want. Her matrifocal staging of this political desire vis-à-vis the reincarnation of Freud and Fanon emerges as the critical force of the narrative's psycho-political critique.

Suzanne imagines herself in the space of a colonial subject, which implies her desire for a political identity and a place within the framework of revolutionary politics. Through the expression of this political desire, Kennedy challenges the boundaries of psychoanalytic thought by pointing to Suzanne's dissatisfaction with merely occupying the role of wife and mother. Instead, Kennedy "[replaces] women as a category of male fantasy with women subjects having not only an independent voice that could defend and articulate the experience of women but also having knowledge that was previously excluded from the psychoanalytic dialogue" (Schwartz 271). In both Freud's and Fanon's paradigms, women are reduced to desiring, passive subjects who offer little to the discourse of revolutionary politics and are primarily understood through their sexual relationship to men, whether as wife (in the case of Freud) or race traitor (in the case of Fanon). Kennedy subtly explores the displacement of black women from politicized discourses in her 1964 play *Funnyhouse of a Negro,* in which the protagonist, Sarah, simultaneously embodies the personas of Patrice Lumumba and Queen Victoria, unable to authenticate an individual subjectivity between them. Sarah remains outside the nexus of colonial politics, neither able to identify with Lumumba, who symbolizes the liberation of colonial territories, nor with Queen Victoria, whose reign was emblematic of white domination and imperialism. Instead, Sarah commits suicide. Though Sarah's demise is generally read as yet another contemporary manifestation of the tragic mulatto trope, she maintains an in-between status both racially and politically. Kennedy seems to suggest that a woman's place within revolutionary masculinism is barely on the periphery, and that marginal status often manifests itself as some form of madness.

Kennedy's engagement with Freud and Fanon in *Dramatic Circle* both underscores and problematizes the marginalization of black women within Freudian and Fanonian analyses, pointing to the continued invisibility of the black female subject and indicating that this invisibility corresponds to a larger problem of black women's invisibility within black and feminist political discourses. As such, *Dramatic Circle* functions as a fictional response to this exclusion within psychoanalytic discourses and as a poignant critique of its centrality of the male subject.

Portrait of a Young Housewife-Mother-Artist

Kennedy's own anxieties about the ways that marriage and motherhood might remove her from the political sphere are rampant in *People.* Excerpts from the autobiography highlight some of the subtle means by which the protagonist's role in *Dramatic Circle* shapes, informs, and enables male authority. The autobiography facilitates a deeper understanding of the fictional text by illuminating the ways that psychoanalytic and political discourse works to undermine feminine agency. The quandaries that face Suzanne Alexander are informed by Kennedy's frustrations about her own role as wife, daughter, and mother.

Kennedy's 1987 autobiography can best be described as a collage of significant moments and persons that influenced Kennedy both personally and professionally. *People* is divided into six sections: "Elementary School," "Junior High School," "High School," "College," "Marriage and Motherhood," and "A Voyage." Each of these sections maintains a number of subcategories that defy any temporal logic—for example, the "Elementary School" section is subdivided into the following topics: "Fairy tales," "My family," "the radio," "Jesus," "My teachers," "The movies," "dolls," "paper dolls," "Hitler," and "Jane Eyre." The arrangement of Kennedy's autobiography is certainly consistent with the idiosyncrasy, fragmentedness, and apparently schizophrenic nature of her drama (particularly her earlier oeuvre) by violently disrupting the narrative form and disarming the reader of all the creature comforts that normally accompany a paradigmatic autobiographical presentation: stories that maintain a logical beginning, middle, and end, neat resolutions, and a singular perspective. Even though the form of *People* may read as chaotic and irresolute, this structure actually enables a depiction that is more true to the twists, turns, and general inconsistencies that often define life experiences. *People* presents the reader with a series of anxieties, tensions, and issues that confronted the writer at various stages in her life. Yet Kennedy refuses to offer any remedy for the problems she broaches. As such, the autobiography reads as a narrative of anxiety—of troubling moments and questions that offer no path for resolution. Often her remembrances reflect her own questions of esteem and beauty. Of her Great Aunt Ella, she writes, "she died as a young girl and I was the 'spitting image of her,' 'looked just like her,' Aunt Mary Lee and many of my father's relatives in Montezuma said of me. . . . She was a little touched in the head, Aunt Mary told me once. . . . Why I wondered, did I have to look like someone dead who was 'touched in the head?'" (22). Throughout *People,* Kennedy expresses the silent sorrows of women in her family, of women who cried in silence and who suffered from unidentified psychological illnesses. That Kennedy's Aunt Mary Lee would compare her to an aunt who was "touched in the head" informs Kennedy's own narratives of madwomen.

Toward the end of *People,* Kennedy describes the problematic nature of her emerging identities, particularly her marriage to Joseph Kennedy, which she often describes through episodes of feeling overshadowed by her husband's burgeoning academic celebrity. Joseph's research took him to West Africa, where he traveled the region writing about African resistance movements, with a specific focus on Fanon. Because Kennedy was pregnant at the time, she was often unable to accompany her husband on these journeys. The solitude Kennedy experienced during the period clearly had a significant effect on the playwright, so much so that those recollections became the subject of *Dramatic Circle.*

In the final moments of *People,* Kennedy recalls, "*The United States Army (1953):* We were newly married, happy in Colorado for six months until the army intervened. The army caused me to enter a *state of anxiety* I had never known before sending my husband to Korea. Now I was pregnant. 'Can't I go?' I begged. 'I could live nearby.' But off he went. We were separated for a year . . . the year of the birth of our child" (77, original emphasis). This sense of desertion and social dislocation haunts Kennedy not only because the government forced the separation of their family, but also because it highlights the extent to which Joseph's role as a man would allow him meaningful experiences and a sort of relevance that might never be available to her. The "state of anxiety" she experiences when her husband leaves for Korea is echoed in other moments throughout the autobiography, in which she wrestles with her place within social and familial structures. Once their son Joe is born, Kennedy finds herself faced with the overwhelming task of attempting to manage the work of a mother and wife as well as an emerging (and much desired) identity as a writer. In the entry titled "*Winston Churchill and myself*," she writes:

> My husband admired the many dimensions of Churchill's career: author, statesman, soldier. I often wondered how I, as a woman, could have a "destiny" (like Churchill). Careers with great destiny all seemed to be for men. It didn't seem possible that I would be a Marie Curie or a Marian Anderson or an Eleanor Roosevelt. . . . Although I had stories, poems, and one and a half novels and a play, was I even capable of being an author? I wanted a "destiny." But no one seemed to see me in this light. At twenty-six, even though I had studied for two years at Columbia General Studies writing my novel and had gone to the New School and had tried to read my way through the Modern Library and had acquired an agent at MCA, people still (very often) asked me only: Would I like to help plan the kindergarten Halloween party? Would I be part of a group of mothers taking the kindergarteners to the Boat Pond in Central Park? I seemed bland and mediocre to myself. I often felt miserable. (*People* 93–94)

While Kennedy identifies women who have lived out what appears to be "a destiny," such as Curie and Roosevelt, she fails to imagine herself as someone able to fulfill such a distinguished social role. Her literary ambition seems to emerge from this complex negotiation of maternal obligation and artistic and intellectual respectability.

At the time that Kennedy was busy negotiating her place within her family and a larger Black Arts and Black Power movement, second-wave feminists were challenging Freudian-based familial structures that regarded women as a "strange, inferior, less-than-human species" (Friedan 100). Betty Friedan's hugely popular *The Feminine Mystique* (1963) exposed the insidious ways in which Freudian conceptions of family rested on the notion that "'normal' femininity is achieved . . . only insofar as the woman finally renounces all active goals of her own, all her own 'originality,' to identify and fulfill herself though the activities and goals of husband, or son" (113). Given Kennedy's anxieties about marriage and motherhood, Friedan's text among other important feminist works of the period would have resonated with, shaped, and confirmed her burgeoning fears of irrelevance.[6] Indeed, Kennedy's coming-of-age as a writer was framed by narratives of resistance to conventional female roles. Her seeming desire to live out a maternal and matrimonial fantasy appears strangely at odds with the kind of fierce autonomy required of the artist. This insecurity is exacerbated once Kennedy and her husband travel to Africa as part of his graduate research. The space of Africa offers Kennedy artistic inspiration, but at the same time, her second pregnancy forecloses the possibility of living in equanimity with her husband, and further removes her from her ambition to become an accomplished playwright.

> *My husband and myself:* "I had never seen my husband less than I did now that we were in Africa. He left very early before daylight and was often in the bush two or three days. And now that I was pregnant, I would not be able to travel freely with him over Ghana. The doctor advised that I travel little until the fifth month of pregnancy. All this produced growing tensions and unhappiness in me. It was now that I felt increasingly that I was just accompanying another person as he lived out his dreams. . . . I was 29 years old and a failure in my eyes. And although Africa had ignited a fire inside me and we looked forward to the birth of our second child, I felt (after being together ten years) that I was acquiescent to another person's desires, dreams and hopes. The solitude under the African sun had brought out a darkness in me. (*People* 122)

This passage reveals Kennedy's painful lack of recognition both socially and within the context of her marriage. The adventure they set out on as partners quickly relegates Kennedy to the role of a housewife, which she desires to reject. Her acquiescence to her husband's "desires, dreams, and hopes" reads, as Betty Friedan describes, as the prototypical state of "role crisis" in which women find themselves as a result of not being able to "accept or gratify their basic need to grow and fulfill their potentialities as human beings, a need which is not solely defined by their sexual role" (69). The passage also evokes Kennedy's conflicted attitude about being a wife and mother, because even as she eloquently juxtaposes the African sun with an internal darkness, she admits to looking forward to the birth of her child, suggesting that her ambivalence about marriage does not necessarily translate into antinatal sentiments. In fact, throughout the autobiography Kennedy writes about her pregnancies and her sons in genuinely positive terms. Her feelings coincide with the black community's counternarrative to second-wave feminism's antimaternal discourse. Lauri Umansky argues, for example, that "in the mid-1960s, black activists and intellectuals focused considerable energy on defending the black family" (78). Because Black Power activists framed their struggle within the context of both oppression and *extermination,* African Americans "were enjoined to resist by drawing themselves into father-dominated families and having many babies, for 'procreation is beautiful, especially if we are devoted to the Revolution'" (Umansky 81). However, Kennedy's desire to integrate herself within this dynamic Black Arts and Black Power moment also meant facing its raging patriarchy. The logic of black nationalism left little space to explore the gendered politics within the movement. For black women activists, political engagement required a certain allegiance to black masculinism. In *People,* Kennedy deftly articulates the ambivalent space she occupies as a black woman with feminist inclinations that do not necessarily coincide with the larger Black Arts collective of which she is also a part.

Taken alone, each section reads as an account of Kennedy's momentary frustration with her husband's emerging success and what appears to be a stagnant phase of her own writing career. But collectively, they reveal a mounting anxiety and angst with her husband's absence and Kennedy's sense that her roles as mother and wife would consistently usurp her status as a writer. Though the longevity of Kennedy's career as a playwright attests to her importance as an artist, she re-creates the anxieties and insecurities she experienced during the early stages of her career through the life of Suzanne Alexander, the fundamental self at the center of her 1992 oeuvre, *The Alexander Plays.* Despite Kennedy's ardent denial that Suzanne functions as an alter ego, Claudia Barnett notes that Kennedy "has increased the level of autobiographical referents in her work" and that her "creation of Suzanne Alexander has been integral to this unmarking; Kennedy has simply transferred the marks to Suzanne, thereby establishing invisibility for herself" ("Evasion" 160). Through Kennedy's self-conscious projection of anxiety, *Dramatic Circle* can be read as a dialogic drama in which she contextualizes her own anxieties as a wife, mother, and emerging artist within the sociopolitical context of colonialist resistance. Perhaps in response to her own perceived one-dimensionality, Kennedy's *Dramatic Circle* functions as a palimpsest of the competing desires, emotions, and tensions she experiences in the attempt to reconcile the rival roles she must play.

The Politics of Identification

The force of *Dramatic Circle* resides in the circumstances of Suzanne and David's separation. His presence in the play comes only in the form of his letters to Suzanne and Alice, which are generally romantic accounts of the war in Algeria. Though David recognizes the dangers inherent in his mission, he writes enthusiastically: "Even the sky is constantly changing. Some days ago we saw a sunset that turned the robe of heaven a bright violet. Today it is a very hard red that the eye encounters. At Tessalit we cross French military camps. We must work fast, time passes, the enemy is still stubborn, he does not believe in military defeat but I have never felt victory so possible, so within reach. We only need to march and charge. We have mobilized furious cohorts, loving combat, eager to work. We have Africa with us" (183). The letters Alice and Suzanne receive from David not only note his devotion and investment in Fanon and the project of anticolonialism, but also they locate David within a community of resistance and purpose. This preoccupation with purpose is one that Kennedy makes apparent in her own autobiography, and it emerges similarly as a matter of concern for Suzanne. Like Joseph Kennedy, David is driven by a purpose larger than that of fulfilling the roles of husband, brother, and soon, father. And like Adrienne Kennedy, Suzanne responds to David's devotion to Algeria's liberation from the French with tinges of sadness and regret: "I would like as much as possible to see you, to live quietly, I could do other things but fight, but duty comes before all else. All my life I have sacrificed everything, tranquility, my own desire, my happiness, my destiny (*Sigh.*)" (183). Suzanne is sympathetic to the anticolonialist project but she must witness the revolutionary shift from afar, while David is an active participant against the colonialist regime. Alice explains, "she had always missed David when he traveled to do research. David and Suzanne had always traveled together but his research on Fanon, the trips the research required, were trips he forbade her to take" (183). In David's absence, Suzanne develops symptoms of anxiety similar to those of the Algerian soldiers with whom her husband travels, "states of agitation, rages, immobility, tears, attempted suicides, lamentations, appeals for mercy" (179). Suzanne's and David's disparate gender and social roles are concretized around Algeria's fight for liberation. Because of her inability to physically participate in Algeria's revolution, Suzanne takes on an imagined role in the colonial drama in order to lessen the distance between herself and David, as well as to establish her social and political desires. In *The Interpretation of Dreams,* Freud theorizes that identification is: "a highly important factor in the mechanism of hysterical symptoms. It enables patients to express in their symptoms not only their own experiences but also those of a large number of other people; it enables them, as it were, to suffer on behalf of a whole crowd of people and to act all the parts in a play single-handed. I shall be told that this is not more than the familiar hysterical imitation, the capacity of hysterics to imitate any symptoms in other people that may have struck their attention—sympathy, as it were, intensified to the point of reproduction" (149). Although Suzanne only mimics symptoms of colonial trauma, there exists for her and for the soldiers a struggle for recognition, for independence, and for the achievement of one's own destiny. In the process of inserting herself in the space of the colonial subject, Suzanne both imagines herself as the object of her husband's desire and moves from experiencing her grief as an individual subject to assuming group identification. It is significant that in not being able to travel with David, Suzanne is not only separated from her husband but also excluded from actively participating in Algeria's political revolution. In this sense, Suzanne's longing reads both as a desire to be with her husband and as an indication of a political want, or more specifically, a political identity. As Kennedy has demonstrated time and again, black female subjectivity is often rendered invisible in multiple and overlapping discourses of race, gender, and politics. This is where and why Kennedy's invocation of Fanon becomes significant within the framework of *Dramatic Circle*. While Suzanne demonstrates her allegiance to the colonialist struggle, there exists an inherent critique of the way that she, as a black woman, is excluded from the processes of colonial change.

Suzanne's symptomatic appropriation of the Algerian soldiers' colonial trauma could easily be read as a manifestation of grief given the danger David is in. But Suzanne's identification with the soldiers as a way to cope with her husband's absence seems more pathological than curative, which would mean that Suzanne's "melancholy" ultimately acts as a disabling force. I invoke the term *melancholy* here because of the circumstances of Suzanne's grief; her response to the absence of David, coupled with her identification with Algerian soldiers, coincides with Freudian definitions of a melancholic condition. Referring to Freud's notion of identification, specifically the idea that identification emerges from the ego's attempt to compensate for a lost loved one or object, Anne Anlin Cheng explains that "Freud explains melancholic incorporation as a procedure whereby the bereft recuperates and 'takes in' the lost object by 'identifying' with it. Identification is thus a form of cannibalism and/or duplication. A fundamental relationship has been set up between identification and the compensation of loss. As such, identification may in fact be said to be, literally, an expression of grief" (177–78).[7] A psychoanalytic interpretation of melancholy could satisfactorily describe Suzanne's condition: her husband is in the midst of Algeria's struggle for independence and, because of her gender (and her pregnancy), she must be separated from him. Yet I want to continue to pursue her colonial anxiety or melancholy as a function of political desire because the object of "loss" with which she identifies is not David but the Algerians, or more precisely, Algerian women.

Underscoring the import of psychoanalytic structures to Kennedy's dramatic work, the final lines of *Dramatic Circle* are taken directly from Frantz Fanon's *The Wretched of the Earth*: "But the war goes on; and we will have to bind up for years to come the many, sometimes ineffaceable, wounds that the colonialist onslaught has inflicted on our people" (Fanon 249; *Dramatic Circle* 196). This statement opens Fanon's chapter "Colonial War and Mental Disorders," which offers readers various case studies of individual Algerian and French citizens who have been afflicted by traumas due to the war. By narrowing his focus from the general to the specific, Fanon expertly articulates the variant ways in which the Algerian war has "become a breeding ground for mental disorders" (251). The war that ensues once the French have been defeated is one that takes place in the psyche. The "ineffaceable wound" is not one of the body, but in Freud's very definition of trauma, a "wound of the mind."[8] Although *Film Club*, Kennedy's precursor to *Dramatic Circle*, links Suzanne's symptoms of colonial trauma to those experienced by Algerian soldiers, Fanon's text attributes these symptoms to Algerian women refugees. Fanon specifically identifies those symptoms as characteristic of a psychological condition known as "puerperal psychoses." By quoting directly from Fanon's text, Kennedy indicates her familiarity with his work, which makes her misdirection of Suzanne's symptoms rather suspicious. The fact that Suzanne's symptoms are associated with the male soldiers demonstrates, as I have noted, a desire for a political subjectivity but they also seem to indicate a desire for autonomy, authority, and agency that appears to be the exclusive domain of the masculine subject. Perhaps Kennedy's misdirection is, in some way, linked to Suzanne's own misdirected desire to assume a space of male agency. Interestingly, "puerperal psychoses" as defined by Fanon are "mental disorders which occur in women around childbirth. Such disorders may appear immediately before or some weeks after giving birth" (Fanon, *Wretched* 278). The primary causes of puerperal psychoses are thought to be "the upsetting of the functioning of the endocrine glands and the existence of an 'affective shock.' The latter heading, though vague, covers what most people refer to as 'violent emotion'" (278).

The symptoms that Suzanne is said to experience are those suffered by Algerian women refugees. The notion of "violent emotion" is essential to articulating the source of Suzanne's anxiety, such that the expression of her political desire emerges, symptomatically, through puerperal psychoses. Claudia Barnett has argued that "throughout her dramas, Kennedy presents pregnancy and motherhood not as traditional symbols of life and growth, but as signs of madness and death" ("Fundamental Challenge" 142). It is befitting, then, that Suzanne's mental lapse is tied to her pregnant body—a consistent theme in Kennedy's work. Through Suzanne's imagined affliction with puerperal psychoses, she also takes on an "acquired" refugee status. In *The Refugee in International Law,* Guy Goodwill-Gill explains that international policy regarding refugee women implies that "'*all* violence against women is political, or in its slightly less radical variant, that all violence against women should be presumed to be political unless and until the State is shown to provide effective protection. Thus, it is argued, being a woman is a sufficiently political statement in itself, as far as violence against women, domestic, sexual or public, is part of the process of oppression" (363, original emphasis).

That the mere fact of womanhood indicates a political status is key to understanding the extent to which Kennedy attempts to inscribe black women within the framework of revolutionary politics. The very unevenness of gender relations emerges from a self-consciously established political hierarchy, which clearly seams raced women into the fabric of the political state. Goodwin-Gill goes on to assert that "gender is used by societies to organize or distribute rights and benefits; where it is also used to deny rights or inflict harm, the identification of a gender-defined social group has the advantage of external confirmation" (365).

While Goodwin-Gill's interpretation primarily emerges from an ongoing dialogue about women and domestic violence, the notion that as refugees women are deemed political subjects by virtue of their gender seems especially relevant to this discussion of political desire. Suzanne uses identification as an entrance into the complex web of colonialist struggle. As a pregnant woman distanced from the site of battle, Suzanne's procured refugee position enables her to establish relevance as a political subject and to become part of a larger social and political community. Not only does Suzanne assume a politicized status through this identification, but also her gender within the context of "refugee" validates and confirms her political positioning. Identification, in this case, functions as a simultaneous site of desire and resistance. In Diamond's "The Violence of 'We': Politicizing Identification," identification is interpreted as the appropriation of the Other, and it also functions as a means of "incorporation," which is a useful way to think about Suzanne's chosen objects of identification. Suzanne's psychic life is formulated around the subjectivities of Algerian refugees, whose very circumstances enable an inherently politicized position. Diamond reads Kennedy's relationship to Freudian psychoanalysis as one that does not merely capitulate to a Freudian schema, but that "press[es] psychoanalysis on precisely this question: what social and cultural meanings are embedded in acts of identification?" ("Rethinking Identification" 87). Broaching the social and cultural significations of *identification* makes its political import equally salient. Psychoanalysis defines identification as a simultaneous process of assimilation and transformation, which speaks to the dangerous nature of Suzanne's mimicry; the process of identification enables Suzanne's attempted transformation as a political subject.

If we read Goodwin-Gill's insight as a lens through which to understand Suzanne's desire for communal belonging, the fact that she imagines herself among a group of women who are extricated from the actual battleground of political struggle yet remain political subjects gives credence to the drama's complex configuration of race, gender, and the psychoanalytic subject. Kennedy's direct appropriation of Fanon's language to describe (or diagnose) Suzanne's psychological condition points to the drama's subtle interrogation of the complex processes of gender and colonialism. By echoing and decontextualizing Fanon, Kennedy subtly revises the terms of psychoanalytic language to account for its displaced subjects. Suzanne's pregnant body becomes an overtly politicized space that prevents her participation within this critical revolutionary moment and simultaneously serves as a site of mental decline; hence, the violent emotion she experiences is inextricably tied to her biological fate.[9] It is important to recognize that Suzanne's identification is not a general or nebulous sympathetic response to the male soldiers with whom her husband travels or even to her husband whose absence serves as the obvious impetus of her grief, but instead reads as a communal identification with pregnant Algerian women who, for reasons outside of their control, exist outside the heterofamilial norm.

Freudenberger, *Dracula,* and the Return to the "Normal"

Suzanne's covert identification with pregnant Algerian refugees places her within an identifiable political community, yet it also points to the extent to which this community exists in the absence of male authority and dominion. In this respect, such a female-dominated space becomes a dangerous site where the normative familial matrix is disrupted. Such disorganization within the familial structure naturally leads to a drastic and unnatural social structure. This is where Dr. Freudenberger's presence in *Dramatic Circle,* and his selection of Bram Stoker's *Dracula,* are particularly instructive. Sigmund Freud would have been familiar with Bram Stoker's *Dracula,* which was written in 1897—at the same time Freud became interested in psychopathology (E. Jones 198). In *Dracula,* the novel's protagonist, Jonathan Harker, visits

Transylvania and the home of Count Dracula to settle the count's purchase of an estate in London. Jonathan begins to take note of Dracula's eccentricities, notably his "peculiarly sharp teeth," "pale" ears of which the "tops were extremely pointed," and "hairs in the centre of the palm" (23–24). Harker realizes during the course of his visit that Dracula has strategically made him a prisoner. Though he attempts to write letters to his fiancée, Mina, to inform her of his dangerous situation, Dracula mysteriously intercepts his correspondences, leaving Mina in London to worry about his fate. In order to distract herself from Jonathan's absence, Mina plans an extended visit to Whitby, the home of her best friend, Lucy Westenra. Mina soon must serve as a nursemaid, as she is charged with guarding Lucy, who is prone to sleepwalk. In fact, it is during one of her sleepwalking episodes that Lucy becomes one of Dracula's victims. Harker and Mina then join a group of men whose mission is to slay Dracula and to kill Lucy, who has begun to kidnap young children to drink their blood.

While Mina and Lucy's adventures in the novel are fantastical compared to the circumstances of Alice and Suzanne, there exists a similar set of anxieties exists among these characters. Christopher Craft describes Stoker's *Dracula* as "a book whose fundamental anxiety, an equivocation about the relationship between desire and gender, repeats, with a monstrous difference, a pivotal anxiety of late Victorian culture" (444). Recent *Dracula* scholarship indicates that it is because of Lucy's overt sexuality that she becomes victim to Dracula's bite.[10] Her death at the hands of her best friend and former suitors may be interpreted as her deserved punishment for her would-be sexual transgression.[11] Given Kennedy's fascination with the Victorian era, it is not surprising that her twentieth-century iteration of Lucy and Mina reveals a more nuanced anxiety about the relationship between gender and desire.[12] Joining Mina's and Harker's endeavor to murder Lucy and Dracula are Van Helsing and Dr. Seward, who also happens to run an "immense lunatic asylum" (*Dracula* 56). Although Stoker may not have been familiar with Freud's particular methods, Seward's character does reflect the late-nineteenth-century fascination with the "new profession of psychiatry" (Dracula 57, n.9). The relationship between Lucy's voracious sexuality and Dr. Seward's courtship suggests psychiatry's, and perhaps Stoker's, preoccupation with the regulation of female sexuality. However, Lucy's refusals of Dr. Seward's proposals both to marry him and to be his analytic subject suggest his inability to curb Lucy's appetite. In a letter to Mina, Lucy describes Dr. Seward as "absolutely imperturbable," noting "what a wonderful power he must have over his patients." Yet Lucy resists Dr. Seward's pathologization by telling Mina that "he has a curious habit of looking one straight in the face, as if trying to read one's thoughts. He tries this on very much with me, but I flatter myself he has got a tough nut to crack. . . . He says that I afford him a curious psychological study, and I humbly think I do." Lucy defies Seward's attempts at analysis and proves herself to be impervious to the psychoanalytic gaze. We can interpret this refusal of the subjugating gaze as the very event that makes inevitable her impending death.

Kennedy's revision of this tale takes a different turn as the subject of analysis, Suzanne, proves a more willing patient. There is, however, one brief moment that intimates Suzanne's suspicion of Freudenberger, in which she asks Alice, "Do you trust Dr. F?" (*Film Club* 178). While Suzanne's nicknaming Freudenberger "Dr. F" suggests a certain intimacy with the analyst, her question (which is dismissed by Alice) shows a recognition that she may be acquiescing to a program she does not entirely endorse. Moreover, Kennedy's caricatural naming of Freudenberger may intimate that Freud, as a symbol of heteronormative values, is both flawed and anachronistic. Just as Lucy's victimhood is canonically interpreted as the result of her voracious sexuality, we can similarly read Suzanne's impending doom to be the result of a dangerous political desire. Dr. Freudenberger emerges as an intervening presence who works to thwart Suzanne's burgeoning identification with colonized Algerians. Though Freudenberger emerges in the narrative as a figure meant to subjugate Suzanne's anxiety (that is, politicism), it is Alice who orchestrates the meeting. She explains to Freudenberger that she has sought help because of Suzanne's sleepwalking, and since their arrival in London Suzanne "has inexplicable dreams of historical characters and speaks as the characters in her sleepwalking. I have written down what she said last night for you to read" (*Dramatic Circle* 185). Alice, like Mina, occupies an idealized feminine position. She reads Suzanne's desire and melancholy as a dangerous ensuing madness, and it is she who seeks out Dr. Freudenberger and transcribes the details of Suzanne's sleepwalking speech. Though Alice seems to care for Suzanne a great deal and also worries about the dangers David may face, the two women do not engage in direct dialogue with each other during the play. Rather, Alice speaks to Freudenberger and maintains meaningful contact with David, while Suzanne's position is generally articulated through Alice. This critical distancing of the drama's two female characters insinuates Suzanne's resistance to Alice's desire to normalize her through a therapeutic relationship with Freudenberger. Instead, Suzanne's imagining herself as part of a political community of Algerian women is a form of resistance to Alice and Freudenberger's political policing.

Lucy's sleepwalking makes her vulnerable to Dracula's "kiss," which translates into Lucy's loss of chastity. Craft reads the novel's adulation of Mina and consequential fear of Lucy as indicative of a "proleptic fear" that "indirectly acknowledges woman's dangerous potential" (452). Suzanne's sleepwalking makes her vulnerable to desire as well. Alice enlists Freudenberger to quell Suzanne's political identification with the soldiers, and together they reinscribe Suzanne's maternal and matrimonial roles. Once Alice and Suzanne join Freudenberger's dramatic circle, he invites her to read directly from the text:

> Suzanne Alexander: Lucy sleepwalks to the suicide seat on the last cliff. (*She reads breathlessly.*)
> Dramatic Circle: Yes.
> Suzanne Alexander: Dracula drinks her blood for the first time. She receives a blood transfusion. The wolf, Berserker, escapes from the zoo, breaks a window providing a passage to Lucy again. Lucy dies.
> Dramatic Circle (After each sentence): Yes.
> Suzanne Alexander: She is buried in a churchyard near Hampstead Heath. (Sobbing.) (Rain.)
> Alice Alexander: The passage made me cry too. We broke the circle then and said good night. . . . We continued going to the embassy each morning. The ambassador said we would be leaving London soon. (*Dramatic Circle* 193)

By playing the character of Lucy, Suzanne is made to articulate the terms of her own death should her sleepwalking activities persist; sleepwalking in both *Dracula* and *Dramatic Circle* acts as a metaphorical expression of desire. Suzanne's sadness can then be interpreted as a fear of her impending death, but also and perhaps more accurately as the potential loss of an emerging political consciousness. The lines immediately following support this conclusion further, indicating Suzanne's forthcoming departure from London and reminding us of her refugee position. Given Kennedy's astute attention to matters of the psyche, it is no accident that Freud is invoked as the figure most apt to save the Alexanders' heteronormative familial matrix. Suzanne's attempt to become politicized through identification represents a threat to normative gender distinctions and consequently to patriarchal hegemony. Franco Moretti explains that "a sociological analysis of *Frankenstein* and *Dracula* reveals that one of the institutions most threatened by the monsters is the family. . . . Lucy is the only protagonist who falls victim to Dracula. She is punished, because she is the only one who shows some kind of *desire*" (438–39, original emphasis). Like Lucy, Suzanne suffers because she shows desire, and Kennedy's comingling of Lucy's and Suzanne's characters suggests the indistinguishable nature of sexual and political desire. That Freudenberger has the group read *Dracula* is not surprising, given the anxieties about moral decline revealed in the text. As such, it seems that Freudenberger has Suzanne recount the last moments of Lucy's life partly as an admonition, partly as a warning to repress her political desire lest she suffer similar consequences. In this way, *Dracula* is a cautionary tale for Suzanne, whose political desire threatens to destroy her family.

Despite being made to recite Lucy's lines, Suzanne attempts to negotiate her own desire for a political subjectivity, which is uniquely expressed in a brief moment during the play in which Suzanne spontaneously recites lines from David Diop's poem "The Vultures." Depicting the atrocities of colonization, this poem provides an effective mask for Suzanne's attempt to "return" to Africa to join the struggle for liberation and shows her resistance to the role of Lucy that Freudenberger has designated for her. However, at the moment that Suzanne takes up Diop's poetry, she is informed that her stay in London will end since her husband will soon return to London. Suzanne's imaginative attempts to defy social regulation are thwarted at every turn. As she endeavors to carve out a space of social responsibility, she is consistently diverted to act out her domestic responsibility, hence the "vultures" of Diop's poem may refer not only to European colonizers but also to Freudenberger's methods, which are entirely constructed around the subjugation of her desire.

Shortly after joining the dramatic circle, Suzanne learns from the ambassador that her husband is well but that Fanon has been poisoned and died. Fanon's death enables the release and return of David, but it also signals the end of Suzanne's identification with her imagined political community. Once Freudenberger learns of David's impending arrival, he begins to appear in Suzanne's garden each night disguised as an old, feeble man. Alice finds him there one evening and inquires,

> Alice: Sebastian, why have you walked in the garden at night, limping, hair white, almost as an apparition?
>
> Dr. Freudenberger: I wanted to appear as an apparition. . . . To prepare Suzanne's mind for the darkness I knew she must face. The moment I met Suzanne I fell in love with her. I had a premonition that David, like Jonathan Harker, was going through bad times and she, like Lucy, would become the victim of an unfair, tragic plot. I'd hoped that my dramatic circle would help her and you on this difficult journey. (*Dramatic Circle* 196)

It is significant that Freudenberger appears as an apparition of Suzanne's husband because he means not only to prepare her for his return but also to return her to social position as wife and mother. Within the Freudian schema, subjectivity is constituted by one's status within the matrix of the nuclear family. Freudenberger's haunting of Suzanne is not truly altruistic, as it serves to regulate her sexuality. While Freudenberger's circle addresses one of Suzanne's anxieties—the solitude that drives her to sleepwalk—his method only helps Suzanne prepare for the return of her husband who, at the conclusion of the play, is presumed to have been the victim of physical and psychological violence. Freudenberger's psychoanalytic resolution for Suzanne effectually mirrors Freud's reading of the normative Oedipal circumstance in which the female subject must remain passive, submissive to the male subject, and masochistic. Freudenberger altogether forecloses the possibility for Suzanne to develop a politicized consciousness by offering her the role of Lucy and reinscribing her to a conservative heteronormative space of female submission. Alice speaks the play's final words, informing the audience that "in months David would recover. The book on Fanon would be powerful" (196). The play's conclusion suggests that now that David has returned, the familial order is restored and the social order is no longer threatened. It is also assumed that Suzanne's anxieties are no longer of concern; she has been cured by the arrival of her husband, as Mina is cured by the death or destruction of her desire through the killing of *Dracula.*

Kennedy's invocation of psychoanalysis in her rendering of Freud and Fanon calls attention to the way that black writers have considered psychoanalytic culture integral to the social and political lives of black people. Not only are Freud and Fanon a testament to Kennedy's interest in psychoanalytic culture, but also she takes up these figures to broach the drama's larger questions of subjectivity, experience, and representation. That Kennedy looks to psychoanalysis to address the politics of race and gender speaks to her singularity among Black Arts writers, for whom psychoanalysis was at best an inappropriate methodology for interpreting the complexities of black interiority. Indeed, Kennedy juxtaposes psychoanalytic and Black Power discourses as a way to underscore their historical contradictions and to begin to imagine the reconciliation of the political, the social, and the psychic, through the lens of black female subjectivity.

6

Racial Sincerity and the Biracial Body in Danzy Senna's *Caucasia*

When published in 1998, Danzy Senna's novel *Caucasia* emerged as a curiosity in its attempt to recoup and redefine the racial passing narrative. Novels in which racial passing is the primary theme had not been published in the past seventy years. But since 1990 we have witnessed a boom in the publication of fictional and nonfictional texts situated around the politics of multiracial identity.[1] From the onslaught of literary criticism delineating the interstices of race, class, sexuality, and gender in passing narratives to the mass production of sociological studies examining the lived experiences of biracial and multiethnic subjects, the move to think seriously about what it means to occupy two (or more) racialized positions signals more than a trend. The effect of this critical exchange has led to a reconsideration of the ways in which blackness and whiteness serve (or fail to serve) as effective categories of representation. The notion that the "fate of the mulatto in history and in literature . . . will manifest the symptoms that will eventually affect the rest of the nation" would suggest that *Caucasia* aims to add a new space on the literary continuum of the passing novel in general, and its representation of the "mulatto" figure in particular (*Caucasia* 393). A more pressing question is what Senna's recuperation of this theme says about the shifting perspectives of racial definition and identification for the mixed-race subject. By situating the protagonist, Birdie Lee, as a not-so-tragic mulatto, what statement does *Caucasia* make about the dilemma of the contemporary biracial figure? Senna's tongue-in-cheek passage on mulattoes in the new millennium in which she satirically claims that, "America loves us in all of our half-caste glory," certainly offers a different conception of multiracial identity in American culture and literature than earlier representations of the familiar "tragic mulatto" trope.[2] Though Senna presents a fantastical account of a world dominated by biracial subjects, her underlying notion that "hybridity is in" is astute.

Psychoanalytic thought has been employed to respond to an exterior logic of race. Despite the differences among them, the texts I discuss in earlier chapters posit a similar relationship between the raced subject and psychoanalytic discourses; specifically, each contains a certain "inevitability" of blackness. In these narratives, blackness functions as a static site of subjectivity that is normalized, made invisible, tragic, and/or subjugated within a psychoanalytic context.[3] However, *Caucasia*'s concern with the contemporary politics of mixed-race subjectivity enables a reconsideration of blackness as shifting and multivalent, proposing a new relationship between psychoanalytic discourse and racial subjectivity, one that is concerned with the interiority of race. Such a privileging of racial interiority marks the distinct way in which *Caucasia* inspires a new direction in the confluence of race and psychoanalysis that moves beyond the idea of the social construction of race and takes seriously the notion of racial "choice."[4] Using John L. Jackson Jr.'s concept of racial sincerity as a starting point, I consider *Caucasia*'s formulation of race as one that privileges psychic, rather than bodily, representation.

Jackson produces an interesting distinction between racial sincerity and models of racial authenticity, noting that "sincerity privileges intent—an interiorized intent that decentralizes the racial seer" (18). He adds: "With sincerity as a model, one still does not see into the other, one still does not know if one can trust the other's performances; however, one recognizes that people are not simply racial objects (to be verified from without) but racial subjects with an interiority that is never completely and unquestionably clear. Racial subjects demand a mutual granting of autonomy and interiorized validity that outstrips authenticity's imperfect operationalizations" (18). Useful in Jackson's conceptualization of racial sincerity is the priority he assigns to the racial subject's interior claims to a particular racial self. The idea that one's self-articulated racial identity is not fixed but rather continuously shifting is intrinsic to Jackson's notion of racial sincerity. Yet however unstable this self-assigned racial designation may appear, the subject's perception of his or her racial self trumps the authenticity model, in which the racial seer reserves the right to "name" the racial object. Jackson seeks to clear a space "for intersubjectivities that presume the agency and interiority of one's interlocutors" (24). His formulations resonate with Hortense Spillers's call for attention to deeper modes of self-reflexivity, or rather what she calls an "interior intersubjectivity," in African American cultural analysis (383).[5] Jackson contends that the entire framework of passing, for example, is predicated on "a certain privileging of authentification" which "demands hard, fast, and absolute surefootedness" (21, 18). Authentification also requires a seer, the "subject" of the gaze, an authenticator or verifier, one who legitimates, names, and in doing so, dominates. Similarly, Spillers explains that naming "becomes destiny, to the extent that the social formation, or individual communities within it, more accurately, comprehend themselves, almost entirely, as an innocence or a passivity worked upon, worked over, by others" (383). The model of racial sincerity grants authority to the racial subject to self-signify, rather than allowing the authenticating subject the power to decide his or her "destiny." Not unlike racial sincerity, Spillers locates "interior intersubjectivity" as "the locus at which self-interrogation takes place" (383). As such, "interior intersubjectivity" is "persistently motivated in inwardness, in-flux, it is the 'mine' of social production that arises, in part, from interacting with others, yet it bears the imprint of a particularity" (Spillers 383). The agency that emerges from (or during) the process of self-interrogation clearly resonates with Jackson's articulation of racial sincerity as an intensely personal self-analysis that deserves public recognition. Interior intersubjectivity as a mode of racial subject formation does not function in opposition to social and cultural formations, but is produced from them. However, the racial subject, while a product of his or her environment, does not have to be defined or confined by it. If a subject were able to assume any racial identification of his or her choosing, regardless of his or her bodily markings, then the act of passing would not be possible, because authority would be granted to the subject and not to some larger social force that dictates his or her racial status.

In its imaginative representation of the way that race functions as an interior site of subjectivity, *Caucasia* intensifies critical discussions concerning racial futurity. In *Caucasia,* the protagonist's challenge is to make an interior blackness legible through a body that reads as white. The concept of race as an interior rather than social construction suggests an innovative approach to interpreting and destabilizing the terms of race itself. Such focus on interiority also coincides with Kalpana Sheshadri-Crooks's notion that one possible method to destabilize the terms of race would be to adopt an "adversarial aesthetic" that would allow for a consideration of "identity in tension with our usual habits of *visual* categorization of individuals" (*Desiring* 160, my emphasis). To remove racial meaning from its visual trappings necessitates that race be reassessed as a largely psychic mode of subjectivity. What is at stake in this chapter, then, is the novel's intention to subvert visible racial characteristics as the primary element of racial identification while at the same time preserving race as a crucial yet unstable and ambiguous marker of individual and communal identity.

Biracial Is the New Black

Caucasia takes place from the late 1970s to the mid-1980s, when Birdie Lee's parents, Sandy (a white social activist) and Deck (an African American intellectual), struggle with their opposing roles in a waning Black Revolution. The novel begins moments before the dissolution of Sandy and Deck's marriage, and we witness Sandy's effort to raise their two "black" daughters, Birdie and Cole, while Deck tries to assuage his conscience for marrying a white woman during an era of Black Power. When Deck leaves the family home, Sandy becomes a more active crusader for social justice by harboring political refugees and allegedly stockpiling illegal weapons. Her work reaches a frightening climax when she learns that the "Feds" may have discovered her subversive activities and could capture and imprison her. In response to the perceived threat of Sandy's incarceration, Deck and Sandy make a crucial decision: Deck will flee to Brazil with Carmen, his girlfriend, and the dark-complexioned Cole (read: *coal*), whereas Sandy will take Birdie to New Hampshire. They justify the splitting of their family, especially their daughters, because they surmise that the government will be searching for a white woman accompanied by two black girls. Because of Birdie's "general phenotypic resemblance to the Caucasoid race" (128), Sandy reasons that Birdie should pass in order to save their lives. The story unfolds with a careful examination of Sandy and Birdie's experience in exile, tracing Birdie's psychological development as a once-black girl from Boston who must now adjust to a white existence, first in a women's commune in Aurora and then in the homogeneously white environment of New Hampshire. The novel concludes in Berkeley, California, where mulattoes are a "dime a dozen" and where Birdie reconnects with Cole as they prepare to reintegrate their lives (411). After living unsuccessfully as a black girl in Boston and as the white Jesse Goldman in New Hampshire, Birdie finds what appears to be an inner sanctum in Berkeley, where multiracials maintain a pervasive presence. The conclusion of the text positions Berkeley as a multiracial haven where mixed-race persons like Birdie and Cole no longer have to suffer the isolation and rejection that has defined their experiences in other geographic spaces. That Senna would choose Berkeley as a racial utopia for her biracial protagonists makes sense, given that California maintains the largest multiracial population in the contiguous United States, and it also served as the origin of the multiracial movement. Although *Caucasia* was published in 1998, the events in the novel span the period from the mid-1970s to the early 1980s. These dates are significant because the *Loving v. Commonwealth of Virginia* landmark appeal, which "held that miscegenation statutes adopted by Virginia to prevent marriages between persons solely on basis of racial classification *violate* equal protection and due process clauses of the Fourteenth Amendment" (my emphasis), immediately precedes the birth dates of Cole and Birdie Lee, 1964 and 1967, respectively.[6] Cole and Birdie Lee represent the "first generation of canaries" to survive the passage of the law that legitimated their existence (392).[7] The *Loving v. Commonwealth* decision is credited with producing the "biracial big boom," which also accounts for the contemporary interest and debates surrounding multiracial identity politics.[8]

Because Birdie and Cole happily reconcile in Berkeley, the conclusion of the novel suggests that the ability to live freely as a multiracial person is ideal. This ending has largely structured the way in which critics have interpreted the text's racial motives. For example, Brenda Boudreau postulates that Birdie's "identity will never be complete until she owns both her blackness and whiteness and claims her biracial body" (68). However, I read the novel's intention differently. While proponents of the multiracial movement have been the most vocal in advocating for the consideration of "multiracial" as a separate and distinct racial category, Senna represents another camp of biracials who choose to retain their connectedness to the African American community. In a 2002 interview, Senna notes the extent to which "multiraciality has become fetishized in the media and in popular discussions on race" (Arias 448). Further, she admits to being "suspicious of adding a new category to the Census," primarily because it "upholds a simplistic, scientific vision of race" (448). Rather than continually creating new racial categories, Senna is more concerned with "deconstructing the premise of race itself" and is "wary of sanctifying any group based on race, or romanticizing the so-called mulatto" (448). "The Mulatto Millennium" offers a satirical account of a nation in which mulattoes have taken over. However, in the conclusion of that essay she expresses her own stance toward a "mulatto millennium" and admits that, for her, blackness is a "privilege" and not a choice.

Despite *Caucasia*'s celebratory overtones of multiracialism, it remains immersed in a sentimentalized politics of blackness that ultimately works in opposition to a multiracial sociopolitical agenda. The contemporary politics surrounding the recognition of biracial and multiracial persons has been affected by a number of organizations, including the Association of Multi-Ethnic Americans (AMEA), Project RACE, and I-Pride, whose agendas included the recognition of mixed-race persons as a separate racial class. These groups were largely responsible for the multiracial classification on the 2000 census, which allowed persons to choose more than one racial category in an effort to increase the political visibility of multiracials in the United States. While initiatives like this are largely symbolic, the social implications of such efforts have been challenged by U.S. Senator Diane Watson and State Senator Charles Walton, the Civil Rights Division of the Department of Social Justice, the Equal Employment Opportunity Commission, and most recently the University of California Board of Regents, who claim that the loss of representation by formerly "black" people would "harm the case for civil rights enforcement and diminish the number of valid claims of the patterns of discrimination that result, under federal law, in compensatory programs such as affirmative action" (Daniel 130).[9] In addition, conservatives have taken up the multiracial cause to promote an agenda of color blindness and thereby undermine the fact that race continues to be a defining social and political category.[10] But multiracial advocates argue that the right to acknowledge all parts of one's racialized self without disavowing one group or the other is central to one's self-esteem and the development of a coherent sense of identity. Maria P. P. Root writes that "in essence, to name oneself is to validate one's existence and declare visibility. This seemingly simple process is a significant step in the liberation of multiracial persons from the oppressive structure of the racial classification system that has relegated them to the land of 'in-between'" ("Within" 145). More progressive multiracial advocates imagine mixed-race persons as the group that will most effectively construct a bridge between an era of biological race and a future of racelessness. G. Reginald Daniel notes that "the proponents of the 'constructive' postcolonial perspective . . . posit a multiracial identity as a form of 'racial transcendence' that acknowledges a more inclusive identity based on a multiplicity of ancestral backgrounds." Daniel further asserts that "the new multiracial identity is part of a broader postcolonial social transformation and consciousness, although it does not in and of itself dismiss the concept of race. It does, however, challenge essentialist and reductionist notions of race and de-centers racial categories that originate in the dominant Eurocentric paradigm by pointing to the ambiguity and multiplicity of identities" (11).

In "The Face of America and the State of Emergency," Lauren Berlant critiques arguments like Daniel's that imagine multiracial identities as enabling social or personal transformations or as providing a challenge to racial essentialism. In her reading of *Time* magazine's 1993 cover story "The New Face of America," Berlant argues that the computer-generated image of

America's new face, the fusion of several races accomplished by morphing technology, does not suggest progressive possibilities for a "posthistorical," "postwhite" future (200). Instead, she reads *Time*'s "mixed-race but still white enough" face of futurity as the sign and symbol of an amnesiac ambition. *Time*'s postracial "cyborg" possesses "no narrative of identity." Through the symbolic wiping-away of the nation's racial, ethnic, gendered, and economic complexity, the "face" represents the erasure of "African American history to American culture by predicting its demise; it sacrifices attention to the concrete lives of exploited immigrant and native people of color by fantasizing the future as what will happen when white people intermarry, thus linking racial mixing to the continued, but masked, hegemony of whiteness" (207). In short, multiraciality does not necessarily signal a new direction for a more progressive racial future, but can camouflage insidious attempts to elide the inequities that result from racial hierarchies operating under the guise of colorblindness.

Senna's aversion to racial labeling affirms her discomfort with the visual as a signifier of racial identity, but she also signals an intention to reformulate blackness as dynamic and multivalent. Lori Harrison-Kahan has asserted that Senna "queer[s] our understanding of mixed race identity, affirming that race—even whiteness itself—is not clear-cut and fixed but multiple and 'in motion'" (27). Indeed, Senna's novel constructs more comprehensive articulations of blackness, rather than encouraging the potential reification of more racial categories, including a nebulous "multiracial" category. Though racialized categories, particularly blackness and whiteness, are generally read as fixed binaries and static subject positions, Senna disrupts this paradigm by pointing to the complexities of such subjectivities. *Caucasia* examines blackness through a classed, gendered, sexualized, and even transnational lens. The narrative is more sympathetic to complicating existent notions of blackness than to constructing a "border identity" that rests between two racial positionalities.[11] Reading biraciality as blackness may appear as a reversion to the arcane one-drop rule evident in nineteenth-century works like Charles Chesnutt's *The House Behind the Cedars* and Frances Harper's *Iola Leroy*, in which the protagonists choose not to pass as white or claim a white identity as a matter of guilt or racial pride and solidarity. But multiracial writers like Senna, Lisa Jones, and Rebecca Walker lay claim to blackness as a move toward affirming a new black self. In *Bulletproof Diva*, Lisa Jones explains, "I call myself African-American, which means, to me, a person of African and Native American, Latin, or European identity," and "by claiming

African American and black, I also inherit the right to ask questions about what this identity means" (31).

Though multiracial discourses offer the possibility of providing a new language and framework to discuss race, the conversation surrounding the social constructedness of race in general and multiraciality in particular remains grounded in largely static notions of blackness and whiteness, thereby reproducing the very essentialisms the discourse seeks to escape.[12] Discourses of racial authenticity assume that one's racial identity is determined by the gaze of the Other. Such an assumption leaves little space to examine the way that complex processes of race become internalized in the mixed race body.[13] *Caucasia*'s highly psychological resonances make clear that racial identification, as shown especially in Birdie's claims to blackness, is less a matter of epidermal darkness than one of psychic interiority. In order to capture the extent to which the psychoanalysis of race emerges in *Caucasia,* I provide a comparative analysis of Senna's text with Fanny Howe's *The Deep North,* as Senna explicitly draws on the psychological constructions of race in Howe's novel to shape her own protagonist's racial subjectivity.[14] Though *Caucasia* does not admit to any explicit psychoanalytic claims, its connection to Howe's novel demonstrates how Senna's formulations of contemporary multiracial identity are inextricably tied to psychological interpretations of identification.[15] The complex interstitial elements of desire, race, family, and individual subjectivity in *Caucasia* significantly illuminate the process of racial becoming in the narrative.

Passing through *The Deep North*

In a December 1999 interview, Senna claims her indebtedness to Nella Larsen and Ralph Ellison, whose themes of invisibility and passing provide the governing framework for her own novel. In the interview Senna notes that her first choice among books she would carry with her into the new millennium would be Ellison's *Invisible Man*: "One of the things that I worry about in the new millennium is that people will assume that we've somehow got distance on the past, and on what has happened in the twentieth century. This book is to remind us about the proximity of the past. We aren't in the future yet. We are still living in the present" (Aronson). Senna's selection of *Invisible Man* offers a useful context to consider her project of re-articulating the terms of blackness in *Caucasia.* Robert Reid-Pharr identifies Ellison's work as "challen[ging] notions of an already decided black identity" and working to reveal blackness as thoroughly modern and consistently in process (33).

In the same way that Ellison's invisible narrator must shed the contents of his suitcase in order to release himself from the social and cultural signifiers of blackness, Senna's protagonist must formulate the terms of her racial self. In addition to Ellison's text, Senna adds that she "would also bring my mother, Fanny Howe's, novel, which is still in print by Sun and Moon Press. It's called *Deep North* (1990), and it's an amazing story, dealing with race and gender, of a white woman crossing out of her world and passing as black in the sixties. . . . And James Baldwin's *Giovanni's Room,* a book about a white bisexual man living in Paris and struggling with his sexual identity. It's a beautiful book and a daring one. It touches on my obsession with passing; it's about sexual passing, really" (Aronson).

Senna's favorites are all concerned with the negotiation of seemingly fixed boundaries of race and sexuality, yet the influence of Howe's novel is perhaps the most compelling. The narrative centers on the life of a young woman, Gemma, who is from a well-to-do white family in Boston. The postmodern narrative is told primarily through Gemma's point of view but is interspersed with more abstract poetic musings that capture the intense moods of Gemma and her family as they face the familial struggles of infidelity, divorce, infirmity, and, death. Surrounded by a bourgeois, self-centered mother, a nervous academic father, and a manipulative brother, Gemma emerges as the innocent loner among the group, and attempts to act as a stabilizing presence in this group of eccentrics. In addition to her calm persona, Gemma is distinguished from her family by the color of her skin.

While the family is racially white, *The Deep North* consistently references Gemma's darker hue. As a child, her brother forces her to play the role of an escaped slave: "Pretend, he said, we are slaves escaping. You're the slave and I'm the master's son. You said I want to go to the North with you, so I took you with me late one night. You were actually the illegitimate daughter of the master, too, by a slave woman who had very pale skin" (10). References to Gemma's epidermal difference punctuate the narrative; even the black maid, Darlene, whom Gemma eventually befriends, "called G 'the dark little white girl' and so did Ron, her fiancé, whom she had followed to Boston" (25). Once Gemma reaches adulthood, she begins to take frequent train trips throughout Boston and discovers there is life beyond the confines of her wealthy and neurotic home. She eventually meets Adam, a budding young psychoanalyst, and the two marry and quickly divorce. During the course of their relationship, Adam converses with Gemma in primarily psychoanalytic terms, which eventually emerge in the narrative as emotional abuse:

> The way they talked to each other was frightening to her—he in the language of Freud, of Wilhelm Reich, of others who saw the psychological subject as being the whole person. This was his field, and he was young in it and couldn't resist explaining herself to herself in those terms. 'You are functioning with a diminished libido and a fear of separation bordering on psychosis,' he might say. Or: 'You suffer from an enlarged super-ego which dominates the infantile aspects of your personality. This keeps you at a level of suspended and unfulfilled genital fixation.' He told her that the Civil Rights movement was a misplaced rebellion against the father on the part of adolescents. (*Deep North* 34)

Adam uses a psychoanalytic vocabulary to subjugate Gemma and produce within her feelings of intellectual and emotional inferiority. Once the inevitability of their divorce becomes apparent, his "words [become] nasty, and cruel (*schizoid, paranoid, autistic, catatonic, psychotic*), the opposite of Hope Chest, the dowry of her divorce." Adam's verbal attacks are effective: "Little flashes of resistance, which she held up like shields before them, were flattened at once" (85). Adam experiences the world almost exclusively through a psychoanalytic lens, and Gemma becomes the victim of Adam's psychoanalytic gaze. His complete detachment from the social world is evidenced by his "analysis" of the civil rights movement, in which he interprets African Americans as "adolescents" who rebel against the father (white hegemony).

Gemma dreams of leaving Adam and moving to New York, but an unexpected encounter with a young African, Augustine, changes her course. After distracting a young white mob and perhaps saving Augustine's life, Gemma shares a cab with him, answers affirmatively when he asks whether she is either West Indian or Cape Verdean, and decides to try to change the course of her life. Gemma decides in that moment with Augustine to pass as black. His belief that she is "a person of color, meeting him that night with her August tan high on her arms, legs, and face, and her kinky hair flying" allows her the possibility of escaping her family and her former life once and for all (107). She clumsily attempts to assimilate the language of blackness: "She cross-examined Augustine and others on African colonialism and literature, in the effects of oppression and racism on the Third World, and so on" and moves into an apartment complex inhabited solely by black tenants in a lower class section of the city. Gemma believes that her "passing" enables her to be "liberated from the sense of being on the wrong side of history," and to enter a world that would have forever remained foreign had she not crossed the color (and class) line (117). Gemma appropriates blackness as her defense against Adam's insults.

This act articulates a broader relation between psychoanalysis and black subjectivity. Adam's psychoanalytic prowess defeats the shy, "white" Gemma, who holds no form of resistance against his insults, but the West Indian Gemma "let[s] her freedom carry her forward into territories where she forgot herself" (117). The territories to which she refers are both physical and psychological spaces. Gemma reformulates Adam's terms to create a psychic space of blackness that can free her from both her dysfunctional family and Adam's insults. The use of a psychological blackness to deny the trappings of a visibly white body emerges as the central theme in both Howe's and Senna's texts. For Gemma: "The lie about her race made her see the world fresh the way you do on the first October day which is clear and blue. . . . The pavement glittered with a mica unnoticed before, and the squirrels ate nuts with focused relish. Grains of sugar seemed larger than ever; cream was sweeter; and the smell of the air anywhere was human and familiar. It was like being in love with the new person that she now was" (116). The experience of becoming black in both *The Deep North* and *Caucasia* emerges as a highly romanticized process that occurs at the psychic level. Though Gemma is racially white and Birdie is biracial, their investments in blackness are not articulated merely through performance. Gemma and Birdie consciously construct a racialized interiority that, in both texts, ultimately calls into question the normative terms of race. The opening of *The Deep North* reveals Gemma's desire to "locate the process that underlay the surface image, to put [her] hand under the top without looking at what I let out," indicating a disjuncture she imagines between the interior and exterior self (9).

Part of Howe's and Senna's projects to reformulate racial paradigms include the disruption of whiteness. Howe's and Senna's unfavorable rendering of whiteness and glorified portrayals of the Black Power movement are central to both narratives' undermining of the logic of racial hegemony. In the introduction to *The Wedding Dress,* Howe recalls the ways in which the Black Power movement forced white Americans to rethink their place in the social order. She explains: "Blackness became the club that many whites longed to join. The raised fists, the street signals, the attitude, the rhetoric, the music, all these produced a change in white consciousness that had the effect of making whites defensive and aggressive on the one hand, or yearning for conciliation on the other. Black Power forced individual whites to see themselves as unstable and isolated social products, people who had come to the end of the line, and not the transcendent and eternal beings that they were raised to believe themselves to be. It was a terrible blow to a mass ego" (xiii). Howe articulates the impact of the Black Power movement on white

American consciousness in psychological terms. She credits the Black Power movement with exposing the myth of whiteness.

Caucasia explores this sociopsychological shift from white superiority to black power in the context of a nuclear interracial family structure, primarily through the lens of Birdie Lee. The construction of whiteness as a fluid and an "isolated" racial space is instructive to both novels' troubling of what is generally understood as an uncomplicated racial binary, the effect of which is not only a repositioning of whiteness, but a more complex rendering of blackness. However, *The Deep North* probes the issue of passing in particular and race more generally through the lens of authenticity. Gemma is ultimately forced to abandon her newfound blackness because she is "outed" during a visit by her visibly white brother. She fails the test of authenticity and is never able to recover. Conversely, Birdie's allegiance to blackness surfaces as a more "sincere" psychic space of racial belonging that acts as a form of resistance against authenticating narratives.

"Mirroring" Blackness and the Logic of Racial Interiority

Caucasia insists upon broader, alternative locations of racial identity and challenges the black-white binary inherent in most narratives of racial passing. Birdie passes as white in appearance only; her act of passing is not confused with the appropriation and privileging of white identity. Because Birdie's primary identification is with her older, darker sister, the impetus of Birdie's desire is to become racially visible, meaning visibly black, to garner love from her father. Though Birdie's fantasy of blackness is never fully realized, it does broach the important subject of desire, which is crucial to this (and any) discussion of identification and recognition. After their parents' separation, Birdie realizes that her father fails to see her during his visits because of her white features, and he privileges Cole because of her visible blackness. Birdie recognizes that blackness is directly correlative to the amount of love and attention she will receive from her father. In the eyes of young Birdie: "Cole was my father's special one. I understood that even then. She was his prodigy—his young, gifted, and black. At the time, I wasn't sure why it was Cole and not me, but I knew that when they came together, I disappeared. . . . Cole was his proof that he had indeed survived the integrationist shuffle, that he had remained human despite what seemed like a conspiracy to turn him into stone. She was his proof of the pudding, his milk chocolate pudding, the small dusty body, the burst of mischievous curls (nappier than his own), the full pouty lips (fuller than his own). Her existence told him he hadn't wandered quite so far and that his body still had the power to leave its mark." (55–56) Although it is Birdie who internalizes their father's Black Power rhetoric, he consistently rejects her due to her white appearance. As a result, Birdie recognizes whiteness as invisibility long before she actually passes as white. Given the persistence of the one-drop rule, both Cole and Birdie are racially marked as black, but the epidermal distinction (which is exacerbated by their father's favoritism toward Cole) exposes an intraracial politics of color within the novel as well. Despite his frequent affirmations of blackness, Deck needs Cole in order to validate his own tenuous racial identity. The dismantling of the Lee family occurs largely because Deck is unable to reconcile his marriage to a white woman while attempting to establish himself as a major scholar on race theory. Rather than engage in more grassroots activism like Sandy, Deck uses blackness as a way to construct his intellectual identity. His blackness has to be reaffirmed through his fetishized attachment to Cole and his superficial relationship with Carmen, who possesses "glowing, mocha-brown skin" (89).

Deck's decision to move to Brazil so that he may be free from U.S. racial limitations resonates with the character Brian Redfield in Nella Larsen's 1929 novella, *Passing*. Though Brian Redfield is a relatively minor figure in the text, he reemerges in a more realized form as Deck Lee in *Caucasia*. In *Passing*, Brian represents a persistent threat to the social, economic, and familial security of the protagonist, Irene, due to his growing desire to escape U.S. racism and move to Brazil. Brian never leaves Harlem, but Deck capitalizes on Sandy's fears of imprisonment and moves to Brazil with Cole and Carmen in an attempt to start anew with his refigured "black" family. This decision is curious, considering that miscegenation was and still is encouraged in Brazil. Deck's obsession with Brazil recalls the widespread construction of Brazil in the early-twentieth-century African American cultural and literary imagination as a racial democracy, making it an idealistic environment for those who wished to evade the pressures of U.S. racism and heterosexism.[16] However, the reality was that although Brazil lacked American forms of racism, similar problems existed nonetheless. Senna translates Brian Redfield's desire into Deck Lee's reality, but the fact that he returns disappointed with the experience also discloses the inescapability of the dilemma of race. Eventually, Cole tells Birdie that the scenario in Brazil was not much different than the one in the United States. Cole explains that they "had gone to Brazil with such high expectations. But over those first few months in Rio, it had slowly dawned on them that poor people living in the favellas resembled Africans, the rich people in power resembled Europeans, and everyone in the middle was obsessed with where they and their children would fall on the spectrum of color" (*Caucasia* 406).

When Deck realizes that Brazil's problem has manifested in a conflict of color as opposed to race, he comes back to the United States, where the racial situation is not obfuscated with semantics. Racial difference, in fact, is not only what informs Deck Lee's academic work, but also what consumes him. For Deck, to exist in the absence of race would be counterproductive, and he leaves Brazil with the understanding that there is no such thing. Though he asserts that "race is a complete illusion," Birdie exposes his hypocrisy by telling him that "you gave me to Mum 'cause I looked white" (391). Generally, the passing figure is presented outside of his or her racial community and family, but *Caucasia* illustrates that the kinship between mother and daughters, fathers and daughters, and sisters is not immune to the contagion of the racial order in the home or abroad. Deck's insecurities lead to the lessened value he assigns Birdie, which is evident in one of the narrative's most significant but unacknowledged dilemmas: if Deck flees to Brazil because he perceives it to be a racial democracy, why doesn't he take Birdie as well? The distance between Birdie and her father widens once he becomes involved with Carmen, who makes Birdie feel that the physical differences between herself and her father and Cole are "deeper than skin" (91). Carmen's ill-treatment of Birdie forces her to consider whether her phenotypic "whiteness" signals a psychic difference as well as a biological or epidermal difference. Despite the fact that Birdie and Cole are sisters, Birdie's white body discredits her as an authentic black subject in the eyes of an authenticating Carmen.

Deck's favoritism of the darker daughter, Cole, is responsible for Birdie's desire to be like her sister in order to receive the same attention and love from their father. Birdie realizes that to accomplish this, she must also be racially visible as a black person and identify with Cole. Identification is understood as the "psychological process whereby the subject assimilates an aspect, property or attribute of the other and is transformed, wholly or partially, after the model the other provides" (Silverman 205). Birdie's mirroring of Cole highlights the narrative's almost obsessive privileging and sentimentality of blackness. In addition, Birdie's reading of Cole as a mirror image demonstrates the narrative's partiality to an interior logic of race: "Before I saw myself, I saw my sister. When I was still too small for mirrors I saw her as the reflection that proved my own existence. Back then, I was content to see only Cole, three years older than me, and imagine that her face—cinnamon-skinned, curly-haired, serious—was my own. It was her face above me always, waving toys at me, cooing at me, whispering to me, pinching me when she was angry and I was the easiest target. That face was me and I was that face and that was how the story went" (*Caucasia* 5).

Through this mirroring relationship with Cole, Birdie internalizes blackness. Gwen Bergner produces a persuasive model for interpreting the formation of a racial subjectivity in terms similar to that of gender identity formation. Locating a visual experience at the center of the process of subject formation, Bergner argues that "individuals internalize ideologies of race and gender by way of the psychic processes of symbolic accommodation" (xxiii). In this moment between Birdie and Cole, the novel confirms its thesis that blackness is not fixed; it is psychically formed. Because Birdie immediately recognizes (i.e., misrecognizes) Cole as her mirror image, she naturally identifies with her sister and thus desires to be "cinnamon-skinned" and "curly-haired" as well. By adopting Cole's image as the ego ideal, she implicitly rejects the fair-skinned and straight-haired image that her mother, Sandy, embodies. Birdie recognizes Cole as the image that promises her racial unity and fulfills Birdie's epidermal void or "lack" due to her white complexion. Sandy serves as an inadequate model for her black children, which further signals what Senna portrays as an unbridgeable gulf between mother and child. Both Freud and Lacan understand the role of the mother as "the initial object of desire both for the male and female objects—the first object, that is, which is loved as something distinct from the self" (Silverman 190). However, Birdie fails to identify with her mother and, instead, looks to Cole to fulfill this role. Cole's displacement of Sandy in the role of mother is further exemplified by the fact that Sandy fails to name Birdie, whose birth certificate still reads "Baby Lee." It is the three-year-old Cole who gives Birdie her name. In the Oedipal relationship, the female child in particular identifies with her mother. Yet instead of the natural identification the child experiences with her mother, Birdie rejects her mother in favor of identification with her dark sister, who does not possess the "white" lack found in herself and their mother. Birdie's desire to be visibly black emerges in her image of Cole: taken out of context, the "before I saw myself, I saw my sister" passage may simply read as a younger sister's desire to emulate her older sibling. However, the passage marks what is only the beginning of Birdie's unfulfilled desire to be "black" like Cole.

Birdie's rejection of her white mother and desire for the black father points to the novel's (and Birdie's) general tendency to romanticize blackness. In *Caucasia,* blackness signifies wholeness, and because Birdie does not look black, she finds it necessary to affirm a black consciousness or psyche that is never presumed because of her complexion. Before the collapse of her family, Birdie's world is saturated with images and rhetoric of the Black Power movement. This is exemplified by the influx of political prisoners who become an everyday part of Birdie's domestic life after her enrollment at the Nkrumah school. Although Sandy is well-intentioned, her untiring work for social justice goes relatively unappreciated by Birdie, who internalizes her father's more theoretical response to the revolution. Birdie is portrayed as an ambivalent body that is out of place in Nkrumah (the Afro-centric school she attends in Boston) because of her "Sicilian" features, as well as in New Hampshire, where she imagines herself as a "spy" infiltrating the white world. In fact, Birdie envisions her act of passing as potential research material for her father's book, which she playfully titles "What White People Say When They Think They're Alone," or even more comically, "Honkified Meanderings: Notes from the Underground" (189).[17] She interprets her racial transgression with a great deal of levity as an act that functions within the framework of her relationship with her father. Even in Deck's absence, she never collapses her white appearance with an appropriation of white identity. In fact, Birdie never truly refers to herself as Jewish—she merely wears a necklace with the Star of David and relies on others to "read" her accordingly.

Though Birdie is not accepted at Nkrumah and suffers rejection from her father's girlfriend and subsequently her father, she clings to images of her black life, like the Sambo-inspired Golliwog doll she embraced as a child. Birdie's desire for blackness can be viewed as a natural instinct for one who seeks to reclaim what she has lost. For Birdie, blackness represents a constructed yet valued site of subjectivity that cannot be forcibly maintained or easily rejected through the act of passing. But in the novel's romanticized view, blackness becomes a racial position that would fulfill Birdie's fantasy of wholeness. Birdie's desire stems from an early identification with Cole, but due to Cole's absence throughout the crucial years of Birdie's identity formation, her desire to be black like Cole remains unfulfilled (as are all notions of desires that operate within a psychoanalytic context). In an imaginative reversal of the dominant racial order, in which blackness rather than whiteness functions as the desired racial identity—Birdie lacks visible blackness, and Sandy desires a black man, Deck—blackness acts as the "phallus" for the novel's female characters. Birdie must realize that her blackness is not like Cole's or her father's, but her blackness (like theirs) will have to be invented.

While Birdie's identity formation is actualized through the desire to be like her sister, Cole's blackness is also largely constructed, despite her dark appearance. At Nkrumah, Cole tells Birdie of the importance of "talk[ing] like black people"—to say "tell de troof" instead of "tell the truth" (53). At home, however, Cole enjoys the scones and marmalade their mother prepares while Birdie prefers grits and greasy sausage from Aku-Aku, the tiki restaurant favored by their father. Though Birdie's story acts as the center of the narrative because of her ambiguous appearance, Cole's struggle with biracialism is no less intriguing. *Caucasia* is ripe with moments that demonstrate Cole's dilemma as a biracial child with a black appearance, including the strange looks she receives when in public with Birdie and their mother; her maternal grandmother's rejection; and her father's inability to see her beyond the color of her skin. But Birdie's split racial self points to the complex interplay of racial and sexual identification and desire in that this tension manifests itself through identification with her "black" sister and aggression toward her white mother. The contrast between Birdie and Cole is notable because it demonstrates the extent to which multiraciality functions as a complex, multilayered site of subjectivity that does not read the same for every multiracial subject.

Birdie comes into existence through a psychic mirroring relationship with Cole, but also through a linguistic kinship. Before Birdie passes as white, she becomes well-versed in the craft of linguistic fluidity through the tales she and Cole share of the make-believe Elemenos, who speak their own language and are "constantly changing their form, color, pattern, in a quest for invisibility" (7). Birdie describes the Elemeno language as "a complicated language, impossible for outsiders to pick up—no verb tenses, no pronouns, just words floating outside time and space without owner or direction" (6). Though Birdie actively participates in these changing games, Cole invents and orchestrates them. The link between language and subjectivity is such that within the context of psychoanalysis, "there can be no imaginary relation or ego function without desire, and when we invoke the term 'desire,' we are always in the realm of language and the symbolic" (Silverman 33). In alignment with the Oedipal stages of development, the way in which the subject enters the symbolic order in the Oedipal stage is identical to how she enters the symbolic order with respect to language and speech. According to Kaja Silverman, Lacan formulates the Oedipus complex as a "linguistic transaction," attributing to it "the same determinative role as that of language in the constitution of the unconscious, subjectivity, and symbolic order" (181). Birdie and Cole's conception of an alternative language points to the inadequacy of preexisting language systems for their unique form of communication, but it also marks their precarious racial position within a black-white binary.

By inventing their own language, they remove themselves from the realm of signification and live out—in their imaginary world—an agential existence defined by their own forms of meaning and signification.

In the same way that their race is consistently imposed onto them, Birdie and Cole face a similar struggle in terms of language. At Nkrumah, they feel compelled to speak black dialect as a way to fit in with their peers, and Deck drills them with phrases to repeat like catechisms. When Deck asks Birdie and Cole to evaluate particular events in popular culture, Birdie's automatic response is typically "diluting the race" or "Jigaboo Time" (*Caucasia* 73). Conversely, Sandy's mother rebukes their attendance at Nkrumah, describing it as "crazy, child abuse" (106). Within a Lacanian framework, subjects participate in a linguistic practice that depends entirely upon historical and cultural conventions. By inventing their own language, Birdie and Cole refuse to enter the (racially) symbolic order, as demonstrated by their preference to exist "outside time and space without owner or direction" (*Caucasia* 6). Birdie and Cole's invention of Elemeno takes on a special significance, because they reject two predominant and binary linguistic systems that not only signify a matter of speech but a matter of race as well—standard English and black dialect. Birdie and Cole's relationship to language exemplifies the ways in which the subject takes on the position as signifier and is "defined by a linguistic structure which does not in any way address its being, but which determines its entire cultural existence" (Silverman 166). Birdie and Cole demonstrate their attempts at agency and autonomy by constructing their own linguistic structure, thereby establishing themselves outside the realm of predetermined signification and the symbolic order. The girls' conception of an independent and free-floating language system complicates their relationship to systems of power and authority.

Birdie continues to explain that Elemeno is more than a language; it is a place and a community of people: "[Cole] said they were a shifting people, constantly changing their form, color, pattern, in a quest for invisibility. According to her, their changing routine was a serious matter—less a game of make-believe than a fight for the survival of the species. The Elemenos could turn deep green in the bushes, beige in the sand, a blank in the white snow, and their power lay precisely in their ability to disappear into any surrounding. As she spoke a new question—a doubt flashed through my mind. Something didn't make sense. What was the point of surviving if you had to disappear?" (7–8). The world of the Elemenos mirrors Birdie's own life, in which she believes that her survival depends upon her racial mutability. At this particular moment, Senna sets forth the existential dilemma that will plague her protagonist throughout the text. However, it is clear that Cole, not Birdie, invents this language, and that both sisters internalize it quite differently. For Birdie, invisibility and existence work in contradiction to one another because she fails to see the power of invisibility, especially as a "white" subject who lacks Cole's overt racial markers. Cole, on the other hand, recognizes the precariousness of her racial positionality, particularly in her reference to the Elemenos's invisibility as crucial to the "survival of the species." One can only speculate as to the nature of this particular species, but I would argue that Cole considers herself and Birdie as part of an endangered class of subjects who refuse categorization and are in many ways unknowable. Because the subject is constituted in language and because language precedes the individual, Birdie and Cole are always required to enter the symbolic order as dictated by forces outside of her control. The fact that Birdie and Cole invent their own language prevents them from entering an established social, symbolic, or racial order without complication, and allows them the space and possibility to conceive of an existence without preexisting signifiers.

Birdie's refusal to submit to conventional categories of race and language is further demonstrated in her confrontation with Samantha Taper—the only visibly black girl at her school in New Hampshire. The two girls maintain a tense relationship in that each is aware of the other's blackness, yet each refuses to acknowledge the other. The dynamic between Samantha and Birdie is visible in numerous passing narratives in which the passer encounters a person from her "former" racial group. The perceived black person does not "out" the passing subject but in some slight verbal or nonverbal form makes the passing subject aware that she has not crossed the color line entirely. Birdie breaks the bond of silence between her and Samantha by asking her, "What color are you?" to which Samantha replies, "I'm black like you" (286). This exchange reveals a twisted instance of mirroring and misrecognition for Birdie that sharply contrasts with her initial mirroring with Cole. As the two girls face each other—one phenotypically white and the other black—the expectation of identification falls dramatically short. Samantha's image does not fulfill the same sense of gratification that Birdie experienced during the mirroring of Cole. Instead, Samantha's visage distorts Birdie's own self-image, and she immediately recognizes her image as reflected in Samantha as a lie. The dialogue provides the impetus for Birdie to run away from New Hampshire and to search for her father and sister. Samantha's words release Birdie (a.k.a. Jesse Goldman) from her false inhabitation of a singular white body. In novels like Nella Larsen's *Passing*, the death experienced by the passer is literal, indicative of the punishment for his or her racial transgression or the impossibility of peaceably reconciling the worlds of black and white. But Birdie's decision to end her white performance marks the symbolic death of her passing identity, Jesse Goldman. When Birdie decides to no longer pass as white, she describes the process as "killing one girl in order to let the other one free. It hurt, this killing, more than I thought it would, but I kept walking, repeating a pattern of words under my breath, words that I no longer understood but whispered just the same. *Kublica marantha boda. Lasa mel kin*" (289). Birdie's reversion to Elemeno signals her intent to reclaim the distinct yet nebulous space she once occupied with her sister.

In a 2002 interview, Senna notes that "with Birdie, her authentic racial self is only what she makes it" (Arias 449). Therefore, racial authenticity is not left to the gaze of the other but, for Birdie, is self-determining, and if we take Senna's statement seriously, then racial authenticity is shifting as well. After leaving New Hampshire, Birdie recalls: "Samantha had told me what color I was. She had said I was Jewish, but she had been joking, just playing along with what she knew to be a gag. Later she had told me that I was black like her. At least that's what I heard. Those words had made something clearer. Made it clear that I didn't want to be black like Samantha. A doomed, tragic shade of black. I wanted to be black like somebody else" (*Caucasia* 321). Though Cole has functioned as Birdie's primary object of identification, it remains unclear whose blackness she would like to emulate. Birdie does not express a desire to be "black like" Cole but "like somebody else." This is a significant moment in the text because it signals a potential break from Cole and her father as objects of desire. Instead, the blackness she seeks to model in this scene is one of her own choosing but is not yet knowable or nameable. Cole seems to provide an adequate biracial model for Birdie, but the physical difference between the two girls does not allow the possibility for them to experience a "black" identity in the same way. Birdie never desires whiteness but rather a legitimate racial space where her brand of blackness is both validated and recognized. Thus she traverses the fantasy of blackness as represented by her father because she realizes that though she is not fully white, she does not desire a blackness that excludes her whiteness.

Upon abandoning Birdie, Deck and Cole leave her with a box of "Negrobilia" as a reminder of her blackness. The box contains "a black Nativity program from the Nkrumah School, a fisted pick (the smell of someone's scalp oil still lingering in between the sharp black teeth), a black Barbie doll head, an informational tourist pamphlet on Brazil, the silver Egyptian necklace inscribed with hieroglyphics . . . and a James Brown eight-track cassette with a faded sticker in the corner that said 'Nubian Notion,' the name of a record shop on Washington Street. That along with Cole's Golliwog, was all that was left of them" (127). Well aware that his daughter will soon pass into a new world of whiteness, Deck tries to empower Birdie with reminders of her black life in Boston with himself and Cole. However, the items compiled by Deck and Cole are nothing but empty signifiers of what he believes constitutes black identity. At the time the family separates, Birdie is apparently eight years old. The items in the box are not indicative of Birdie's experiences but rather of Deck's and Cole's. Birdie never felt as though she belonged at Nkrumah, so the black Nativity program can only serve as a reminder of her exclusion. Birdie's experience at the school only exacerbates her difference from Cole and the other visibly black children. The greasy pick she receives is reminiscent of Cole's hair issues, since Birdie's fine, straight hair does not need to be picked or oiled. When the sisters arrived at Nkrumah, Cole realized that as a black girl (or one that has been deemed black) she should conform to certain elements of beauty and style. After her mother unsuccessfully braided her hair in a fashion similar to the child sitcom star Keisha Taylor, Cole convinced her father to pay for the expensive hair salon braiding by feeding into his "black guilt" by convincing Deck that "Mum just doesn't know how to handle raising a black child, Papa" (55). While this hair experience is largely Cole's, Birdie celebrated Cole's affirmation of blackness when she returned from the salon with braids that were perfectly decorated and aligned. However, this incident forms another moment that distinguishes the sisters, since when Birdie attempts to braid her hair in a similar fashion, the texture refuses to hold the braids in place. The items in the box of Negro memorabilia are designed to serve as memories for Birdie, but they also serve as signs of the constructedness of her black identity, which is supposedly summed up by a black Barbie doll head and a cassette by the "Godfather of Soul," James Brown. The items in the package are presented in a way to suggest that this is all Birdie needs to keep her blackness intact.

The package of Negrobilia is reminiscent of the suitcase that Ralph Ellison's invisible narrator continuously fills with objects that represent the series of roles he embodies at various points in *Invisible Man*. To escape his past and light his way to what will become his border area, the narrator must burn the objects in his suitcase, which are also meaningless signifiers of an identity that was never truly his. Yet instead of burning these mementoes upon leaving New Hampshire, Birdie adds them to her box of Negrobilia. In deciding to leave and to quit passing as Jesse Goldman, she adds the necklace with the

Star of David, a snipping of Samantha's hair, a Jim Rice baseball card, and other trinkets to her box, signaling her increasing ability to invent a blackness that speaks to her experience as Birdie Lee *and* Jesse Goldman. Unlike Ellison's invisible man who destroyed the objects that defined him, Birdie (whether consciously or not) understands her identity as a cumulative process that is marked not by erasure but by layers of experience. That the box now contains memories of her life in Boston as well as in New Hampshire points to the evolution of Birdie's subjectivity.

When Birdie finds her father, he reveals the results of his latest scholarly endeavor: a chart titled "Canaries in the Coal Mine." This chart "depicted a row of pictures of mulattos throughout history. . . . I recognized Alexander Pushkin, Phillipa Schuyler, Nella Larsen, Jean Toomer—Xeroxed photographs of their sallow faces above the dates of their lives, and beneath that their 'fates,' brief descriptions of their desolate and violent deaths . . . The last column of the chart was a snapshot of Cole and me when we were eight and eleven" (392). In Deck's formulation, the fact that Birdie and Cole are "alive" signals a disruption in the historical logic of race, especially as it pertains to mixed-race subjects who were largely constructed as impotent bodies. According to Werner Sollors, "the North American cultural maxim to prevent racial mixing was that culturally unacceptable consent relations were considered punished by a lack of descendants, an ideological exaggeration of the general fear of losing a generation. . . . The products of consent relations across dramatic boundaries were, well into the twentieth century, considered to be exclusively and negatively shaped by one aspect of their descent. In the United States, the country of consent, mulattos were not to be viewed as architects of their own fates" (*Beyond* 226). Sollors points to a historical and cultural tradition of racial classification in which mixed race subjects were, and to a large extent remain, unable to define the terms of their identities. The conclusion of *Caucasia* finds Birdie imagining herself on a passing school bus, "just a blur of yellow and black in motion" (419), signaling her desire for a dynamic black identity not fixed by predetermined models. If Birdie remains in motion, she can continue to construct her identity as a constantly shifting and open set of identifications. She is ultimately disappointed by her mother's resignation to live out what was supposed to be a passing game in New Hampshire and is disgusted with her father's lack of interest in their long-awaited reunion. Birdie's disillusionment with Deck's latest scholarly project is significant because after years of attempting to win his approval, she finally realizes that the blackness she once associated with wholeness contains a certain lack as well. Birdie realizes that Deck, like her, suffers from his own anxieties about race, which he then attempts to displace by transforming his children into theoretical objects.

Upon finding Cole, Birdie muses, "I had believed all along that Cole was all I needed to feel complete. Now I wondered if that completion wasn't overrated" (406). In this way, Birdie is able to traverse the fantasy of racial wholeness and recognize the lack in both Cole and her father. Though the story begins with Cole and Birdie as children struggling to dictate their own racial identities, the novel's final scenes find them removed from both parents, armed with the promise to become "architects of their own fates" (*Beyond* 226). Senna's rendering of Berkeley may be read as a multiracial utopia, where Birdie and Cole are able to live out fully their singular forms of blackness without conflict or question, but a more progressive reading of the text might suggest that Berkeley is yet another space on the continuum and that Birdie must travel further still in her quest to reconcile a racialized interior with the external gaze.[18]

The notion of race as a matter of psychic interiority could signal a new future for both psychoanalysis and critical race studies. In contemplating the state of psychoanalysis in contemporary society, Eli Zaretsky questions, "Do our new insights into race, nation, and gender obviate the need for individuals to understand their own unique individuality?" (347). Yet rather than read "race" and one's "unique individuality" as mutually exclusive, I wonder if cultural understandings of race can function in tandem with the expression of one's own distinctive racial formation or formations. Such creativity would entail destabilizing the binary logic of race, but more significantly, require that race become less "social" and more "sincere."

Postscript

In the 1949 film, *Home of the Brave*, a young black soldier, Pvt. Peter Moss (James Edwards) suffers from shell shock that leaves him paralyzed and plagued with short-term memory loss. The film, directed by Mark Robson and based on the play by Arthur Laurents, centers around Moss's interactions with an army analyst who attempts to discover the root cause of the soldier's psychological break. The analyst finds that during a special mission, Moss fights with his white best friend, Finch, and in a fit of anger calls Moss a "yellow-belly nigger." Shortly after the incident, Finch is shot and killed, and Moss discovers that he can no longer walk. In the course of his therapy sessions, Moss reveals to his analyst that, for a moment, he was "glad" that Finch was killed in retribution for calling him a "nigger." However, the doctor convinces Moss that neither race nor racism has anything to do with his feelings of guilt; instead, Moss was simply glad that he was not the victim of the fatal bullet. The analyst notes that Moss has experienced a feeling common to many men who have witnessed the death of a fellow soldier.

Instructive in this scene is the therapist's (and the film's) insistence that the racist attacks Moss has endured throughout the course of his life have led him to become hypersensitive to *any* encounters with whites, even when they are not hostile, and it is this racial sensitivity that Moss must somehow learn to overcome. The film's final triumph emerges when Moss realizes that he is different (yes!) but also that *everybody* is different, and because of this, there is no reason for him to move through the world with a "chip on his shoulder." Moss is able to reach this epiphany only after being chastised by a white soldier, Mingo (Frank Lovejoy), who lost an arm during their mission. Mingo berates Moss for crying—literally—after another soldier directs a racial epithet toward him. Mingo identifies his new disability as something that now makes him "different" too, though ironically, no different from Moss. Not only does Moss emerge as a victim of his own self-perceived and self-constructed "tragedy," but he can be "cured" of his racial sensitivity only by succumbing to a rhetoric of universalism that the model of psychoanalysis (and Hollywood) readily provides. A comprehensive analysis of this film's problematic glossing of the vicious and ubiquitous racial violence enacted upon black soldiers in World War II, not to mention its depiction of black men more generally (Moss is a former high school basketball star and he makes some mean fried chicken), as well as its representation of (white) psychoanalytic authority over the weak black body (paralysis) and mind (amnesia), would warrant another full chapter. However, I use *Home of the Brave* as an example here to point to one of the many reasons why cultural critics have been reticent (rightfully so) to consider psychoanalysis a particularly useful or compelling methodology to examine the black subject. In its totalizing, the film makes it impossible to address racial identity and the subsequent problems it conjures. Despite the film's heroic conclusion, with Moss and Mingo figuratively walking into the sunset, the universality of the film is ultimately destructive in that it forecloses the possibility for psychoanalytic and racial discourses to coexist. Hence, critical suspicion of the pitfalls associated with psychoanalytic inquiry is not without cause.

I embarked upon this project in the hope of complicating this formula. I was curious as to whether psychoanalysis and race were truly fundamentally and diametrically opposed: when psychoanalysis encounters the subject of race, does it work only to subjugate or liberate? In the process of writing this book, I had hoped that the final product would reveal an emergent interconnectedness between black intellectual and psychoanalytic communities that would lend this project a triumphant narrative arc. Instead, the carefully plotted trajectory I attempted to project onto *Freud Upside Down* collapsed into a fragmented compilation of black literary and print interventions framed within, outside, and against mainstream psychoanalytic discourses. The interactions that I examine in this book resisted this oversimplified plot, and revealed a far more complex set of negotiations. What I have attempted to demonstrate in constructing this relatively eclectic collusion is that throughout the course of the twentieth century, black subjects persistently engaged with psychoanalytic thought that has been integral to the working out and working through matters of race, gender, and sexuality. The first chapter of this book illustrates the sometimes contradictory uses to which psychoanalysis was put—even within the context of a single text. The *Messenger* deployed a Freudian paradigm of repression to condemn interracial violence and, at the same time, to advocate interracial love. That chapter also demonstrates the extent to which, in the early 1920s, psychoanalysis was deeply enmeshed within black popular, print, and political cultures. This is an engagement that has endured, to varying degrees, throughout most of the twentieth century and into the twenty-first century.

Many of the arguments against the deployment of psychoanalysis in reading black texts have stemmed from the claim that psychoanalytic practice is yet another assertion of Western hegemony over black psychic life, and psychoanalytic theory as a literary methodology has proved largely illegible as it "mystifies rather than clarifies [the African American] condition, making it possible for a few people who know that particular language to control the critical scene" (Christian 15). While Barbara Christian's essay, "The Race for Theory," has been heralded as an antitheory manifesto, that same essay acknowledges the necessity for a theory that is "prescriptive" and "remain[s] open to the intricacies of the intersections of language, class, race, and gender in the literature" (13). Although psychoanalytic theory is certainly guilty of the critical murkiness of which Christian speaks, that very theory translated (relatively rapidly) into a significant cultural phenomenon that has heavily influenced the black literary and artistic scene. To disaggregate black cultural and artistic production from the theoretical roots by which many artists were inspired would continue to create the critical lacuna that this very project seeks to fill.

From Thomas Jefferson's assertion that African Americans hid "expressions of every passion" behind "that immoveable veil of black" (138), to James Brown's insistence that all black folks possess "soul," the vocabulary of interiority has been consistently bound to cultural, scientific, and personal formulations of blackness. Of interest in Jefferson's claim is the notion that before psychoanalysis emerges as a discipline—before Lacan, before Freud—black people were imagined as having an unknowable interior. How African American intellectuals and artists have addressed the question and, to some, the conundrum of black interiority since the turn of the twentieth century (it was, after all, Du Bois who made the claim about the "souls of black folk" decades before Brown) serve as the fundamental motivation of this project. What I have attempted to articulate in *Freud Upside Down* is that the historical and literary dynamic between African American and psychoanalytic culture was not an uncomplicated top-down relation. Indeed, black appropriations of psychoanalytic thought have been varied in purpose and form, and many of these interventions emerged as playful revisions of psychoanalytic models rather than strict and restricting reproductions of psychoanalytic paradigms. Fundamentally, I am working against the logic that psychoanalytic thought maintains only the power to oppress or liberate when it encounters raced bodies or psyches. I am more interested in interpreting the diverse and vital ways that people with raced bodies have been thinking about psychological ideas for over a century. I have written this book in the hopes of foregrounding the dialogic relation between racial and psychological thinking, specifically highlighting the extent to which this dynamic has been mutually informative and (consciously) constitutive.

Let's fast forward fifty years from *Home of the Brave* to the HBO series *In Treatment,* which features a black navy pilot, Alex (Blair Underwood), who has reluctantly sought the assistance of a therapist, Paul (Gabriel Byrnes). This relationship between analysand and analyst is remarkably different than that presented in *Home of the Brave*; Alex consistently attempts to assert his control over the therapy sessions by testing Paul with dilemmas to which he has already formulated an appropriate response, buying an espresso machine so that he (Paul doesn't drink coffee) can have gourmet cappuccinos during their sessions, and paying his bill in cash at the end of each meeting. Theirs is not a relationship without tension, but notable in this interaction is that despite Alex's assertiveness and Paul's position as analyst, neither possesses authority over the other. Unlike the dialogue between Hubert Harrison and Carl Jung outlined in this book's introduction, in which each theorist directed his psychological claims to a particular racial and professional community, the relationship between Alex and Paul is decidedly intersubjective. Alex's careful speech and Paul's profound listening creates a space of vulnerability in which they engage in a dialogue that ultimately transcends race—they speak of broken marriages, new loves, friendship, children, the loss of a parent. The interaction between Alex and Paul reveals a complex symbiotic relationship in which psychoanalysis neither exploits nor elides completely the subject of race. Perhaps this is the triumphant arc for which I had been waiting.

The dynamic between Alex and Paul provides new ways of thinking about the relationship between psychoanalysis and race in the realm of literature (though the genre of film appears ripe for this kind of investigation), specifically, allowing for a critique in which the language of psychoanalysis enlightens rather than distorts. Recent appropriations of psychoanalytic thought in black texts, as demonstrated in Danzy Senna's *Caucasia,* are intimately bound to the formation of race yet are not entirely explicit about the origins of their inspiration. Much like the way in which psychoanalytic language has become part and parcel of the contemporary American vernacular, its presence in African American literature has taken on a more diffuse quality. The challenge moving forward will be a matter of approaching psychoanalytic thought in "raced" works with less critical suspicion and more attention to ways in which articulations of race rely upon theories of interiority for their very existence, and conversely, recognizing how theories of interiority are entirely dependent on the subject of race.

Notes

Introduction

1. For more information on Harrison, see Jeffrey Perry, *Hubert Harrison: The Voice of Harlem Radicalism 1883–1918*.

2. Throughout *Freud Upside Down* I use the term *psychoanalysis* broadly to refer to the variant manifestations of psychological ideas, language, and methodologies initiated by Sigmund Freud. I am aware, however, that *psychoanalysis, psychiatry, and psychology* represent three distinct yet interrelated approaches to therapy and treatment. These distinctions also represent the contentious history between psychoanalysts and psychiatrists that culminated in the fissure between the two fields in the late 1950s. Nathan Hale Jr. explains that the "psychoanalyst's and psychotherapist's case histories, the basis for claims of therapeutic success and the source of data for theory were dismissed as merely subjective anecdotes, tainted by preconceptions and inadmissible in the courts of 'true science'" (301). However, in the 1940s, psychoanalysts and their methods, with the assistance of Adolph Meyer, were positively received in the medical field. The rather seamless convergence of psychoanalysis and medicine led to the "rapid rise of psychoanalytic psychiatry after World War II" (Hale 167).

3. I begin this study in the Harlem Renaissance because it was the first historical moment in which a critical mass of black writers and intellectuals engaged psychoanalysis as a way to consider racial and cultural formations. However, the relationship between black literary circles and psychological communities can be traced to the influence of psychologist William James on W. E. B Du Bois and Pauline Hopkins. For more extended discussions of James's influence on both writers, see Dickson Bruce, Cynthia Schrager, and Deborah Horvitz.

4. Despite his claim that "psychoanalytic preoccupations pervaded the new literature of the 1920s" (76), Nathan Hale's definitive text, *The Rise and Crisis of Psychoanal-*

ysis in the United States, fails to make mention of the Harlem Renaissance or of any black writer in the scope of the sixty-eight-year history that the text spans. Similarly, black writers are curiously absent in Frederick Hoffman's *Freudianism and the Literary Mind* (1957) and Joseph Schwartz's *Cassandra's Daughter* (2001). Most recently, Eli Zaretsky's *Secrets of the Soul* (2004), offers a cursory examination of the role of psychoanalysis in the Harlem Renaissance, explaining that "Harlem intellectuals were . . . grappling with Puritanism in the form of Booker T. Washington's ideology of self help and respectability . . . [and] the deep embeddedness of the African-American family in African-American society encouraged the attempt to understand the unconscious roots of American culture, including its background of trauma, violence, and betrayal" (154). While Zaretsky offers more in the way of acknowledging black cultural and intellectual engagement with psychoanalytic culture, the extent of this recognition begins and ends in the Harlem Renaissance, with a gesture toward the work of Richard Wright and Ralph Ellison. This exclusion is not entirely surprising. In *Prozac on the Couch,* Jonathan Metzl notes that it "took thirty years . . . for persons of color to appear in pharmaceutical advertisements in the AJP [*American Journal of Pharmacology*], and, when they did appear in the mid-1970s, they did so only as patients in antipsychotic medication advertisement—either as medicated in-patients on psychiatric wards or as assaultive and belligerent, threats to society during an era when the journal pathologized the 'Black Power class of reactions'" (29). Metzl provides a more extended discussion of African American encounters with the psychiatric institution in his more recent text, *The Protest Psychosis.*

Chapter 1. The Politics and Production of Interiority in the *Messenger* Magazine (1922–23)

1. See Hutchinson ("Mediating 'Race'"), Vogel, and Wilson.

2. In *Fair Sex, Savage Dreams,* Jean Walton notes that "the late nineteenth and early twentieth centuries saw a proliferation of psychologies of the inferiority of the 'dark races' elaborated in the service of colonialism and slavery, with their accounts of pathologies assumed to be specific to the 'Negro' or 'native'" (1). See also Pfister, "Glamorizing."

3. I am referring to Freud's characterization of women, presumably white women, as a "dark continent," a mysterious geography that puzzled him throughout his career. See Freud, "Question of Lay Analysis." Despite the enigma that the white female body presents, the black female (or the black male, for that matter) body does not register in Freud's analysis.

4. The November 1922 promotion in the *Messenger* for Calvin's forthcoming editorial positions Calvin as an insightful lay analyst who will provide in-depth examinations of some of the era's most visible race leaders. Perhaps most interestingly, the advertisement suggests that the audience will gain access to the psychology of Calvin's subjects by informing them that they will have an opportunity to "fairly look

through: James Weldon Johnson, Chandler Owen, W. E. B Du Bois, A. Philip Randolph, Marcus Garvey, William Pickens, George W. Harris, and all the other 'upper 10s.'" (516).

5. Calvin left the *Messenger* in 1924 to write his editorial column for the *Pittsburgh Courier,* the largest and most significant black newspaper in the United States between 1924 and 1966. Calvin's post at the *Pittsburgh Courier* was undoubtedly the outcome of his successful run at the *Messenger,* which helped to legitimize Calvin's ability as a frank, thorough, and intellectual critic. Calvin's articles set the precedent for contributors to the *Messenger* to use psychoanalysis in further legitimating their political ends.

6. The *Crisis* and *Opportunity* also featured numerous "sepia beauties" on their covers, but not as consistently or frequently as the *Messenger.* The most successful black women's magazine of the period, *Half Century,* contested black masculine ideas about black female standards of beauty by featuring "large-boned, dark-skinned women" on its covers (Rooks 75). Caroline Goeser discusses the import of mixed-race identities in the Harlem Renaissance era, focusing on Charles D. Johnson's short-lived magazine *Ebony and Topaz,* published just once in 1927. Goeser interprets illustrations created by Charles Cullen and Richard Bruce Nugent from the periodical's single issue to suggest that by this moment, many Renaissance writers and artists had relaxed on the issue of racial uplift and were more interesting in conveying the racial and sexual fluidities within African American community.

7. Pfister refers to "psychological identity" as "an identity conferred upon one who recognizes and refers to himself or herself as determined by, or sometimes beset by, distinct 'psychological' processes, patterns, and problems. This mass-cultural and high-cultural 'psychological' spin in the formation of subjectivities was in certain respects something new in American culture" ("Glamorizing" 167).

8. Anne Elizabeth Carroll's *Word, Image, and the New Negro* and Martha Nadell's *Enter the New Negroes* provide excellent critical analyses of black print culture in the 1920s, showing in particular the ways in which editors and artists attempted to use images to deepen and reformulate representations of black identity. Carroll offers a thorough analysis of image making in the first two essays of her text, which focus on the *Crisis* and *Opportunity.*

Chapter 2. The Anxiety of Birth in Nella Larsen's *Quicksand*

1. In Rank's theory of birth trauma, the artist "creates human beings after his own image, that is, he brings forth his work in ever new, constantly repeated acts of birth, and in it brings forth himself amid the maternal pains of creation" (*Trauma* 156).

2. Barbara Johnson uses Heinz Kohut's theory of "self-psychology" to provide an explanation for Helga Crane's self-described "lack." She explains Helga's repetitive self-destructive behaviors as the products of "negative mirroring" and consistent invalidation. Johnson's explication reproduces, in some ways, Rank's ideas of birth

trauma, particularly the sense that the subject will repeat episodes of anxiety until he or she finds an effective mirror. Rank's and Kohut's accounts differ, however, in that Rank envisions artistic practice as the "cure" for such pathology, since art serves as a mirror for the subject and guards against the death drive.

3. The phases are also the titles of chapters in *Trauma of Birth.*

4. Helga's room is vividly portrayed as an ornate inner sanctum that she uses to distance herself from the outside world. The novel begins with Helga "alone in her room, which at that hour, eight in the evening, was in soft gloom. . . . It was a comfortable room, furnished with rare and intensely personal taste, flooded with Southern sun in the day, but shadowy just then with the drawn curtains and single shaded light. Large, too. So large that the spot where Helga sat was a small oasis in a desert of darkness. . . . This was her rest, this intentional isolation for a short while in the evening, this little time in her own attractive room with her own books" (1). The creation of a pleasurable prison is, for Rank, a common sign of a neurotic suffering from birth trauma. He writes that "even the most horrible forms of punishment which man could imagine and which he directs against himself in the physical symptoms of neurosis, are clothed in the form of the first and strongest pleasure experience of the intrauterine life. . . . This explains to a large extent the pleasurable character of certain neurotic symptoms, in which the patient makes himself a prisoner by withdrawing into a room which he locks, or by pessimistically phantasying the whole world as a dungeon and thereby unconsciously feeling comfortable in it" (*Trauma* 136).

5. George Hutchinson underscores the centrality of interracial identity in *Quicksand,* specifically noting that "in place of the Oedipal drama and the incest taboo (as ubiquitous in tragic mulatto tradition as in psychoanalysis), Larsen turns to a female-centered drama figuring the abandonment of woman under patriarchy, death in childbirth, the enslavement of the body to procreation of racial subjects alienated from themselves and their mothers by national ideologies of racial and class identity" ("Subject to Disappearance" 190). What strikes me about Hutchinson's analysis is his attention to the maternal aspects of the narrative, especially those concerning Helga and her mother. This aspect of *Quicksand* is consistently overlooked apart from critical assertions of the psychological violence that the mother's marriage to a white racist has brought upon Helga.

6. For biographical information on Rank, I relied primarily on Esther Menaker's *Otto Rank.*

7. Rank's theories of birth trauma also provide a new conceptual framework in which to interpret family dynamics in "tragic mulatto/a" narratives, specifically those in which the female protagonist undergoes a violent separation from the mother. In "passing" narratives (where blacks pass for white) or in narratives with biracial protagonists, the tragic mulatto/a figure most often identifies with the absent father, who acts as the source of the interracial female child's racial and sexual lack. In short, the female child's desire lies within the half of her racial self signified by the absent parent, which in most cases is the father. As is the case with numerous passing nar-

ratives or narratives featuring mulatto or mulatta figures, the protagonist, Helga, must bear the psychological implications of separation and rejection from both the mother and father. Rank's attention to the mother in the child's repetition compulsion allows for a more comprehensive analysis of the roles that the absent father and lost mother independently and interdependently contribute to the anxiety and inevitable tragedy experienced by mixed-race protagonists.

8. Rank asserts that "whether it is the primitive hut covered with foliage (nest) or the 'altar' which originates from the hearth fire (warmth from the mother), or the prototype of the temple (such as the Indian cave temple) which represented the roof or house as protection for this fire . . . everywhere it is creative shaping of approved objects, approximating in form to the substitution of the primal situation" (*Trauma* 187).

Chapter 3. Art's Imperfect End: Race and Gurdjieff in Jean Toomer's "Transatlantic"

1. Critics have maintained that "by the mid-twenties, when the Harlem Renaissance was in full flower, Toomer had abandoned black writing and had traveled to Europe in the pursuit of the mystical wisdom of Georges I. Gurdjieff" (Rusch 115).

2. For information on Gurdjieff, I rely primarily on Sophia Wellbeloved, *Gurdjieff.*

3. In "'Taking Myself in Hand': Jean Toomer and Physical Culture," Mark Whalan notes that "Toomer's disdain for racial essentialism . . . hardened into a principle of not being identified publicly as African American by 1924. This decision was also influenced by his contact with the Armenian mystic Georges Gurdjieff, a relationship which led to what many have seen as Toomer's idealistic and millennial predictions about the end of racial categorization in the western world—a type of hazy thinking and bland transcendence of social actuality and social organization which has incurred much criticism" (597–98).

4. The foundation of Gurdjieff's principles is the idea that most people exist in a state of mechanicality; they are unable to think objectively and do not possess the ability to know or comprehend the interior self. Gurdjieff believed that people could not live harmoniously with one another because most people lacked self-knowledge, which almost ensured utter disregard for others. He was not against the idea of politics or self-reform for its own sake. But as he once explained to his disciple A. R. Orage, who asked for Gurdjieff's opinion of his economic theory of social credit, "men in their mechanical state could not communicate well enough to establish a lasting peace. Once enough people were awakened, real communication—and a corresponding hope for peace—would be possible" (quoted in Shirley 82).

5. Jon Woodson characterizes "Transatlantic" as exemplary of Toomer's desire to emulate Gurdjieff's "objective" writing form, which is defined by six qualities: "(1) it is conscious; (2) the artist creates knowing what is being done and why; (3) it makes an identical impression on everybody, with variations depending on the level of

personal development; (4) it contains exactly what the artist wants; (5) its purpose is the illumination of truth through the recipient's emotional experience; and (6) it originates from objective consciousness" (6).

6. Paul Gilroy's concept of "planetary humanism" refers to the "deliberate and self-conscious renunciation of 'race' as a means to categorize and divide humankind" (17). A course of "planetary humanism" would do away with all aspects of race thinking.

7. According to Toomer's biographers Kerman and Eldridge, Toomer wrote "Transatlantic" in seventeen days while in residence at Fontainebleau-sur-Avon (188).

8. Langston Hughes to Jean Toomer, Nov. 17, 1953, box 4, folder 111, Jean Toomer Papers.

9. For a more sustained discussion of the genealogy of the black intellectual from the turn of the century to the 1960s, see Ross Posnock's "How It Feels to Be a Problem: Du Bois, Fanon, and the 'Impossible Life' of the Black Intellectual." In it, Posnock argues that in the late nineteenth century, the "social role of the intellectual [was] founded on a refusal of the ideology of the authentic," and that Du Bois and Fanon in particular "fashion[ed] a performative cosmopolitanism that anticipated the contemporary moment of postidentity" (325). Although Posnock makes no mention of Toomer, I would locate Toomer's struggle to exist as a "postracial" subject within the larger framework of the crisis of the black intellectual. George Hutchinson also provides some insight on Toomer's desire to exist outside the conventions and confines of racial language: "With Nella Larsen, Toomer has come to be regarded as one of the chief 'tragic mulattoes' of American literary history because . . . he insisted upon a self-naming that threatened racialist discourse, along with the rich structures of knowledge, identity, and power to which that discourse is inextricably bound" ("Jean Toomer" 375).

10. In an unpublished essay, Toomer responds to C. G. Jung's *The Secret of the Golden Flower*, in which Jung surmises that neurotic behaviors are epitomized in individuals who are governed by the unconscious. What appears to be of most significant interest to Toomer is Jung's statement that "there could be no greater mistake than for a Westerner to take up the direct practice of Chinese yoga, for then it would still be a matter of his will and consciousness, and would only strengthen the latter against the unconscious, bringing about the very effect which should have been avoided." Toomer read Jung's diagnosis quite differently and was apparently miffed by Jung's disapproval of cultural border-crossing. Instead, Toomer thought that the "professional eye is prone to see people too much in these terms, too little in terms of the wonder that is in each and every individual. Perception of the actual observation tends to prohibit perception of the potential marvel of the human being" ("Meditation on Jung" 4).

11. "Autobiographical Sketch," 1933, drafts, box 311, folder 343, Jean Toomer Papers.

12. Toomer's contact with Fontainebleau was largely mediated through Gurdjieff's assistant Ethel Thurston, who apparently was charged with seeking funds for the Institute. In a letter to Toomer, Thurston writes: "My dear Mr. Toomer, Is there any

possibility of sending any money? I know you've been hoping to send $300, but even $150 or $200 would help me out of this month's straits. . . . Gurdjieff is in one of his restless not-sleeping-at-night phases and can't write or do anything, and is longing to get away, but has not enough money. It is [at an] impasse because if he doesn't go away he can't write, he can't because he has no money, and he can get no money if he doesn't write" (letter to Jean Toomer from Ethel Thurston, n.d., n.p., box 3, folder 96, Jean Toomer Papers). The monetary and physical demands placed upon Gurdjieff's students in addition to their required intense devotion led many to consider Gurdjieff a cult leader or a mystic rather than a legitimate therapist. Even biographies sympathetic to Gurdjieff describe him as "a con man from his youth on," "a fraud, liar, and cheat" (Rauve 48). Upon Toomer's arrival to Gurdjieff's Institute in 1924, he was "summarily forbidden to write at all and was assigned chores—hard, physical labor" (Woodson 32). Nonetheless, Toomer remained devoted to the institute and continued to lead sessions throughout the United States and to send money back to the institute in support of its mission and founder.

13. Although there is no indication of the surname of Toomer's addressee, we can assume that Toomer is writing to his longtime friend Paul Rosenfeld. Letter to Paul from Jean Toomer, Oct. 19, 1949, box 3, folder 96, Jean Toomer Papers.

Chapter 4. "A genuine cooperation": Richard Wright's and Ralph Ellison's Psychoanalytic Conversations

1. Letter from Frantz Fanon to Richard Wright, 6 Jan. 1953, MS, box 97, folder 1324, Richard Wright Papers.

2. I borrow liberally here from Francoise Verges's "To Cure and to Free," in which Verges defines Fanon's projects of "decolonized psychiatry as one that insisted on "the importance of the cultural context in which symptoms appear" (83). Fanon believed that "medical practitioners must know the historical and social conditions of formation of the society in which they practice, as well as its cultural practices and beliefs" (96). I use Verges's conception of decolonization and its link to psychiatric and psychoanalytic practice as a way to think more precisely about the imperatives of the Lafargue Clinic and Ellison and Wright's vision of psychoanalysis as a vehicle for individual and social transformation.

3. For more information about the origins of the mental hygiene movement see A. Rossi.

4. Benjamin Karpman to Richard Wright, MS 1942–45, box 100, folder 1416, Richard Wright Papers.

5. Ibid.

6. For a more sustained discussion of the relationship between psychoanalytic therapy and celebrity culture, see Jonathan Freedman.

7. Karpman to Wright, MS 1942–45.

8. In Claudia Tate's *Psychoanalysis and Black Novels,* she notes that Wright's li-

brary contained "Karl Abraham's Selected Papers on Psycho-Analysis, Clifford Allen's Sexual Perversions and Abnormalities, Josef Freuer and Sigmund Freud's Studies in Hysteria and Anna Freud's Ego and the Mechanisms of Defense" (206 n.7). Tate also indicates that Wright's library contained all of Freud's major works, including all five volumes of his collected papers, and all of Frederic Wertham's texts.

9. Karpman to Wright, MS 1942–45.

10. Frederick Whiting provides a nice discussion of the ways in which the pathologization and criminalization of sexual behaviors emerged as a central concern for psychoanalysts in the years during and immediately following World War II. Specifically, Whiting notes that "to the extent that psychoanalysis helped recast popular notions of criminal behavior during this period by pathologizing it, it did so in the public mind by means of a pathology that was ultimately, and indicatively, sexual in nature" (150).

11. In the 1916 essay "Criminals from a Sense of Guilt," Sigmund Freud theorizes that subjects commit criminal acts from an overwhelming desire for punishment. Indeed, Freud links the guilt criminals experience to the Oedipal complex, noting that those who engage in certain criminal acts are motivated by wanting to be punished for their Oedipal desires (Freud "Some Character-types"). Freud returns to this idea in *The Ego and the Id* (1923), in which he writes that "it was a surprise to find that an increase in this Ucs. sense of guilt can turn people into criminals. But it is undoubtedly a fact. In many criminals, especially youthful ones, it is possible to detect a very powerful sense of guilt which existed before the crime, and is therefore not its result but its motive" (52).

12. Wright and Ellison's friend Dr. Frederic Wertham was a forerunner in studies on the relationship between sexuality, violence, and criminality. His 1941 text *Dark Legend* narrativizes the matricidal impulses of a young man who kills his mother to punish her for what he perceives as her promiscuous behavior and to avenge his father. In *Show of Violence* (1949), Wertham compiles and analyzes a series of "case studies" of murders and links them to Greek tragedies. His most famous text, *The Seduction of the Innocent* (1954), suggests that comic books negatively influence children to engage in deviant sexual and criminal behaviors as adults.

13. In 1940, the same year that Wright published *Native Son,* Karpman's "Principles and Aims of Criminal Psychopathology" was published. In the years following his correspondence with Wright, Karpman published approximately fifty articles on sexuality and criminality, as well as essays that emphasized the integral relationship between psychoanalytic psychiatry and sociology and psychoanalytic study and the law. Some of these articles include "A Psychiatrist Looks at the Social Scientists," "Dream Life in a Case of Transvestism: With Particular Attention to the Problem of Latent Homosexuality," "A Case of Paedophilia (Legally Rape) Cured by Psychoanalysis," "A Psychoanalytic Study of a Case of Murder," and "Psychosomatic Neurosis as Expression of a Barrier against Indulgence in Craved but Prohibited Sexual Drives." The introduction to Karpman's 1951 article "Sexual Psychopath" states that "he had

made the study of criminality his life work," and that he "pioneered" the study of sexual psychopathology with his initial case study on the topic in 1923 (184).

14. Karpman to Wright, MS 1942–45.

15. Robert Corber's *In the Name of National Security* nicely explicates how homosexuality became criminalized and was constructed as threat to national security in the 1950s.

16. In Shelly Eversley's "The Lunatic's Fancy and the Work of Art," she refers to a newspaper headline that reads "They're Crazy Anyway," published in response to the opening of the Lafargue Mental Hygiene Clinic in March 1946. The idea that African Americans were inherently inferior, intellectually and emotionally, was a common cultural perception. On the exclusion of African Americans from mental health services, Martin Grossack notes that "problems of sex and aggression are frequent in Negro life. Unconscious aggression towards whites frequently is misdirected into the Negro group to sow increasing amounts of disunity. Illegitimacy is commonly followed by neglected children" (72). In "Psychoanalysis and the Negro Problem" (1956), Charles Glicksberg cites Erik Erikson's "Black Identity" in *Childhood and Society* as one example of how psychoanalysis can go wildly astray when it indulges in untested and irresponsible theoretical speculation (42—43). Specifically, Erikson claims that "Negro babies often receive sensual satisfactions which provide them with enough oral and sensory surplus for a lifetime, as clearly betrayed in the way they move, laugh, talk, sing. Their forced symbiosis with the feudal South capitalized on this oral-sensory treasure and helped to build a slave's identity: mild, submissive, dependent, somewhat querulous, but always ready to serve, with occasional empathy and childlike wisdom" (quoted in Glicksberg 43). Glicksberg criticizes Erikson, referring to Erikson's interpretations as a "curious mixture of penetrating psychological insight and unsupported and sometimes dangerous mumbo jumbo" (43).

17. In what appears to be one of the final letters from Karpman to Wright, Karpman refuses Wright's request to allow him to read Karpman's criminal cases. He writes, "[Wertham] expressed himself so clearly and unequivocally in the article about free associations that unless I don't know how to read English, it can mean only one thing; that he is analyzing you or having some sort of therapeutic contact with you. Under the circumstances, professionally or otherwise, it is just impossible for me to give you any material that deals with analytic situations, even if it does not deal with you directly." Benjamin Karpman to Richard Wright, Nov. 10, 1944, MS 1942–1945, box 100, folder 1416, Richard Wright Papers.

18. One of the fundamental arguments in Gilles Deleuze and Félix Guattari's *Anti-Oedipus* is that the schizophrenic not only defies the logic of Freudian psychoanalysis but also resists hegemonic power, including capitalism. As such, the schizophrenic is regarded as a subversive figure within the context of a capitalist and oppressive system.

19. Ralph Ellison to Richard Wright, Sept. 5, 1944, box 97, folder 1314, Richard Wright Papers.

20. Lawrence Rodgers describes Ellison's *Invisible Man* as "the most formally innovative and ambitious examination of what it means for a migrant to be displaced from the roots of southern culture" and refers to northern migration as a "dynamic, dialectical process offering the possibilities of both transcendence and madness, liberation and enslavement" (157).

21. Ellison's biographer, Lawrence Jackson, alludes to Ellison's reliance on Hegel's dialectic to craft his insights on the failures of American democracy and "the psychological repression in the white unconscious mind." According to Jackson, Ellison's essay "Beating that Boy," written for *New Republic,* served to solidify his role as an intellectual and critic who was at the very least on par with Wright. In "Beating that Boy," Ellison "had satisfactorily meshed the theories of Hegel and Freud, and his self-confidence showed" (322).

22. Frederic Wertham to Richard Wright, May 12, 1953, box 108, folder 1677, Richard Wright Papers.

23. Sander Gilman explains that psychological discourses that argued that madness was endemic to black character emerged in the nineteenth century. Citing Samuel Cartwright's 1851 essay in the *New Orleans Medical and Surgical Journal,* Gilman notes that "manifestations of the blacks' rejection of the institution of slavery were fitted into the medical model of insanity . . . specifically [that] the physiology of blacks . . . predisposes them to mental illness" (*Difference* 138–39).

24. "Harlem Is Nowhere" drafts, box 222, Ralph Ellison Papers, Ralph Ellison Collection, Library of Congress, Washington, D.C.

25. In addition to the crucial evidence pointing to the damaging effects of segregation provided by Drs. Kenneth Clark and Mamie Clark, Wertham's study of thirteen children at the Lafargue clinic proved invaluable because it used both black and white children as its subjects to prove the detrimental effects of segregation for people of all races. Using a number of experiments, including individual interviews, mosaic tests, and group observation, psychiatrists at the Lafargue clinic found that segregation resulted in the black children having feelings of inferiority, insecurity, and alienation and bred strong sentiments of racism and prejudice with the white children. After the study, Dr. Wertham concluded that segregation "created a massive public health problem [and] create[d] in the mind of the child an unsolvable conflict" (Kluger 443–44). The results of the study were later instrumental for the NAACP attorneys, who relied heavily on psychological evidence in the *Brown v. the Board of Education* case before the U.S. Supreme Court. In addition, the findings of Wertham and the Clarks pointed to ways in which racism is internalized, thereby refuting popular and long-standing scientific (biological and anthropological) claims of black inferiority.

Chapter 5. Maternal Anxieties and Political Desires in Adrienne Kennedy's *Dramatic Circle*

1. The scene in *The Slave* in which Walker refers to the "psychological novel" as being "the worst thing that ever happened to the West" comes after Gracie and Eas-

ley's "analysis" that Walker has come to murder them out of a misguided heroic effort to save his children from "whiteness" (70). Easley goes on to compare Walker's revolutionary army to the Nazis, claiming that "when the Nazis were confronted with Freud, they claimed his work was of dubious value" (70). Further, Eldridge Cleaver's *Soul on Ice* describes his negative experience with an analyst who theorized that he "hated [his] mother." He writes, "How he arrived at this conclusion I'll never know, because he knew nothing about my mother, and when he'd ask me questions I would answer him with absurd lies. What revolted me about him was that he had heard me denouncing the whites, yet each time he interviewed me he deliberately blocked all my attempts to bring out the racial question, and he made it clear that he was not interested in my attitude toward whites. This was a Pandora's box he did not care to open. After I ceased my diatribes against the whites, I was let out of the hospital, back into the general inmate population just as if nothing ever happened" (24). Cleaver's example illustrates psychoanalysis's historic inattention to matters of race and further exemplifies how psychoanalytic models have been inadequate in attempting to address black subjectivity.

2. Diamond has also argued that because "Kennedy's texts borrow the metaphorics of hysteria to pose the political question of race identity in the United States," her works allow for "a rethinking of identification for political ends" ("Rethinking Identification" 93). Diamond takes up this notion of a politically motivated identification in his readings of *The Owl Answers* and *Funnyhouse of a Negro,* whose protagonists are victims of both racial and political oppression and respond to this subjugation with madness. However, their madness takes the form of identification as each character assumes the persona of a figure of oppression, for example, Queen Victoria.

3. Kalpana Sheshadri-Crooks offers a nuanced perspective to the debates surrounding Fanon's apparent misogyny. Rather than locate her analysis on one side or another, Crooks emphasizes that Fanon's masculinism was not "anti-feminist," but rather that Fanon's revolutionary politics offered "an overhauling of the place of sexual difference in the visioning of the social good and the party's political aims" ("I Am" 94). Sheshadri-Crooks also asserts that "Fanon's political masculinism is actually part of a larger struggle for the decolonization of all" and that "at the moment of his writing political struggle and national sovereignty were unimaginable without a rehabilitation of masculinity" (96).

4. Despite Diamond's compelling thesis, which interprets identification as a political act, she reads *Dramatic Circle* as a play about "Suzanne's terror over the absence of her husband" ("Rethinking Identification" 98).

5. In a 2005 interview with Claudia Barnett, Kennedy seemingly became frustrated with Barnett's questions inviting the playwright to discuss the origin of particular characters. Barnett's inquiry regarding Kennedy's shift from the male protagonists in her earlier plays to the female protagonists of her later works was met with the response, "I have no idea. You're making me angry. I'll tell you why. Because I hate it when people analyze my work like that. That's why I don't even teach my work. I have no idea" (Barnett, "Evasion" 162).

6. Shulamith Firestone's *The Dialectic of Sex: The Case for Feminist Revolution* (1970) and Kate Millet's *Sexual Politics* (1968) were also influential texts with which Kennedy would have been familiar.

7. I refer to Cheng's definition here, rather than Freud's, because of her reference to cannibalism, which is useful in considering my discussion of Bram Stoker's *Dracula* later in this chapter.

8. For an extended discussion of Freud's theory of trauma, see *Beyond the Pleasure Principle.*

9. Through her imagined experiences of "puerperal psychoses," Suzanne acts out, in a paradigmatic fashion, Freud's theory of identification.

10. See Nancy Armstrong and Phyllis Roth.

11. Anita Levy interprets Lucy's "risqué speech" as a signification of "the sensuality which characterizes Lucy as a vampire. What she later becomes—a sexually aggressive (and therefore 'abnormal') woman—is seen as implicit in her behavior even before Dracula arrives in England. Lucy's sexual aggressiveness . . . will be seen as her greatest crime and will provoke a combined male assault and assertion of dominance" (164).

12. Kennedy's earlier works portray characters or make explicit references to the Victorian period, notably Queen Victoria Regina in *Funnyhouse of a Negro.* She who is Clara Passmore in *The Owl Answers* is a clear allusion to the character Ayesha, also known as "She-who-must-be-obeyed," in H. Rider Haggard's 1887 novel *She.*

Chapter 6. Racial Sincerity and the Biracial Body in Danzy Senna's *Caucasia*

1. Much of the discourse of multiraciality has been explored within the realm of cultural studies, sociology, and critical race theory. These theoretical methodologies have proved fruitful in terms of unearthing the sociopolitical complexities multiraciality presents in a postmodern world. But these largely sociohistorical analyses that often problematize the "one-drop rule" and the conservative call for colorblindness rarely engage the psychical aspects of multiracial identity. Recent texts that explore biracial and multiracial subjects are Kathleen Odell Korgen's *From Black to Biracial: Transforming Racial Identity among Americans,* Kerry Ann Rockquemore and David Brunsma's *Beyond Black: Biracial Identity in America,* and Suki Ali's *Mixed-Race, Post-Race: Gender, New Ethnicities, and Cultural Practices.* Jayne O. Ifekwunigwe's *"Mixed Race" Studies: A Reader* collects essays devoted to issues concerning multiracial persons, specifically interpretations of the U.S. census, historical essays that trace the origins of miscegenation in the United States, and speculations about the future of racial identification. Each text takes a social-scientific approach to the discourse of multiraciality.

2. In "The Mulatto Millennium," Senna writes, "Strange to wake up and realize you're in style. That's what happened to me just the other morning. It was the first day of the new millennium, and I woke to find that mulattos had taken over. They

were everywhere. Playing golf, running the airwaves, opening restaurants, modeling clothes, starring in musicals with names like Show Me the Miscegenation! The radio played a steady stream of Lenny Kravitz, Sade, and Mariah Carey. I thought I'd died and gone to Berkeley. But then I realized that, according to the racial zodiac, 2000 is the official Year of the Mulatto. Pure breeds (at least black ones) are out; hybridity is in. America loves us in all of our half-caste glory. The president announced on Friday that beige will be the official color of the millennium" (12–13).

3. Robert Reid-Pharr employs the term *inevitability* to highlight the traditional ways in which blackness has been interpreted in both popular and academic discourse. Specifically, he challenges the "sense of inevitability" by questioning how we became comfortable with "this strange situation in which we all agree upon the 'fact' of the social construction of race while nonetheless never really accepting the idea that this construction might be dismantled" (9).

4. I am interested in Robert Reid-Pharr's idea that race, or blackness in particular, is and has been historically a matter of "choice." He writes that "as it became increasingly apparent that race was immaterial, it became that much more apparent that its maintenance was, in fact, a matter of the performance of individual and communal will, a matter of choice" (22).

5. For more information on Spillers's notion of interior intersubjectivity, see "All the Things You Could Be By Now."

6. Sollors describes the case as follows: "In June 1958, two residents of Virginia, Mildred Jeter, a Negro woman, and Richard Loving, a white man, were married in the District of Columbia pursuant to its laws. Shortly after their marriage, the Lovings returned to Virginia and established their marital abode in Caroline County. At the October Term, 1958, of the Circuit Court of Caroline County, a grand jury issued an indictment charging the Lovings with violating Virginia's ban on interracial marriages. On January 6, 1959, the Lovings pleaded guilty to the charge and were sentenced to one year in jail; however, the trial judge suspended the sentence for a period of 25 years on the condition that the Lovings leave the State and not return to Virginia together for 25 years" (*Interracialism* 28). After a series of appeals, in 1967 the U.S. Supreme Court declared state laws banning interracial marriage unconstitutional. Chief Justice Earl Warren delivered the opinion of the court that "the freedom to marry has long been recognized as one of the vital personal rights essential to the orderly pursuit of happiness by free men. Marriage is one of the 'basic civil rights if man,' fundamental to our very existence and survival" (26).

7. In *Caucasia,* Deck Lee refers to his biracial children as "canaries" whose existence will determine the poisonous state of U.S. race relations (393).

8. See Maria Root for a more extensive discussion of the biracial "big boom."

9. In a 12-1 vote in 2004, the University of California Board of Regents decided not to add a multiracial box to application forms, explaining that such an initiative would make it more difficult to collect data on ethnic minorities. See "California Regents Vote."

10. MAVIN Foundation founder Matt Kelley was awarded the Points of Light distinction in 2001 by President George W. Bush for his service to the multiracial community. MAVIN is a not-for-profit organization that "creates innovative projects that celebrate and advocate for mixed race people and families to create a cohesive, multicultural society." http://www.mavinfoundation.org/about/mission.html, accessed May 2, 2005.

11. In *Beyond Black*, Kerry Ann Rockquemore and David Brunsma identify a "border identity" as one of the four ways in which black-white biracials understand their racial status. The other three categories are a singular identity, a protean identity, and a transcendent identity. Biracials who identify exclusively with either a black or a white racial group despite their mixed-race status are determined by the authors to maintain a singular identity. According to the findings of Rockquemore and Brunsma, 13 percent of the individuals they interviewed considered themselves black, which is no doubt due in large part to the pervasiveness of the one-drop rule. The concept of a singular identity works in direct opposition to a transcendent identity, in which individuals attempt to adopt a nonracial identity and refuse to be categorized as a result of fallacious and historically overdetermined constructions of race in American society. Those who perceive themselves as racially transcendent are "more likely to be found among biracial people who identify with and reference themselves in both white and black communities in roughly equal amounts than among those who feel more comfortable in the company of other mixed race people" (51). Those who feel free to shift their racial identity depending on their environment assume what the authors identify as a "protean identity." Conceivably, a biracial person who understands his or her racial identity as fluid can maintain both black and white racial positions within a given day. Rockquemore and Brunsma define a border identity as one that is "exclusively biracial," which is further broken down by validated and invalidated borders. The validity or invalidity of biracial identity is pertinent to the study of biracials in American literature, especially since "tragic mulatto" figures emerge as classic examples of those who hold an "invalidated border identity[ies]." This group, in particular, "experiences an internalized social dislocation because of its continual oscillation between having its self-understanding validated by some and invalidated by others" (45).

12. Walter Benn Michaels argues that "the very impulse to preserve race reveals the degree to which those who imagine that their accounts of race are 'antiessentialist' or 'performative' remain, in fact, committed to racial essentialism" (125). Given this assertion, one may challenge whether or not Birdie actually passes, since she never identifies with whiteness. Her experience of passing is restricted to how she is read by others and what her parents force upon her rather than an assertion, or performance, of white identity. From this perspective, the novel challenges the notion of passing as it merely reinforces the authenticity of race—the very thing that the text is working to disrupt.

13. To illustrate this point, John Jackson refers to the case of white supremacist

Leo Felton, who had been described in the press as a "lean, tall, imposing man with tattoos up and down each arm and the word 'skinhead' inked into his shaved scalp in inch-high Gothic letters" (Tough 42). Felton is presently serving a twenty-one-year sentence for plotting to commit terrorist acts that would "spark and ignite a racial war . . . that would bring about this new, all-white nation." The irony of Felton's case is that he is biracial—the product of a "short-lived and idealistic late-60s marriage between a white former nun named Corinne Vincelette and a black architect named Calvin Felton" (42). Despite Leo Felton's biological reality, there is no doubt that he really believes that he is white. While Felton's circumstance may be extreme, it provides an interesting challenge to claims of racial authenticity and it also allows for thinking about race beyond matters of biology and social construction.

14. Christopher Lane observes that his edited collection, *The Psychoanalysis of Race,* addresses "what it means today to invoke 'race' and 'ethnicity' as concepts organizing our identifications and lives" (2). In a similar vein, this chapter is interested in the way that multiraciality complicates the necessary identifications the protagonist and her sister attempt to use to understand their positions in the social and racial order.

15. Howe's relationship to psychoanalysis was both personal and intellectual. In the introduction to *The Wedding Dress,* Howe admits to experiences of extreme poverty ("we lost our house, we had no money and nowhere to go, and made daily visits to the dismal welfare office and food stamp offices") and notes that a breakdown was thwarted due to her friendship with Daryl Utz, a young female African American psychiatrist, who worked at a neighborhood clinic. Howe explains that Utz was "a brilliant and gentle counselor through this bad time. . . . We shared champagne at New Year's Eve; we became friends; she told me: 'You married your mother!'" (xxi–xxii). Utz eventually committed suicide, and her death gave Howe "the impetus to leave Boston." Howe further recounts that the budding relationship between her and then-husband Carl Senna deepened due to their shared admiration of and interest in the work of Frantz Fanon.

16. Zita A. Nunes argues that South America acted as "a discursive formation that derives from an African-American literary imaginary of the 1920s presented to us in Larsen's text [*Passing*] as well as in the black press of the United States and Brazil" (51).

17. The novel's references to the underground speak to *Caucasia*'s intertextuality with the works of Ralph Ellison and Fyodor Dostoyevsky, who Senna identifies as influences on her work. The strongest commonality among the three authors is that despite the fact that they maintain marginalized positions in their given environments, these invisible locations also afford them a critical space from which to view, evaluate, and interpret the worlds they inhabit.

18. Sandy and Birdie's experience in Aurora is significant in that it is constructed in direct opposition to the Afro-centric, phallic (marked by Deck) space of Boston. In addition, Aurora is a community of transient women who Birdie believes are, like she and her mother, "in a perpetual state of reinvention" (136). In Aurora, Sandy finds

love with Bernadette, and Birdie develops a friendship and semisexual relationship with a young girl, Alexis, but these relationships don't last. Sandy leaves Aurora over a disagreement with the founder of the women's commune, which is partially fueled by Sandy's reference to feminism as "an excuse for 'white, bourgeois bitches to complain about something" (55). Despite her friendship with Alexis, Birdie does not appear to mind their abrupt departure. For Birdie, the time at the commune leaves her feeling "incomplete—a gray blur, a body in motion, forever galloping toward completion—half a girl, half-caste, half-mast, and half-baked, not quite ready for consumption" (137). Though Birdie feels incomplete, she claims to find a strange sense of comfort in that incompletion. Aurora is the first space Birdie enters as Jesse Goldman and the space where she sexually experiments with another girl. In this way, her state of incompletion at Aurora suggests her ambiguous racial and sexual identities. In the same way that Birdie vacillates between blackness and whiteness, she also maintains sexual (though never consummated) relationships with Alexis at the commune and Nick Marsh in New Hampshire. The linked sexual and racial indeterminacy speaks to the novel's governing theme of the difficulty of locating a comfortable space on the border between races and sexualities. The Aurora experience in particular broaches a possible relationship between racial and sexual indeterminacy in the novel.

Bibliography

Ali, Suki. *Mixed-Race, Post-Race: Gender, New Ethnicities, and Cultural Practices.* Oxford: Berg Publishers, 2003.

Arata, Stephen. "The Occidental Tourist: Dracula and the Anxiety of Reverse Colonization." In Stoker, *Dracula,* 462–70.

Arias, Claudia M. Milian. "An Interview with Danzy Senna." *Callaloo* 25:2 (2002): 447–52.

Armstrong, Nancy. "Feminism, Fiction, and the Utopian Promise of Dracula." *Differences: A Journal of Feminist Cultural Studies* 16:1 (2005): 1–23.

Aronson, Amy. "Novel Companions." *Ms. Magazine,* December 1999. http://www.msmagazine.com/dec99/books-senna.asp.

Avery, Sheldon. *Up from Washington: William Pickens and the Negro Struggle for Equality, 1900–1954.* Newark: University of Delaware Press, 1989.

Bagnall, Robert. "The Madness of Marcus Garvey." *Messenger* (March 1923): 638, 648.

———. "A Psychoanalysis of Ku Kluxism." *Messenger* (August 1923): 789–91.

Baraka, Imamu Amiri. *"Dutchman" and "The Slave," Two Plays.* New York: Morrow: 1964.

Barnett, Claudia. "'An Evasion of Ontology': Being Adrienne Kennedy." *TDR: The Drama Review: A Journal of Performance Studies* 49:3 (2005): 157–86.

———. "'This Fundamental Challenge to Identity': Reproduction and Representation in the Drama of Adrienne Kennedy." *Theatre Journal* 48:2 (1996): 141–55.

Beaty, Bart. *Fredric Wertham and the Critique of Mass Culture.* Jackson: University Press of Mississippi, 2005.

Bell, Derrick. *Race, Racism, and American Law.* Boston: Little, Brown, 1992.

Bender, Bert. *The Descent of Love: Darwin and the Theory of Sexual Selection in American Fiction, 1871–1926.* Philadelphia: University of Pennsylvania Press, 1996.

Bennett, J. G. *Is There "Life" on Earth? An Introduction to Gurdjieff.* New York: Stonehill Press, 1973.

Berg, Allison. *Mothering the Race: Women's Narratives of Reproduction, 1890–1930.* Urbana: University of Illinois Press, 2002.

Bergner, Gwen. *Taboo Subjects: Race, Sex, and Psychoanalysis.* Minneapolis: University of Minnesota Press, 2005.

Berlant, Lauren. *The Queen of America Goes to Washington City: Essays on Sex and Citizenship.* Durham, N.C.: Duke University Press, 1997.

Besley, Tina. *Counseling Youth.* Boston: Sense Publishers, 2006.

Blazer, Dan. *The Age of Melancholy: 'Major Depressions' and Its Social Origins.* New York: Routledge, 2005.

Bogues, Anthony. "Imagination, Politics, and Utopia: Confronting the Present." *Boundary 2: An International Journal of Literature and Culture* 33:3 (2006): 151–59.

Boudreau, Brenda. "'Becoming' White in *Caucasia.*" *Modern Language Studies* 32:1 (2002): 59–70.

Brown, James. "Soul Power." *Revolution of the Mind.* Polydor Records, 1971.

Bruce, Dickson D., Jr., "W. E. B Du Bois and the Idea of Double Consciousness." *American Literature* 64:2 (1999): 299–309.

Byrd, Rudolph P. *Jean Toomer's Years with Gurdjieff: Portrait of an Artist, 1923–1936.* Athens: University of Georgia Press, 1990.

"California Regents Vote against Adding 'Multiracial' Box to Application Forms." *Black Issues in Higher Education* (Dec. 16, 2004): 13.

Calvin, Floyd J. "The Mirrors of Harlem: Psychoanalyzing New York's Colored First Citizens." *Messenger* (December 1922–March 1923).

Capeci, Dominic. *The Harlem Riot of 1943.* Philadelphia: Temple University Press, 1977.

Carby, Hazel. *Race Men.* Cambridge, Mass.: Harvard University Press, 1998.

Carroll, Anne Elizabeth. *Word, Image, and the New Negro: Representation and Identity in the Harlem Renaissance.* Bloomington: Indiana University Press, 2005.

Cheng, Anne Anlin. *The Melancholy of Race: Psychoanalysis, Assimilation, and Hidden Grief.* New York: Oxford University Press, 2000.

Chesnutt, Charles. *The House behind the Cedars.* 1900. New York: Penguin, 1993.

Christian, Barbara. "The Race for Theory." In *The Black Feminist Reader.* Eds. Joy James and T. Denean Sharpley-Whiting. Oxford: Wiley-Blackwell, 2000, 11–23.

Cleaver, Eldridge. *Soul on Ice.* 1968. New York: Dell, 1991.

Cohen, Cathy. "Deviance as Resistance: A New Research Agenda for the Study of Black Politics." *Du Bois Review: Social Science Research on Race* 1 (2004): 27–45.

Corber, Robert. *In the Name of National Security: Hitchcock, Homophobia, and the Political Construction of Gender in Postwar America.* Durham, N.C.: Duke University Press, 1993.

Craft, Christopher. "Kiss Me with Those Red Lips: Gender and Inversion in Bram Stoker's *Dracula*." In Stoker, *Dracula*, 444–59.

Daniel, G. Reginald. *More Than Black? Multiracial Identity and the New Racial Order.* Philadelphia: Temple University Press, 2002.

Davis, Thadious. *Nella Larsen: Novelist of the Harlem Renaissance.* Baton Rouge: Louisiana University Press, 1994.

Defalco, Amelia. "Jungle Creatures and Dancing Apes: Modern Primitivism and Nella Larsen's *Quicksand*." *Mosaic* 38 (2005): 19–36.

Deleuze, Gilles, and Félix Guattari. *Anti-Oedipus: Capitalism and Schizophrenia.* Trans. Robert Hurley, Mark Seem, and Helen R. Lane. New York: Viking Press, 1977.

Diamond, Elin. "Rethinking Identification: Kennedy, Freud, Brecht." *Kenyon Review* 15:2 (1993): 86–99.

———. "The Violence of 'We': Politicizing Identification." In *Critical Theory and Performance.* Eds. Janelle Reinelt and Joseph Roach. Ann Arbor: University of Michigan Press, 1992, 390–98.

Douglas, Ann. *Terrible Honesty: Mongrel Manhattan in the 1920s.* New York: Farrar, Strauss, and Giroux, 1995.

Elam, Harold J. "August Wilson, Doubling, Madness, and Modern African-American Drama." *Modern Drama* 43:4 (2000): 614–15.

Ellison, Ralph. *The Collected Essays of Ralph Ellison.* Ed. John F. Callahan. New York: Modern Library, 1995.

———. "Going to the Territory." *Collected Essays,* 591–612.

———. "Harlem Is Nowhere." 1953. *Collected Essays,* 320–27.

———. *Invisible Man.* New York: Random House, 1952.

———. "Richard Wright's Blues." *Collected Essays,* 128–44.

English, Daylanne K. *Unnatural Selections: Eugenics in American Modernism and the Harlem Renaissance.* Chapel Hill: University of North Carolina Press, 2004.

Eversley, Shelly. "The Lunatic's Fancy and the Work of Art." *American Literary History* 13:3 (2002): 445–68.

Fabre, Michael. *The Unfinished Quest of Richard Wright.* Urbana: University of Illinois Press, 1993.

Fanon, Frantz. *Black Skin, White Masks.* Trans. Charles Lam Markmann. New York: Grove Press, 1967.

———. *The Wretched of the Earth.* New York: Grove Press, 1961.

Ferguson, Jeffrey. *The Sage of Sugar Hill: George S. Schuyler and the Harlem Renaissance.* New Haven, Conn.: Yale University Press, 2005.

Ferguson, Roderick. *Aberrations in Black: Toward a Queer Critique of Color.* Minneapolis: University of Minnesota Press, 2004.

Firestone, Shulamith. *The Dialectic of Sex: The Case for Feminist Revolution.* New York: Morrow, 1970.

Frazier, E. Franklin. *The Negro in the United States.* New York: Macmillan, 1949.

Freedman, Jonathan. "From *Spellbound* to *Vertigo*: Alfred Hitchcock and Therapeutic Culture in America." In *Hitchcock's America.* Eds. Jonathan Freedman and Richard Millington. New York: Oxford University Press, 1999, 77–97.

Freud, Sigmund. *Beyond the Pleasure Principle.* 1920. New York: Norton, 1989.

———. *Civilization and Its Discontents.* 1930. In vol. 21 of the Standard Edition of the Complete Works of Sigmund Freud. Ed. James Strachey. Trans. James Strachey, Anna Freud, Alix Strachey, and Alan Tyson. London: Hogarth Press and the Institute of Psychoanalysis, 1955, 64–145.

———. *The Complete Introductory Lectures.* New York: Norton, 1966.

———. "Criminals from a Sense of Guilt." In vol. 14 of the Standard Edition of the Complete Psychological Works of Sigmund Freud. Ed. James Strachey. Trans. James Strachey, Anna Freud, Alix Strachey, and Alan Tyson. London: Hogarth Press, 1914–16, 332–33.

———. *The Ego and the Id.* 1923. New York: Norton, 1960.

———. *The Interpretation of Dreams.* 1900. New York: Basic Books, 1955.

———. "The Question of Lay Analysis." In vol. 20, part 4, of the Standard Edition of the Complete Works of Sigmund Freud. Ed. James Strachey. Trans. James Strachey, Anna Freud, Alix Strachey, and Alan Tyson. London: Hogarth Press, 1926, 183–250.

———. "Some Character-types Met with in Psychoanalytic Work." In vol. 21 of the Standard Edition of the Complete Works of Sigmund Freud. Ed. James Strachey. Trans. James Strachey, Anna Freud, Alix Strachey, and Alan Tyson. London: Hogarth Press and the Institute of Psychoanalysis, 1955: 309–33.

———. "The 'Uncanny.'" 1919. In vol. 17 of the Standard Edition of the Complete Works of Sigmund Freud. Ed. James Strachey. Trans. James Strachey, Anna Freud, Alix Strachey, and Alan Tyson. London: Hogarth Press, 1917–19, 219–56.

Friedan, Betty. *The Feminine Mystique.* New York: Dell Publishing Group, 1963.

Friedel, Tania. *Racial Discourse and Cosmopolitanism in Twentieth-century African American Writing.* New York: Routledge, 2008.

Gates, Henry Louis, Jr. *The Signifying Monkey: A Theory of African-American Literary Criticism.* Oxford: Oxford University Press, 1988.

Gilman, Sander L. *Difference and Pathology: Stereotypes of Sexuality, Race, and Madness.* Ithaca, N.Y.: Cornell University Press, 1985.

———. *Freud, Race, and Gender.* Baltimore: Johns Hopkins University Press, 1993.

Gilroy, Paul. *Against Race: Imagining Political Culture Beyond the Color Line.* Cambridge, Mass.: Belknap Press of Harvard University Press, 2000.

Glicksberg, Charles. "Psychoanalysis and the Negro Problem." *Phylon: The Atlanta University Review of Race and Culture* 12:1 (1956): 41–51.

Goeser, Caroline. "The Case of Ebony and Topaz: Racial and Sexual Hybridity in Harlem Renaissance Illustrations." *American Periodicals* 15:1 (2005): 86–111.

Goodwill-Gill, Guy. *The Refugee in International Law.* New York: Oxford University Press, 2007.

Gordon, Lewis R., T. Denean Sharpley-Whiting, and Renee T. White, eds. *Fanon: A Critical Reader.* Cambridge: Blackwell, 1996.

Greenburg, Doris. "New Clinic in City Helps Curb Crime." *New York Times,* 18 June 1949: 8.

Grimké, Archibald. "Inter-Mixture and Inter-Marriage." *Messenger* (August 1924): 260, 263.

Grossack, Martin. "Psychological Research and the Negro." *Phylon: The Atlanta University Review of Race and Culture* 12:1 (1956): 70–73.

Guinier, Lani, and Gerald Torres. *The Miner's Canary: Enlisting Race, Resisting Power, Transforming Democracy.* Cambridge, Mass.: Harvard University Press, 2002.

Hale, Nathan, Jr. *The Rise and Crisis of Psychoanalysis in the United States: Freud and the Americans, 1917–1985.* New York: Oxford University Press, 1995.

Hardwig, Bill. "'A Lack Somewhere': Lacan, Psychoanalysis, and *Quicksand.*" *Soundings* 80:4 (1997): 573–89.

Harrison, Hubert. "Race Consciousness." *Boston Chronicle* (March 15, 1924). Rpt. in *The Hubert Harrison Reader.* Ed. Jeffrey B. Perry. Middletown, Conn.: Wesleyan University Press, 2001, 116.

Harrison-Kahan, Lori. "Passing for White, Passing for Jewish: Mixed Race Identity in Danzy Senna and Rebecca Walker." *MELUS: The Journal of the Society for the Study of the Multi-Ethnic Literature of the United States* 30:1 (2005): 19–48.

Hoffman, Frederick J. *Freudianism and the Literary Mind.* Baton Rouge: Louisiana State University Press, 1957.

Home of the Brave. Dir. Mark Robson. Screen Plays Corp. 1949. Videocassette. Republic Pictures, 1998.

Hopkins, Pauline. *Of One Blood: The Hidden Self.* Intro. Deborah E. McDowell. New York: Washington Square Press, 2004.

Horvitz, Deborah. "Hysteria and Trauma in Pauline Hopkins' 'Of One Blood; Or, the Hidden Self.'" *African American Review* 33:2 (Summer 1999): 245–60.

Howe, Fanny. *The Deep North.* Los Angeles: Sun and Moon Press, 1988.

———. *The Wedding Dress: Meditations on Word and Life.* Berkeley: University of California Press, 2003.

Hughes, Langston. *The Ways of White Folks.* New York: Vintage Books, 1971.

Hutchinson, George. *The Harlem Renaissance in Black and White.* Cambridge, Mass.: Harvard University Press, 1995.

———. *In Search of Nella Larsen: A Biography of the Color Line.* Cambridge, Mass.: Belknap Press of Harvard University Press, 2006.

———. "Jean Toomer and American Racial Discourse." In *Interracialism: Black-White Intermarriage in American History, Literature, and Law.* Ed. Werner Sollors. Oxford: Oxford University Press, 2000, 369–90.

———. “Mediating ‘Race’ and ‘Nation’: The Cultural Politics of *The Messenger*.” *African American Review* 28:4 (1994): 531–48.

———. “Subject to Disappearance: Interracial Identity in Nella Larsen’s Quicksand.” In *Temples for Tomorrow: Looking Back at the Harlem Renaissance*. Eds. Geneviève Fabre and Michel Feith. Bloomington: Indiana University Press, 2001, 177–92.

Ifekwunigwe, Jayne O., ed. *“Mixed Race” Studies: A Reader*. London: Routledge, 2004.

In Treatment. Prod. Rodrigo Garcia. HBO. Jan. 29, 2008.

Jackson, John L., Jr. *Real Black: Adventures in Racial Sincerity*. Chicago: University of Chicago Press, 2005.

Jackson, Lawrence. *Ralph Ellison: Emergence of a Genius*. New York: John Wiley and Sons, 2002.

Jameson, Fredric. *The Political Unconscious: Narrative as a Socially Symbolic Act*. Ithaca, N.Y.: Cornell University Press, 1981.

Jefferson, Thomas. *Notes on the State of Virginia*. 1781. Ed. William Peden. Chapel Hill: University of North Carolina Press, 1982.

Johnson, Barbara. “The Quicksands of the Self.” In *Female Subjects in Black and White: Race, Psychoanalysis, Feminism*. Eds. Elizabeth Abel, Barbara Christian, and Helene Moglen. Berkeley: University of California Press, 1997, 252–65.

Johnson, Charles. “The Contributions of Harry Stack Sullivan to Sociology.” In *The Contributions of Harry Stack Sullivan*. Ed. Patrick Mullahy. New York: Hermitage House, 1952, 207–14.

Johnson, Miriam M. “Maternal Agency vs. the Brotherhood of Males.” In *Provoking Agents: Gender and Agency in Theory and Practice*. Ed. Judith Kegan Gardiner. Urbana: University of Illinois Press, 1995, 152–66.

Jones, Ernst. *The Formative Years and the Great Discoveries, 1856–1900*. Vol. 1, *The Life and Work of Sigmund Freud*. New York: Basic Books, 1953.

Jones, Lisa. *Bulletproof Diva*. New York: Doubleday, 1994.

Jung, Carl G. *Civilization in Transition*. Ed. Herbert Read, Michael Fordham, and Gerhard Adler. Vol. 10, *The Collected Works of C. G. Jung*. New York: Pantheon Books, 1953.

Kampf, Fay B. *The Psychology and Psychotherapy of Otto Rank: An Historical and Comparative Introduction*. 1953. Westport, Conn.: Greenwood Press, 1977.

Karpman, Benjamin. “A Case of Paedophilia (Legally Rape) Cured by Psychoanalysis.” *Psychoanalytic Review* 37 (1950): 235–76.

———. “Dream Life in a Case of Transvestism; With Particular Attention to the Problem of Latent Homosexuality.” *Journal of Nervous and Mental Disease* 106 (1947): 292–337.

———. “The Principles and Aims of Criminal Psychopathology.” *Journal of Criminal Psychopathology* 1 (1940): 187–218.

———. “A Psychiatrist Looks at the Social Scientists.” *American Journal of Sociology* 53 (1947): 131–40.

———. "A Psychoanalytic Study of a Case of Murder." *Psychoanalytic Review* 38 (1951): 139–57.

———. "Psychosomatic Neurosis as Expression of a Barrier against Indulgence in Craved but Prohibited Sexual Drives." *Journal of Criminal Law and Criminology* 44 (1954): 746–52.

———. "Sexual Psychopath." *American Journal of Psychotherapy* 5 (1951): 584–605.

Kawash, Samira. *Dislocating the Color Line: Identity, Hybridity, and Singularity in African-American Literature.* Stanford, Calif.: Stanford University Press, 1997.

Kennedy, Adrienne. *The Adrienne Kennedy Reader.* Intro. Werner Sollors. Minneapolis: University of Minnesota Press, 2001.

———. *Dramatic Circle.* In *Adrienne Kennedy Reader,* 182–96.

———. *The Film Club.* In *Adrienne Kennedy Reader,* 174–81.

———. *Funnyhouse of a Negro.* In *Adrienne Kennedy in One Act.* Minneapolis: University of Minnesota Press, 1988.

———. *The Owl Answers.* In *Adrienne Kennedy Reader,* 29–42.

———. *People Who Led to My Plays.* New York: Knopf, 1996.

Kerman, Cynthia E., and Richard Eldridge. *The Lives of Jean Toomer: A Hunger for Wholeness.* Baton Rouge: Louisiana State University Press, 1987.

Kluger, Richard. *Simple Justice: The History of* Brown v. Board of Education *and Black America's Struggle for Equality.* New York: Knopf, 1976.

Kohut, Heinz. *The Psychology of the Self: A Casebook.* Ed. Arnold Goldberg et al. New York: International Universities Press, 1978.

Korgen, Kathleen Odell. *From Black to Biracial: Transforming Racial Identity Among Americans.* Westport, Conn.: Praeger Publishers, 1998.

Kornweibel, Theodore. *No Crystal Stair: Black Life and* The Messenger *1917–1928.* Westport, Conn.: Greenwood Press, 1975.

Kramer, Robert. Intro. to *A Psychology of Difference: The American Lectures 1924–38,* by Otto Rank. Princeton, N.J.: Princeton University Press, 1996, 3–50.

Lacan, Jacques. *Écrits: A Selection.* 1966. Trans. Bruce Fink. New York: Norton, 2002.

Lake, Obiagele. *Blue Veins and Kinky Hair: Naming and Color Consciousness in African America.* Westport, Conn.: Praeger, 2003.

Lane, Christopher, ed. *The Psychoanalysis of Race.* New York: Columbia University Press, 1998.

Laplanche, J., and J.-B. Pontalis. *The Language of Psycho-analysis.* Trans. Donald Nicholson-Smith. New York: Norton, 1974.

Larsen, Nella. *"Quicksand" and "Passing."* Ed. Deborah E. McDowell. New Brunswick, N.J.: Rutgers University Press, 1986.

Levy, Anita. *Reproductive Urges: Popular Novel-Reading, Sexuality, and the English Nation.* Philadelphia: University of Pennsylvania Press, 1999.

Lieberman, E. James. *Acts of Will: The Life and Work of Otto Rank.* New York: Free Press, 1985.

Menaker, Esther. *Otto Rank: A Rediscovered Legacy.* New York: Columbia University Press, 1982.

"Mental Hospitals Bar Negroes." *New York Amsterdam News*, Saturday, April 27, 1946, 1.

Metzl, Jonathan. *The Protest Psychosis: How Schizophrenia Became a Black Disease.* Boston: Beacon, 2010.

———. *Prozac on the Couch: Prescribing Gender in the Era of Wonder Drugs.* Durham, N.C.: Duke University Press: 2003.

Michaels, Walter Benn. "Autobiography of an Ex-White Man: Why Race Is Not a Social Construction." *Transition* 73 (1998): 122–43.

Millet, Kate. *Sexual Politics.* Urbana: University of Illinois Press, 1968.

"The Mirrors of Harlem." Advertisement. *Messenger* (November 1922).

Monda, Kimberly. "Self-Delusion and Self-Sacrifice in Nella Larsen's Quicksand." *African American Review* 31:1 (1997): 23–39.

Moretti, Franco. "A Capital Dracula." In Stoker, *Dracula,* 431–44.

Morrison, Mark S. *The Public Face of Modernism: Little Magazines, Audiences, and Reception, 1905–1920.* Madison: University of Wisconsin Press, 2001.

Nadell, Martha. *Enter the New Negroes: Images of Race in American Culture.* Cambridge, Mass.: Harvard University Press, 2004.

"The New Negro—What Is He?" Editorial. *Messenger* (August 1920): 73–74.

Nies, Betsy L. *Eugenic Fantasies: Racial Ideology in the Literature and Popular Culture of the 1920s.* New York: Routledge, 2002.

Nin, Anaïs. *The Diary of Anaïs Nin, 1934–1939.* New York: Swallow Press, 1967.

Nunes, Zita A. "Phantasmatic Brazil: Nella Larsen's *Passing,* American Literary Imagination, and Racial Utopianism." In *Mixing Race, Mixing Culture: Inter-American Literary Dialogues.* Eds. Monika Kaup and Debra J. Rosenthal. Austin: University of Texas Press, 2002, 50–61.

Pellegrini, Ann. *Performance Anxieties: Staging Psychoanalysis, Staging Race.* New York: Routledge, 1997.

Perry, Jeffrey B. *Hubert Harrison: The Voice of Harlem Radicalism 1883–1918.* New York: Columbia University Press, 2008.

———. "Race Consciousness." *Boston Chronicle* (March 15, 1924). Rpt. in *Voice of the Negro* 1:1 (April 1927): 3–4.

———, ed. *A Hubert Harrison Reader.* Middletown, Conn.: Wesleyan Press, 2001.

Pfister, Joel. "Glamorizing the Psychological: The Politics of Performance of Modern Psychological Identities." In *Inventing the Psychological: Toward a Cultural History of Emotional Life in America.* Eds. Joel Pfister and Nancy Schnog. New Haven, Conn.: Yale University Press, 1997, 167–216.

———. "On Conceptualizing the Cultural History of Emotional and Psychological Life in America." In *Inventing the Psychological: Toward a Cultural History of Emotional Life in America.* Eds. Joel Pfister and Nancy Schnog. New Haven, Conn.: Yale University Press, 1997, 17–62.

Pickens, William. "Color and Camouflage: A Psychoanalysis." *Messenger* (July 1923): 773–74.

———. *The New Negro; His Political, Civil, and Mental Status, and Related Essays.* New York: Negro Universities Press, 1969; 1916.

Plecker, W. A. "Race Mixture and the Next Census." *Eugenics: A Journal for Race Betterment* 11:3 (March 1929): 3–7.

———. "Virginia's Effort to Preserve Racial Integrity." 1932. *A Decade of Progress in Eugenics: Scientific Pages of the Third International Congress of Eugenics.* Baltimore: Williams and Wilkins, 1934.

Posnock, Ross. "How It Feels to Be a Problem: DuBois, Fanon, and the 'Impossible Life' of the Black Intellectual." *Critical Inquiry* 23:2 (Winter 1997): 323–49.

Rank, Otto. *Psychology and the Soul: A Study of the Origin, Conceptual Evolution and the Nature of the Soul.* 1930. Baltimore: Johns Hopkins University Press, 2002.

———. *A Psychology of Difference: The American Lectures.* Princeton, N.J.: Princeton University Press, 1996.

———. *The Trauma of Birth.* 1929. New York: Harper and Row, 1973.

Rauve, Rebecca. "The Intersection of Interests: Gurdjieff's Rope Group as a Site of Literary Production." *Twentieth-century Literature* 49:1 (2003): 46–81.

Reid-Pharr, Robert. *Once You Go Black: Choice, Desire, and the Black American Intellectual.* New York: New York University Press, 2007.

Relyea, Sarah. *Outsider Citizens: The Remaking of Postwar Identity in Wright, Beauvoir, and Baldwin.* New York: Routledge, 2006.

Rockquemore, Kerry Ann, and David Brunsma. *Beyond Black: Biracial Identity in America.* Thousand Oaks, Calif.: Sage Publications, 2002.

Rodgers, Lawrence. *Canaan Bound: The African American Great Migration Novel.* Urbana: University of Illinois Press, 1997.

Rooks, Noliwe M. *Ladies' Pages: African American Women's Magazines and the Culture that Made Them.* New Brunswick, N.J.: Rutgers University Press, 2004.

Root, Maria P. P. *The Multiracial Experience: Racial Borders as the New Frontier.* Thousand Oaks, Calif.: Sage Publications, 1996.

———. "Within, Between and Beyond Race." In *Racially Mixed People in America.* Ed. Maria P. P. Root. Newbury Park, Calif.: Sage Publications, 1992, 3–11.

Ross, Marlon B. *Manning the Race: Reforming Black Men in the Jim Crow Era.* New York: New York University Press, 2004.

Rossi, A. "Some Pre–World War II Antecedents of Community Mental Health Theory and Practice." *Mental Hygiene* 46 (1962): 78–98.

Roth, Phyllis. "Suddenly Sexual Women in Bram Stoker's *Dracula.*" In Stoker, *Dracula,* 411–21.

Rusch, Frederik L. "Jean Toomer's Early Identification: The Two Black Plays." *MELUS* 13:1–2 (1986): 115–24.

Russell, Thaddeus. "The Color of Discipline: Civil Rights and Black Sexuality." *American Quarterly* 60:1 (March 2008): 101–28.

Schrager, Cynthia D. "Pauline Hopkins and William James: The New Psychology and the Politics of Race." In *The Unruly Voice: Rediscovering Pauline Elizabeth Hopkins.* Ed. John Gruesser. Urbana: University of Illinois Press, 1996, 307–29.

Schwartz, Joseph. *Cassandra's Daughter: A History of Psychoanalysis.* New York: Penguin, 2001.

Senna, Danzy. *Caucasia.* New York: Riverhead Books, 1998.

———. "The Mulatto Millennium: Waking Up in an Age of Racial Ambiguity." In *Half and Half: Writers on Growing Up Biracial and Bicultural.* Ed. Claudine Chiawei O'Hearn. New York: Pantheon, 1998, 12–27.

Sharpley-Whiting, T. Denean. "Anti-Black Femininity and Mixed-Race Identity: Engaging Fanon to Reread Capecia." In Gordon, *Fanon,* 155–62.

Sherrard-Johnson, Cherene. "'A Plea for Color': Nella Larsen's Iconography of the Mulatta." *American Literature: A Journal of Literary History, Criticism, and Bibliography* 76:4 (2004): 833–69.

Sheshadri-Crooks, Kalpana. *Desiring Whiteness: A Lacanian Analysis of Race.* London: Routledge, 2000.

———. "'I Am a Master': Terrorism, Masculinity, and Political Violence in Frantz Fanon." *Parallax* 8:2 (2002): 84–98.

Shirley, John. *Gurdjieff: An Introduction to His Life and Ideas.* New York: Penguin, 2004.

Silverman, Kaja. *The Subject of Semiotics.* New York: Oxford University Press, 1983.

Sollors, Werner. *Beyond Ethnicity: Consent and Descent in American Culture.* New York: Oxford University Press, 2000.

———. *Interracialism: Black-White Intermarriage in American History, Literature, and Law.* Oxford: Oxford University Press, 2000.

Somerville, Siobhan. *Queering the Color Line: Race and the Invention of Homosexuality in American Culture.* Durham, N.C.: Duke University Press, 2000.

Speeth, Kathleen. *The Gurdjieff Work.* New York: Tarcher, 1988.

Spillers, Hortense J. "'All the Things You Could Be By Now, If Sigmund Freud's Wife Was Your Mother': Psychoanalysis and Race." *Black, White and in Color: Essays on American Literature and Culture.* Chicago: University of Chicago Press, 2003, 376–427.

Stoker, Bram. *Dracula: Authoritative Text, Contexts, Reviews and Reactions, Dramatic and Film Variations, Criticism.* 1897. Eds. Nina Auerbach and David J. Skal. Norton Critical Editions. New York: W. W. Norton, 1997.

Sullivan, Harry Stack. "Memorandum on a Psychiatric Reconnaisance." 1941. In *The Fusion of Psychiatry and Social Science.* Ed. Helen Swick Perry. New York: Norton, 1964, 89–95.

Tate, Claudia. *Domestic Allegories of Political Desire: The Black Heroine's Text at the Turn of Century.* New York: Oxford University Press, 1993.

———. *Psychoanalysis and Black Novels: Desire and the Protocols of Race.* New York: Oxford University Press, 1998.

Toomer, Jean. Jean Toomer Papers. Jean Toomer Collection. Beinecke Rare Book and Manuscript Library, Yale University, New Haven, Conn.

———. "Meditation on Jung." Unpublished essay, n.d., box 49, folder 1053, Jean Toomer Papers.

———. "Negro Psychology in *The Emperor Jones*." Unpublished review, n.d., box 48, folder 1999, Jean Toomer Papers.

———. "Three Psychological Classes." Unpublished essay, n.d, box 50, folder 1090, Jean Toomer Papers.

———. "Transatlantic." Unpublished story, 1931, Jean Toomer Papers.

Tough, Paul. "The Black Supremacist." *New York Times Magazine*, May 25, 2003, 42.

Umansky, Laura. *Motherhood Reconceived: Feminism and the Legacies of the Sixties*. New York: New York University Press, 1996.

Verges, Francoise. "To Cure and to Free: The Fanonian Project of 'Decolonized Psychiatry.'" In Gordon, *Fanon*, 86–99.

Vogel, Todd. *The Black Press: New Literary and Historical Essays*. New Brunswick, N.J.: Rutgers University Press, 2001.

Walton, Jean. *Fair Sex, Savage Dreams: Race, Psychoanalysis, Sexual Difference*. Durham, N.C.: Duke University Press, 2001.

Wellbeloved, Sophia. *Gurdjieff: The Key Concepts*. New York: Routledge, 2003.

Wertham, Frederic. *Dark Legend*. New York: Duell, Sloan, and Pearce, 1941.

———. *Seduction of the Innocent*. New York: Rinehart, 1954.

———. *The Show of Violence*. 1949. New York: Greenwood Press, 1969.

———. "An Unconscious Determinant in *Native Son*." In *Psychoanalysis and Literature*. Ed. Hendrik Marinus Ruitenbeek. New York: Dutton, 1964, 321–25.

Whalan, Mark. "'Taking Myself in Hand': Jean Toomer and Physical Culture." *Modernism/Modernity* 10:4 (2003): 597–615.

Whiting, Frederick. "Bodies of Evidence: Post-War Detective Fiction and the Monstrous Origins of the Sexual Psychopath." *Yale Journal of Criticism: Interpretation in the Humanities* 18:1 (2005): 149–78.

Williams, Diana I. "Building the New Race: Jean Toomer's Eugenic Aesthetic." In *Jean Toomer and the Harlem Renaissance*. Eds. Geneviève Fabre and Michael Feith. New Brunswick, N.J.: Rutgers University Press, 2001, 188–201.

Williamson, Joel. *New People: Miscegenation and Mulattoes in the United States*. New York: Free Press, 1980.

Wilson, Sondra K., ed. *The Messenger Reader: Stories, Poetry, and Essays from "The Messenger" Magazine*. New York: Modern Library, 2000.

Woodson, Jon. *To Make a New Race: Gurdjieff, Toomer, and the Harlem Renaissance*. Jackson: University of Mississippi Press, 1999.

Wright, Michelle. *Becoming Black: Creating Identity in the African Diaspora*. Durham, N.C.: Duke University Press: 2004.

Wright, Richard. "Psychiatry Comes to Harlem." *Free World* (September 1946): 45–51.

———. Richard Wright Papers. Richard Wright Collection. Beinecke Rare Book and Manuscript Library. Yale University, New Haven, Conn.

Yu, Eric Kwan-Wai. "Productive Fear: Labor, Sexuality, and Mimicry in Bram Stoker's *Dracula*." *Texas Studies in Literature and Language* 48:2 (2006): 145–70.

Zaretsky, Eli. *Secrets of the Soul: A Social and Cultural History of Psychoanalysis.* New York: Vintage Books, 2004.

Zizek, Slavoj. "Love Thy Neighbor? No Thanks!" In *Psychoanalysis and Race.* Ed. Christopher Lane. New York: Columbia University Press, 1998, 154–75.

Index

Page numbers in italics refer to illustrations.

BADIA SAHAR AHAD is an assistant professor
in the department of English
at Loyola University in Chicago.

THE NEW BLACK STUDIES SERIES

Beyond Bondage: Free Women of Color in the Americas *Edited by David Barry Gaspar and Darlene Clark Hine*

The Early Black History Movement, Carter G. Woodson, and Lorenzo Johnston Greene *Pero Gaglo Dagbovie*

"Baad Bitches" and Sassy Supermamas: Black Power Action Films *Stephane Dunn*

Black Maverick: T. R. M. Howard's Fight for Civil Rights and Economic Power *David T. Beito and Linda Royster Beito*

Beyond the Black Lady: Sexuality and the New African American Middle Class *Lisa B. Thompson*

Extending the Diaspora: New Histories of Black People *Dawne Y. Curry, Eric D. Duke, and Marshanda A. Smith*

Activist Sentiments: Reading Black Women in the Nineteenth Century *P. Gabrielle Foreman*

Black Europe and the African Diaspora *Edited by Darlene Clark Hine, Trica Danielle Keaton, and Stephen Small*

Freeing Charles: The Struggle to Free a Slave on the Eve of the Civil War *Scott Christianson*

African American History Reconsidered *Pero Gaglo Dagbovie*

Freud Upside Down: African American Literature and Psychoanalytic Culture *Badia Sahar Ahad*

The University of Illinois Press
is a founding member of the
Association of American University Presses.

University of Illinois Press
1325 South Oak Street
Champaign, IL 61820-6903
www.press.uillinois.edu